The Watermills and Landscape of the River Great Ouse, Cambridgeshire

Modelling the Impact of Watermilling in a Lowland Valley

Bridget Flanagan and Keith Grimwade

Windgather Press is an imprint of Oxbow Books

Published in the United Kingdom in 2025 by
OXBOW BOOKS
81 St Clements, Oxford OX4 1AW

and in the United States by
OXBOW BOOKS
1950 Lawrence Road, Havertown, PA 19083

© Windgather Press, Bridget Flanagan and Keith Grimwade 2025

Paperback Edition: ISBN 978-1-914427-41-1
Digital Edition: ISBN 978-1-914427-42-8 (epub)

A CIP record for this book is available from the British Library

All rights reserved. No part of this book may be reproduced or transmitted in any form or by any means, electronic or mechanical including photocopying, recording or by any information storage and retrieval system, without permission from the publisher in writing.

Printed in the United Kingdom by Short Run Press

For a complete list of Windgather titles, please contact:

United Kingdom
OXBOW BOOKS
Telephone (0)1226 734350
Email: oxbow@oxbowbooks.com
www.oxbowbooks.com

United States of America
OXBOW BOOKS
Telephone (610) 853-9131, Fax (610) 853-9146
Email: queries@casemateacademic.com
www.casemateacademic.com/oxbow

Oxbow Books is part of the Casemate group

Front cover: 'Houghton Mill, 1893' Fritz B. Althaus 1860–1914 (Frederick B. Kerr 1915–31), reproduced with the permission of the Norris Museum, St Ives, Cambridgeshire, PWD/HOUGH/08. This watercolour, painted by one of the early artist visitors to the area, shows Houghton Mill from the south-east in late winter/early spring.
Back cover: Part of 'Huntyngdon & Godmanchester', a plan of the River Ouse and waterways between Huntingdon and St Ives bridge c. 1515, reproduced with the permission of The National Archives, Kew. The extract shows the River Great Ouse from Huntingdon to St Ives. The watermills at Hartford, Houghton and Hemingford Abbots can be seen.

The Publisher's authorised representative in the EU for product safety is Authorised Rep Compliance Ltd., Ground Floor, 71 Lower Baggot Street, Dublin D02 P593, Ireland.
www.arccompliance.com

Contents

List of figures   v
List of tables   vii
Acknowledgements   ix

1. Introduction   1
2. The physical and historical background   17
3. The first watermills: the Roman period to 1066   27
4. A watermilling 'powerhouse': the Domesday Mills   37
5. The Age of Backwaters: 1086–1350   61
6. River Wars: 1515 – matters come to a head   79
7. The Age of Locks: a 17th century technical solution   97
8. Continuity, disputes and cooperation: 1700–1850   113
9. Decline and romantic appreciation: 1850 to the present day   123
10. Modelling and managing the watermilling landscape   137

Primary sources   151
Bibliography   153
Index   159

List of figures

1.1	Hemingford Grey Meadow, 2022	2
1.2	Houghton Mill, 2022	3
1.3	Study area	3
2.1	The River Great Ouse in Cambridgeshire: single and multi-channel sections	17
2.2	A relict channel with flood water near Buckden Mill, 2024	20
2.3	A horizontal waterwheel, Orkney Dounby Click Mill (artist's impression)	23
2.4	A horizontal waterwheel, Orkney Dounby Click Mill, 2022	23
2.5	The vertical undershot waterwheel at Houghton Mill, 2025	24
2.6	Watermill terminology	25
3.1	Godmanchester: channels, ponds and possible watermill sites	31
3.2	The pre-watermilling landscape, Brampton to St Ives	34
3.3	Lee's Brook, 2023	34
3.4	Portholme Brook, October 2023	35
4.1	The Domesday Watermills on the River Great Ouse in Cambridgeshire	40
4.2	The possible location of the Domesday watermills at Eaton Socon and Eynesbury	41
4.3	LiDAR map of the River Great Ouse at Great Paxton	42
4.4	The probable location of Paxton's Domesday watermills	43
4.5	The possible location of the Domesday watermills at Buckden and Offord	44
4.6	The relict channel crossing Miller's Holme, Offord Common, 2024	45
4.7	Locating Hartford Mills	46
4.8	Locating Wyton Mill	48
4.9	Possible sites for Hemingford Abbots watermill	49
4.10	Brampton, Huntingdon and Godmanchester Mills, AD 1086: mill-leats and tail races	51
4.11	Percentage of land held by religious institutions, 1086	56
4.12	The estates and mills belonging to Ramsey Abbey in 1086	57
4.13	Average value of multiple mill sites (England, 1086)	58
5.1	Houghton Mill Backwater and the Abbot's *rivulus* (leat)	65
5.2	The Abbot's *rivulus* (leat) today	65
5.3	Hemingford Grey Mills Backwater	67
5.4	Hartford Mills Backwater	68
5.5	'Plan of the town of Huntingdon' 1768 by Thomas Jefferys, showing the Huntingdon Mill Overflow Channels	69
5.6	Huntingdon Mill LiDAR, 2023	69

vi *List of figures*

5.7	The impact of Brampton Mills on the Landscape in the 13th century	70
5.8	Map of St Ives by Edmund Pettis 1732, showing 'Mill Hill' windmill	74
5.9	Map of St Ives by Edmund Pettis 1728, showing 'Burleigh Hill' windmill	74
5.10	Map of St Ives by Edmund Pettis 1732, next to a map of St Ives 2020	75
5.11	Map of St Ives by Edmund Pettis 1728, showing 'Mill fours' and 'Bugel moor brook' alongside the 1949 OS map	76
6.1	'Huntyngdon & Godmanchester'. Plan of the River Ouse and waterways between Huntingdon and St Ives bridge, *c.* 1515	91
6.2	LiDAR: Huntingdon to St Ives, 2024	91
7.1	The Location of Watermills on the River Great Ouse in 1600	99
7.2	Map of the Great Ouse *c.* 1689, showing a pound lock	103
7.3	The River Great Ouse Navigation in 1700	105
7.4	Overfall Pit and its associated channels	107
7.5	Overfall Pit 1908 watercolour by Garden William Fraser (1856–1921)	108
7.6	Overfall Pit, December 2022	108
7.7	St Ives, Huntingdonshire *c.* 1835 by James Pettrey Hunter (1791–1867)	109
7.8	The towing-path, 1834	110
7.9	Raised bank, Hemingford Abbots Meadow, 2024	111
8.1	Watermill sites on the Great Ouse in Cambridgeshire, 1700–1850	114
8.2	Huntingdon Mills and Portholme Brook	116
8.3	Portholme Brook, April 2022	116
8.4	The weir immediately downstream of Portholme Brook's confluence with Alconbury Brook, April 2022	117
8.5	The bridge crossing Portholme Brook, April 2022	119
8.6	Fishers Dyke and the railway embankment location map	119
8.7	The weir at the entrance to Fishers Dyke, 2024	120
8.8	The remains of the trestle bridge crossing Houghton Mill's tail race	121
9.1	Houghton Mill by Garden William Fraser (1856–1921)	130
9.2	Houghton Mill by William Watt Milne (1865–1949)	131
9.3	Hemingford Grey Mill, early 20th century	133
9.4	Houghton Mill (west side), 2024	133
9.5	Godmanchester Mills, early 20th century	134
9.6	Buckden Mill Buildings, 2024	134
9.7	Eaton Socon Mill Buildings, 2024	135
9.8	Platinum Jubilee celebration, Hemingford Abbots Backwater, 2022	135
10.1	A model of the impact of watermilling on a lowland river landscape	138
10.2	Elton Mill: county boundary and backwater	139
10.3	The Mill Race at Olney	140
10.4	Westend Mills on the River Itchen	141
10.5	Historic Water Polygons: Brampton to Hemingford Grey, 1086–1700	142
10.6	Historic Water Polygons: Eaton Socon to Buckden, 1086–1700	143
10.7	Godmanchester Fish Weir	146
10.8	The river system today, showing the impact of the artificial channels dug to enable watermilling over a thousand-year period	146

List of tables

2.1	Average value, ploughland and total number of ploughs per manor 1086	22
4.1	The value and ownership of watermills on the River Great Ouse in Huntingdonshire recorded in the Domesday Book	38
4.2	Domesday Book, key statistics	53
4.3	Correlation coefficients, Domesday mills	55
4.4	Mill values within a six-mile radius of selected towns	55
4.5	Ramsey Abbey estates in Huntingdonshire's neighbouring counties	57

Acknowledgements

We are grateful to all the following for their support, advice and encouragement. Dr Simon Draper, Assistant Editor VCH Oxfordshire and tutor at Cambridge University's Institute for Continuing Education at Madingley Hall, guided us through the early stages of our research and gave detailed feedback on the first drafts of the manuscript. Michelle Bullivant, a local historian and landscape archaeologist, provided ideas and encouragement and went above and beyond, walking the meadows in the rain searching for traces of Gumcester Drain. John Lewin, Emeritus Professor in the Department of Geography and Earth Sciences at the University of Aberystwyth, gave freely of his time and knowledge to help us understand the very special physical geography of the landscape. We are indebted to Martin Watts, Director of Research and Engagement, Cotswold Archaeology, for sharing his knowledge of medieval watermills, and of millstones in general. Dr Ruth Shaffrey has contributed her unrivalled knowledge of milling in the Roman period and has kept alive our hopes of finding a Roman watermill in Cambridgeshire. We are extremely grateful to Dr Joe Grimwade, Teaching Fellow in Roman History at the University of Southampton, for his help with the translation of medieval Latin milling terminology and his advice on how to present this. Dr Claire Daunton and Sue Cassells have provided invaluable transcripts of the 1515 Duchy of Lancaster court case, while Martha Carlin and Caroline Barron helped track down the 1591 depositions on the state of Houghton Mill. Nigel Woodcock provided a petrological analysis of the millstone fragments at Godmanchester, shown to us by Christopher Vane-Percy from his garden. We thank both Philip Turon and the late Tony Churchill for giving us guided access to their islands at Hemingford Grey, which helped greatly with understanding the complex sequence of channels on this part of the meadow. We also thank Mike Booker for exploring the backwaters in his canoe, and for his thoughts and suggestions. David Jarrett kindly, and helpfully, gave us access to his late wife Sue's research into Eaton Socon. We thank Charles Looker for his help with the records of the 19th century 'Simpson' case. We are extremely grateful to the ever-helpful staff of the Cambridgeshire Archives, the Bedfordshire Archives, the National Archives, the Norris Museum and the Woburn Estate for maps and records of litigation, which helped us to chart the development of watermilling on the Great Ouse. Thank you, too, to Ruth Beckley, Archaeological Officer with Cambridgeshire County Council, for her help with Cambridgeshire's Historic Environment Record. We also wish to thank the members of many Local History Societies along the Great Ouse in Cambridgeshire who have shared and discussed the development of our findings and theories. And finally, a debt of gratitude goes to Professor Stephen Upex, tutor at Cambridge University's Institute for Continuing Education at Madingley Hall, and the 'Class of 18', for his and their inspiration and ideas.

Publication of this book has been supported by a grant from the Goodliff Fund of the Huntingdonshire Local History Society.

Chapters 4 and 5 are derived in part from an article published in Landscape History 2025 © The Society for Landscape Studies, available online: http://wwwtandfonline.com/ 10.1080/01433768.2025.2503535. All maps and diagrams, unless stated below, were created by the authors using QGIS 3.34 with data obtained from OS Open Zoomstack 2020 and Environment Agency LiDAR DTM 1m 2020 & 2022, Open Govt. Licence v3.0; and the Cambridge Historic Environment Record 2021.

All photographs and illustrations are the authors' unless stated below.

- Figures 4.7 i and 6.1 are reproduced with the permission of The National Archives, Kew.
- Figures 4.7 ii, 4.8 i, 5.8, 5.9, 5.10, 5.11 and 7.7 are reproduced with the permission of the Norris Museum, St Ives, Cambridgeshire.
- Figure 5.2 The Abbot's *rivulus* (leat), is by Mike Wallis, superimposed with authors' notes.
- Figure 7.2 is reproduced with permission of the Suffolk Archives, SA/E2/17/1.
- Figures 7.5, 9.1 and 9.2 are reproduced with the permission of Cheffins Fine Art, Cambridge.
- Figure 9.8 is reproduced with the permission of A.-M. Farmer.
- Figures 10.2, 10.3 and 10.4 are based on OS maps in the archives of the National Library of Scotland, with their permission.
- Figure 10.7 Image courtesy of Huntingdonshire District Council/Matthew Power Photography.
- Every effort has been made to trace the copyright of all works reproduced but if any have been overlooked, the authors would be grateful if you would contact us.

CHAPTER ONE

Introduction

This book grew out of a curiosity to understand the landscape of our home stretch of the River Great Ouse valley in Cambridgeshire. The area is scenically very attractive, where the river and its network of many smaller channels meander across a floodplain of traditionally managed hay meadows (Fig. 1.1). To date, there has been a general assumption that some of these channels were variously used to serve the series of watermills along the river. However, there has been no confirmation of this, nor any examination as to how the channels may have related to the mills, and, if they did so, no detailed explanation of how they functioned. This is where our challenge began.

In 1086 the Domesday Survey recorded 25 watermills on this section of the river. Today, Houghton Mill is the only remaining watermill, owned and run by the National Trust (Fig. 1.2). Like Blair (2007, vi) who wrote of his 'growing conviction during the 1990s, as I worked on the medieval landscape of the upper Thames region, that I was encountering watercourses that were neither natural nor recent, and could only be understood as relict canals', we became increasingly convinced that the many channels and pools we were encountering – previously explained, if explained at all, as natural – could only be understood as the result of watermilling. What we did not know was how exceptional watermilling on the River Great Ouse in Cambridgeshire had been, nor how extensive its influence had been on the formation of the river valley landscape that we see today. And as our research progressed, we realised that our findings had a wider significance for understanding the development of watercourses in other lowland valleys, for explaining deviations in parish boundaries, and for the accurate identification and assessment of heritage assets.

Our study area (Fig. 1.3) covers the River Great Ouse and its valley in the present-day county of Cambridgeshire. This county was established in 1974 by the merger of the old counties of Huntingdonshire, Cambridgeshire and the Isle of Ely. (The boundaries of the old county of Huntingdonshire are now those of the Huntingdonshire District Council.) We refer frequently to Huntingdonshire and use it as an area for statistical analysis – but with two exceptions. We have included Eaton Socon: although it was in Bedfordshire until 1965, it is now in Cambridgeshire and has a possible watermill site at the highest point on the river in the county. Swavesey, in Cambridgeshire, is the parish with the only watermill identified downstream of the former Huntingdonshire/Cambridgeshire County boundary.

The first detailed account of the River Great Ouse in Huntingdonshire is in Fox's *The History of Godmanchester* (1831, iv). His aim was 'to give to a local

FIGURE 1.1. Hemingford Grey Meadow, 2022

history an interest beyond the precincts of the place to which it relates', by presenting the wider significance of the events that had shaped the growth and development of the town. Consequently, his chapter on 'Navigation and Drainage' is of great relevance to our study, because he wrote about what had happened in Godmanchester in the context of wider developments, including watermilling, along the river. His history of the Danes and Romans and his observations on agricultural development are similarly relevant. Fox provided translations of the relevant extracts of the Hundred Rolls – *Rotuli Hundredorum* – and the Quo Warranto Pleas – *Placita Quo Warranto* – which help to explain the channel modifications of the river between Huntingdon and St Ives brought about by the expansion of watermilling in the second half of the 13th century. But key terms can be translated differently, and we will show in Chapter 5 that

FIGURE 1.2. Houghton Mill, 2022

FIGURE 1.3. Study area

revisiting these documents has enabled more, and more detailed, conclusions to be reached. Fox appears to have used the records of the Duchy of Lancaster, which would have been in Somerset House, but he does not cite his sources, so we cannot be sure if he accessed the same documents available today in the

National Archives (TNA DL3/23); probably not, as he does not mention the map of the River Great Ouse from Huntingdon to St Ives that was presented as part of the 1515 Duchy Court case (TNA MPCC 1/9). He transcribed the decree of 1524 (Fox 1831, 200–205), a copy of which is now available in the Cambridgeshire Archives (KPGMD/2913/Z/9/B), but this was a summary prepared a decade after the court case. Our transcription and interpretation of the bundle in the National Archives, and an analysis of the map, has provided much more detail about events and background, and has allowed us to understand some of the major changes to the river that had occurred in previous centuries. Many of Fox's conclusions have been repeated in subsequent histories of Godmanchester through to the present day, but our research, based on new evidence, challenges some of his interpretation.

At a national scale, Bennett and Elton's *History of Corn Milling*, published in four volumes between 1899 and 1904, aimed to bring together in a single, comprehensive analysis the many articles that had been written about milling – archaeological, historical and technological – in the previous century. The second volume, *Watermills and Windmills* (Bennett and Elton 1899), was the first text to address questions asked in this study, with chapters on the 'Introduction of Watermills into Britain' and the 'Domesday Mills'. The authors critically evaluated their sources, disputing, for example, that an Anglo-Saxon watermill was mentioned in a charter dated AD 664 and concluding that the earliest authentic reference was in a charter of Aethelberht of Kent, in AD 762– a finding that still stands today. Their chapter on the Domesday mills was groundbreaking. They included a full schedule of the Domesday mills organised by county, with the name of each manor transcribed (but not translated into its modern equivalent), how many mills the manor owned and their value. However, their focus was very much on interpreting ownership, how rents were paid and disputes about tithes, with little analysis of the location of mills and no consideration of the channel engineering required to make the milling operation possible and successful.

Hodgen's 'Domesday Water Mills' was published in 1939 in the journal *Antiquity*. It is of great significance to an understanding of watermills and the landscape because Hodgen used the Victoria County Histories' translations of the schedule of mill locations published by Bennett and Elton (see above), and other texts as required, to create the first national map of the Domesday mills (Hodgen 1939, 267). (The first county map had been produced by Fowler for Bedfordshire in 1922.) She also identified mill clusters, which she mapped at a national scale, and at selected local scales. In attempting to explain these distributions, Hodgen considered a range of factors, including geology and physical geography, population distribution and the spread of technology. Subsequent research, including our own, disagrees with several of her assumptions and conclusions and has identified more fruitful lines of enquiry, *e.g.* looking at factors such as ploughland and mill value, rather than population, to explain distributions. But Hodgen was rigorous in rejecting her own hypotheses when they were not supported by the evidence, *e.g.* she concluded that 'the counties containing the largest number of people were thus not necessarily the counties containing the largest number of mills' (Hodgen 1939, 272) and was transparent about what – at least at the time – was unknown, *e.g.* 'We have no way of knowing yet why an element of advanced culture (i.e. watermilling) was immediately incorporated into the life of one agricultural community and resisted by an adjoining one' (Hodgen 1939, 277). By mapping the distribution of mills, looking for correlations and analysing the Domesday statistics, Hodgen's paper merits the recognition given to it by Ambler and Langdon (1994, 43) as one of the most notable analyses on this topic.

Two publications, although focusing on the history of river transport on the Great Ouse, provide valuable information about watermilling due to the interdependent and often conflicting relationship between these two uses of the river. The first is Willan's 1946 publication 'The Navigation of the Great Ouse between St. Ives and Bedford in the Seventeenth Century'. He transcribed documents from the Francklin MSS (FN1254) (the Francklin family owned a share of the Navigation in the 18th and 19th centuries) and presented a selection of them, with an introductory essay and a facsimile of a map of the river showing the staunches and sluices in 1690. The extracts cover the agreements and many disputes between the owners of the Navigation and other users of the river. Witness statements graphically explain how the mills obstructed river transport and impacted river levels – all of which we evaluate in Chapter 7. In 1973, Summers published *The Great Ouse: The History of a River Navigation*. She assessed the full length of the river in its geographical and historical context, researching the development of the Navigation through to the mid-20th century. Summers drew heavily on Willan for the 17th century developments but added much useful detail about the locks, staunches and sluices, emphasising throughout that 'In the realm of man-made disabilities there is no doubt that mills were the outstanding obstruction' (Summers 1973, 23).

Any study that involves a consideration of Domesday geographies has to acknowledge the work of H.C. Darby, beginning with the publication of 'Domesday Woodland in East Anglia' (1934). 1952 saw the first edition of his *The Domesday Geography of Eastern England*. However, Darby gave relatively little attention to mills. In the Huntingdonshire chapter they occupied less than two pages, most of which was taken up with a map and table (Darby 1972, 344–346). He noted the number of Huntingdonshire mills and gave their range of values, but he did not appreciate that these figures were exceptional. He mapped the mills, including mill clusters, but commented that 'The distribution of mills raises no special points' (1972, 345), something which we show is certainly not the case. Darby did, however, suggest that some of the Paxton mills were in one of its *berewicks* (a detached portion of land belonging to a manor), which is relevant to our discussion of their location.

Green's history of Godmanchester was published in 1977. He was an experienced archaeologist and local historian whose excavations revealed

Godmanchester to have been an important Roman town, and he wrote an evidenced and authoritative account of this period of Godmanchester's history. However, his account of the Danish Burh (Green 1977, 27–29) has been superseded by more recent archaeological evidence and his conclusion about the location of Godmanchester's three Domesday mills was unevidenced and, as we show, incorrect. Green's slim volume (48 pages) provided important information about a key location on the Great Ouse for watermilling, but it needs, and merits, an update as it is still the most used source for general histories of the town.

Bond's 1979 paper 'The Reconstruction of the Medieval Landscape; the Estates of Abingdon Abbey' was of great relevance to the focus of our study. Bond highlighted that 'The impact of monastic organisation upon the landscape itself has, however, been relatively neglected' (1979, 59). He addressed this issue with an account of the Abingdon estates drawing on documentary and field evidence, covering all components of the landscape, including mills. He found the earliest reference to a watermill on the Abingdon estates in the Chronicles of Abingdon Abbey, which describes how Abbot Aethelwold diverted part of the Thames into a leat, built the mill below the *curia* and cut a tail race to rejoin the main river near St Helen's church, *c.* AD 960 (Bond 1979, 69). Bond deduced from the landscape evidence that this mill stood on the same site as the present Abbey Mill and that 'There is no question of this (the mill-leat and tail race) being simply an enlargement of an existing channel as some writers have suggested'. He put forward explanations for the many other channels on the floodplain and referenced disputes between the abbey's mill and its neighbours about water management. He concluded by emphasising the potential of the broad range of topographical information available from monastic sources, 'generally under-exploited at both local and national level'. Regarding watermills and their impact on the landscape, this potential for research remained unheeded; for example, Bond's book *Monastic Landscapes* was published in 2004, and although he devoted a chapter to Monastic mills drawing on his own research, he was able to quote only two papers by other authors about water-powered corn mills published after his 1979 paper (Bond 2004, 370). Only recently has the Abingdon landscape been revisited and reinterpreted, revealing the complexity of channel engineering in medieval times (Thomas 2022). Our study builds on Bond's findings, highlighting the significant and lasting impact of these medieval engineering efforts and undoubtedly supporting his conclusion that 'The study of the landscape must be multi-disciplinary' (Bond 1979, 71).

Another potential line of enquiry was raised by Aston in 1985 in his book *Interpreting the Landscape*. He noted that the relationship between parish boundaries and watermill sites was an interesting one because 'special arrangements are frequently made to incorporate a mill and its water courses within a particular land unit' (Aston 1985, 42). He cited an example of this from Norton Malreward and Norton Hawkfield, south of Bristol, noting that now the mills have gone, only the parish boundary remains as evidence of their existence. He concluded that 'Such changes should be documented, but few examples seem to be known' (Aston 1985, 42). Aston's suggestion was not widely pursued. However, we have found his hypothesis to be extremely significant, establishing an important general principle.

A major fillip to the study of mills was the publication of Holt's *The Mills of Medieval England* in 1988. This book was the outcome of a four-year project that 'began with the proposition that although mills represented the most complex of the technical innovations of the Middle Ages, they have not hitherto received the detailed attention they deserve from historians' (Holt 1988, ix). Holt considered the number, distribution and value of mills, and focused on ownership, technological developments and economic impact – all themes of great value to our study. However, he said very little about channel engineering and water management.

Ambler's appendix to Ambler and Langdon's paper about early 14th century milling (1994, 43–46) gave fresh insight into the Domesday watermills by examining mill values in real detail, for the first time. He observed that the highest average mill value was in Huntingdonshire, 'a curious feature of the evidence' (1994, 44). To explain this, he followed Holt's argument that this was influenced by a concentration of milling on the major rivers of the Nene and Great Ouse and suggested that the domination of the ecclesiastical estates may have been a factor. He also noted the link between mill values and arable land, and proximity to major towns. Our study investigates this 'curious feature of the evidence' and shows that the explanation is complex and involves a range of factors.

In the first decade of the 2000s, several texts and articles were published that advanced the understanding of the impact of watermills on the landscape, putting forward ideas that we have developed further. Watts' book, *The Archaeology of Mills and Milling* (2002), presented evidence of milling from ancient times using archaeological, documentary, and landscape data. He acknowledged the relative lack of archaeological remains but evaluated thoroughly what does exist, highlighting that watermills were part of the landscape in Roman times and that if they fell into disrepair in the immediate post-Roman period, they were re-established almost certainly by the 7th century. We explore both possibilities as foundations for what we have identified as a watermilling powerhouse on the Great Ouse in medieval times and beyond. Watts addressed the issue of water supply at the end of the Middle Ages, describing a common arrangement of mill-leat/tail race/weir and sluice for supplying water to a mill (Watts 2002, 126–128), which we have developed into a more general model covering the period from the 10th century to the demise of watermilling in the 20th century.

Langdon's *Mills in the Medieval Economy: England 1300–1540* (2004) examined in detail the distribution, economics, and technology of milling during this period. He drew conclusions from a database of mills from 333 manors, considering developments in their socio-economic and political context, which encompassed the Black Death and the Dissolution of the Monasteries. He argued convincingly that milling must be seen as part of the wider manorial economy, *e.g.* fishponds, moats and water control systems (Langdon 2004, 73). His main argument, which our study supports, is that the milling industry from 1300 to 1540 showed consolidation and continuity rather than restructuring. He identified the East Midlands as an anomaly, with the number of mills, and revenues, holding up post-Black Death, as was the case on the Cambridgeshire Great Ouse. He found this 'difficult to explain' (Langdon 2004, 33), and we explore this in Chapter 5. Langdon emphasised the importance of water control systems, although his broader translation of the Latin terms did not allow him to distinguish the full range of component parts of these systems, *e.g.* he translated *stagnum* as millpond (Langdon 2004, 75), whereas it can mean more than this depending on the context.

In 2005, Downward and Skinner published an important paper on the impact of deteriorating river structures linked to watermilling. They emphasized that elements like weirs, sluices, mill-leats, tail races, mill ponds, staunches, and locks are integral to the river system. Removing these can cause bank erosion, block channels, and lead to flooding. They raised important questions for the contemporary management of mill sites and set out three management scenarios, which we evaluate in Chapter 10. They concluded 'it is important to draw attention to these mill sites in view of their continuing deterioration and to highlight the need for the evaluation of the risks associated with deterioration' (Downward and Skinner 2005, 146).

Blair's edited volume, *Waterways and Canal Building in Medieval England* (2007), focused on water transport, but its concepts also apply to channel engineering for watermilling, *e.g.* it is suggested that sometimes navigable waterways were originally mill-leats that have been subsequently adapted (Blair 2007, 6). A central argument, that the impact of this activity on the present-day landscape has been largely unrecognised, was one of the key ideas for our study. Rhodes's chapter in this volume on the physical geography of rivers is of importance to the identification and explanation of river channels that have been modified, or created by, human activity (Rhodes 2007, 133–152). His identification of anastomosing, also known as anabranching, channels in lowland Britain – multi-channelled river systems flowing through fine-grained (silt and clay) sediment, where channel positions are retained over a considerable period – has proved to be a major factor in explaining the success of watermilling on the River Great Ouse in Cambridgeshire, and elsewhere. Of great relevance here is Lewin's 2010 paper, 'Medieval Environmental Impacts and Feedbacks: The Lowland Floodplains of England and Wales', which further explored the link between historically anabranching rivers and watermilling. This is discussed on pages 18–19, but it is worth emphasising that our study has shown that although a river system may look as if it is naturally anabranching on an historic map, that may not be the case. This is because either the multi-channel form is entirely the result of human activity, or because relict anabranching channels have been exploited by human activity.

The value of Lucas's 2014 book *Ecclesiastical Lordship, Seigneurial Power and the Commercialisation of Milling in Medieval England* to our study was an understanding of the significant, but complex and variable, role of religious institutions in the development of milling. He argued that ecclesiastical involvement in the development of the English milling trade was a complex process; that 'Monastic Innovation' was neither universal, nor ubiquitous, involving only some of those houses with the capital to invest; and that ecclesiastical elites did not impose watermills on peasants and townspeople as a means of surplus extraction, *e.g.* up to half of all the milling being conducted throughout England in the late 11th century was being done within the domestic setting of the household, using hand mills and the occasional horse mill. He also drew attention to co-operation between ecclesiastical houses and other significant lords, which we see on the Great Ouse with at least some level of collaboration between the Abbot of Ramsey, the Prior of Huntingdon and the lords of Hemingford Grey. However, he did not list the impact of watermilling on the landscape as one of his four reasons for giving mills more academic attention, which we consider an omission for many reasons, *e.g.* in relation to Lucas's interest in power and commercialisation, the landscape can tell a great deal about the relationship between different landowners.

Keith's 2017 paper 'A study of "Domesday Watermills" in the Cambridgeshire landscape' examined the evidence for the 130 watermills recorded in Cambridgeshire in the Domesday Book. His estimation of waterpower at different sites was a new way of looking at the location and distribution of mills. Keith concluded that there never were that number of separate mills in Cambridgeshire. We reach a different conclusion, *i.e.* that a Domesday 'mill' referred to a small pair of stones requiring minimal power, and that although there were fewer than 130 sites, there was sufficient power for that number of pairs of stones. However, Keith's general approach, with its emphasis on geology and hydrology, has proved helpful to understanding the Domesday mills on the Great Ouse and is to be recommended.

The contributors to Hyer and Hooke's *Water and the Environment in the Anglo-Saxon World* (2017) demonstrated that, to understand Anglo-Saxon watermills, they must be seen alongside the many other uses of rivers, *e.g.* water supply, navigation, fishing and as political boundaries. There are many places in our study where we have taken this into account. Watts's chapter in this volume expanded and updated the material he included in his 2002 book. In particular, he noted that both the documentary and archaeological evidence show that all the principal features of channel engineering – weirs, sluices, dams, leats and ponds – were known in or by late Anglo-Saxon times.

The National Planning Policy Framework is important to our study because watermilling has left a heritage landscape facing many threats. In 2018 Historic England published a report *Historic Watermill Landscapes: A national overview* by Alexander and Edgeworth. Their report focused on the water management systems that deliver water to the mill, rather than the mill building itself. This focus was, and is, very helpful to an understanding of watermilling landscapes because channel modifications often originate some considerable distance from the mill building. The report's purpose was to describe 'the key elements of watermill landscapes, their associations and connections, and … the factors affecting their significance' (Alexander and Edgeworth 2015, 5) to improve the identification and recording of heritage assets and to inform management and planning decisions. In their Chapter 4 the significance of watermilling landscapes was considered, the understanding of which is fundamental to identifying areas for protection. Chapter 6 looked at protection and management issues and set out a range of options. Undoubtedly, the Brampton to Hemingford Grey stretch of our study area meets their significance criteria and would benefit from their recommendations.

Initially, some of the recommendations were taken forward by Historic England commissioning a report on *Historic Watercourses* (Firth and Firth 2020) with the following objectives:

- To seek to increase awareness and integration of the historic character of watercourses in catchment management.
- To examine the scope for engaging members of the public in a better understanding of the historic character of watercourses.
- To develop a method for identifying the historic character of watercourses within a catchment, using the Dorset Stour as a case study.
- To disseminate information on the historic character of watercourses to heritage managers, watercourse managers and the general public.

Firth and Firth developed a method for collecting and recording data that involved interested members of the public, *e.g.* local history societies. They defined and presented watermilling landscapes as Historic Water Polygons (HWPs) in a Geographical Information System (GIS). The advantage of HWPs is that they encompass all heritage features associated with a mill as a single unit, *i.e.* the mill and all relevant watercourses and water management features. We have explored and developed this method (see pages 140–144) and strongly advocate its use. However, there is yet to be a wholesale adoption of this, or the other recommendations in the 2018 report.

The most recent book to be published about mills on the River Great Ouse is Howes's *The Water and Steam Mills of Huntingdonshire's Great Ouse* (2020). He wrote mainly about the 'known' watermills and steam mills – the only 'lost' mills he covered being the ones at Godmanchester and Hemingford Grey. He provided a great deal of detail, making extensive use of the publication *The Miller* from the early years of the 20th century. However, his focus was largely on the mill buildings and the millers themselves, and not on the landscape, so we have been able to add a great deal to this history.

A final work of significance to our study is Boardman and Foster's research into the implications of removing barriers such as weirs, dams and sluices to achieve 'free-flowing rivers'. This was published in 2023 and reflected growing concerns about flood management in a time of climate change and the desire to re-create 'natural' landscapes. Few barriers have been removed in the UK but the process is well underway in the USA and Europe. This has implications for the preservation and management of historic watermilling landscapes, which we explore in Chapter 10.

Our study builds on all this previous research. In doing so, we provide an account of the growth and development of watermilling on one of the country's main rivers, and its impact on the landscape, as it flows through the county of Cambridgeshire. However, our findings have a wider significance to other lowland river valleys, and to watermilling landscapes in general. We will show that the lasting impact of watermilling on the landscape, on parish boundaries and on the growth and development of river navigation, has not been fully appreciated. We will, for the first time, give a full explanation of Huntingdonshire's pre-eminence as a watermilling county in the Domesday Book, and in so doing help with a better understanding of Domesday's recording of mills. And we demonstrate an urgent need for greater awareness of our post-watermilling landscapes. Whilst, on a practical level their management is critical to flood control, these landscapes are also a major heritage asset, and in their unaltered, conserved form are a record of past activity as valuable as any manuscript.

Method and main sources

The research for this study was carried out between September 2021 and February 2025. It draws on many disciplines including local history, historical geography, geomorphology and archaeology, and a range of skills including remote sensing, the use of GIS (Geographic Information Systems), statistical analysis, palaeography, the transcription and translation of historical documents and a range of fieldwork techniques. Key sources of evidence are described below, together with a brief comment on their strengths and limitations.

A LiDAR (Light Detection and Ranging) map was created specifically for this project, using composite DTM (Digital Terrain Model) data at a 1 m spatial resolution, available from the National LiDAR Programme (https://www.data.gov.uk/dataset/f0db0249-f17b-4036-9e65-309148c97ce4/national-lidar-programme). The great advantage of LiDAR is to show the ground surface with the vegetation removed. The data was manipulated to emphasise small-scale features, which enabled former channels, not visible on OS (Ordnance Survey) maps and not easily visible on the ground, to be identified. However, there is a vertical accuracy of ±15 cm and, more significantly, features less than 1 m in size cannot be seen.

Aerial photographs from the 1940s through to the 2020s helped reveal and/or confirm many of the relict channels described and explained in this study.

However, their usefulness is affected by a range of factors, including the quality of the film and camera equipment, the weather conditions, the time of day, the altitude of the flight and the ground conditions (time of year, soil moisture content). And it is to be noted that the absence of a feature on an aerial photograph does not mean that it is not present on the ground.

Historic maps

Maps are a rich source of historical evidence for the landscape historian, but they need careful evaluation and have to be placed in context with other sources such as documentation. And frequently, maps can be as much a disappointment as they can be a treasure, especially when it is found that the purpose for which they were drawn does not include the object of research. However, our research enjoyed the great good fortune of an early 16th century map, drawn in detail specifically to illustrate the river and its channels.

'Huntyngdon & Godmanchester'. Plan of the River Ouse and waterways between Huntingdon and St Ives bridge, 1515 (TNA MPCC 1/9). This is the earliest map of (a part of) the river in our study area (see page 91). It is a remarkable map but must be interpreted with care because scale and direction are extremely, and deliberately, varied. It was a legal document, drawn to explain and support the submission by complainants to the Court of the Duchy of Lancaster about the alleged misuse of the river and resultant flooding caused by the watermills of the Abbot of Ramsey and the Prior of Huntingdon. However, almost all the watercourses shown on the map can be found in the modern landscape, or on the LiDAR, and this gives a high degree of confidence in the detail shown. These watercourses are difficult to survey on the ground – further evidence that the map was drawn by a skilled cartographer who responded well to his brief. This map, combined with its accompanying large amount of legal evidence and documentation, was fundamental to our assessment of information on later maps, and was pivotal to the research project overall.

John Speed: County map of Huntingdonshire (1611–12). This map is much too small in scale to provide detailed information about all the watercourses making up the river system. However, it does show that the multi-channel form of the river between Brampton and St Ives was in existence by the beginning of the 17th century. The accompanying inset map of Huntingdon locates the town's watermill, with a mill-leat and tail race.

William Gordon: Map of the County of Huntingdon, 1730 (KAcc4577/2/11). Gordon's map is the first large scale map of the county. It shows several watercourses and locates some (but not all) watermills, but there are significant limitations to its use. The main focus of the map is the road network and the principal county 'seats'. As a result, the mapping of the river and associated watercourses is incomplete and often inaccurate.

Thomas Jefferys: Map of Huntingdonshire 1768 (KHAC4/4347). This map was commissioned – not surveyed – by Jefferys, the leading map supplier of this period. It was drawn at a scale of two inches to the mile. The map is more accurate than Gordon's and provides invaluable detail, including the location of some (but not all) the mill sites. However, it does not record all the watercourses, and makes errors that can be seen repeated in subsequent maps based on this survey.

Inclosure Award maps, Tithe maps and Terriers, and Estate maps. The majority of land adjoining the Great Ouse in Huntingdonshire was enclosed by Acts of Parliament between the 1760s and the first decade of the 19th century. The Award maps that accompanied the Acts are all available, but some only in draft form. Several provide field name evidence and show useful information about the form of the river and its many channels at the time (KDMC/312, KDMC/325, KDMC/344, KHP64/26/1). Very few tithe maps and terriers have survived, and of these none contain field names relating to watermills. The only surviving relevant estate maps are those of The Earl of Sandwich's estate. The maps for Hartford and St Neots give little information, but those of Brampton help to explain 18th and 19th century developments of watermilling near Huntingdon (KHACo/223/1).

Plan of The River Great Ouze from Bedford to Earith Bridge: Lenny & Croft 1834 (R1/478). This splendid large-scale map (12 chains to the inch) was commissioned to identify the ownership of riverside land belonging to the Proprietors of the Navigation, Sir Thomas Cullum and Richard Francklin, who had rights to tolls for the use of the river and its locks. The map accurately locates and gives the purpose of the main weirs and sluices, *e.g.* it identifies those which functioned as a 'back gate' (safety valve) for the watermills. However, because the focus of the map is limited to the land adjoining the river, there are no details of the watercourses as they cross the floodplain.

OS (Ordnance Survey) maps (National Library of Scotland https://maps.nls.uk/os/). The first large-scale OS maps of the county date from the mid-1880s. They give an accurate and detailed record of the river, its floodplain, watercourses, mills, sluices, weirs and locks. These maps are of great value, especially as they were drawn shortly before the major decline in watermilling. But, as with any map, they cannot detail everything; for example, the function of an intervention, or whether a sluice acted as a back gate. Several other OS map series were consulted, with the 1949 1:25 000 colour series being particularly useful because it defines water features clearly, and was prepared before large-scale gravel extraction interrupted the landscape of the Great Ouse valley.

British Geological Survey 1:50 000 Drift Edition for Huntingdon, 1975. This map is essential to understanding the development of watermilling. Channel creation, maintenance and modification are all highly dependent on the superficial geology and, especially, on the extent of the alluvial floodplain and the river gravels. The map's major limitation is its scale. For example, the precise boundary between alluvium and gravel can be very complex on the ground, yet very significant to how the floodplain can be managed, but the map often fails to be able to show this clearly.

Fieldwork and archaeology

Extensive fieldwork was carried out to locate and observe water courses and control mechanisms, such as sluices and weirs. This was particularly helpful in establishing direction of channel flow – which was often not as might be presumed - and in confirming features identified on the LiDAR, aerial photographs and historic maps. However, not all locations were accessible and the time of year/degree of vegetation also hindered the recognition of features.

Archaeological investigations and remains along the river in the study area are disappointingly few. There is no local stone in this part of Huntingdonshire, so it is presumed that the early watermills were almost entirely wooden structures, as were the sluices and other water control measures. Consequently, there is almost nothing surviving from earlier than the 18th century. Millstones, either intact or recycled as building material, could be expected to remain, but none from the medieval period or earlier have been found *in situ* along this stretch of river. The Cambridgeshire Historic Environment Record has compiled the known data, and this has been checked for finds and investigations. Recent reports from rescue archaeology have also been researched, *e.g.* those associated with the building of the new A14, which crosses the Great Ouse valley between the watermill sites at Brampton and Buckden/Offord D'Arcy.

Documentary evidence

As with the 1515 map, our research had the good fortune to find early, (largely) reliable documentary evidence. This begins with the Domesday Book and its overall account of mill numbers, ownership and values. Other main groups of documentation are shown below – and the largest of these is litigation. The watermills along the Great Ouse in Huntingdonshire were central to innumerable arguments about water rights, navigation, flooding and channel maintenance – and this persisted for at least eight centuries. A considerable amount of this documentation has survived.

The Domesday Book, 1086. The Domesday Book is an unrivalled source for understanding medieval watermilling. It not only gives us a unique insight into the period immediately after the Norman Conquest, but also presents a picture of late Anglo-Saxon England because, for example, the 6,000 plus mills listed in the Domesday Book had been built over a period in the preceding decades and centuries. Commissioned by William I, it has been suggested that the Domesday Book's purpose was more than an instrument of taxation (Higham and Ryan 2015, 437). For example, it includes non-taxable assets such as ploughlands, but this focus on agricultural production makes sense given the context of the survey, *i.e.* the need to supply an army in the face of a reported invasion from Denmark. For a study of water, and waterpower, it is invaluable because the agents who carried out the survey had a standardised list of questions, which included 'How many mills and fishponds?', reflecting the importance of these assets to the late Anglo-Saxon and early Norman economy.

It is beyond the scope of this book to give an account of the rich seam of research by historical geographers based on the Domesday Book since H.C. Darby's pioneering paper 'Domesday Woodland in East Anglia' (1934). However, it is important to set out the Domesday Book's main limitations for this study. Specifically, a 'mill' is not defined; value is not always given in monetary terms, *e.g.* it is sometimes presented as a combination of cash and 'sticks' of eels from the millpond; the values are rounded; fractions of mills reflect shared ownership, which has resulted in some duplication of records; and not all mills were valued in Essex, Suffolk and Norfolk. London, Winchester, Bristol, Tamworth, Northumberland, Durham and much of north-west England were not covered by the Domesday Book.

The statistical analysis presented in this book comes with its own limitations. It is based on the raw data provided by The Hull Domesday Project, which produced a freely available electronic and fully encoded text of Great and Little Domesday, a database of major Domesday statistics for all people and places, and a scholarly commentary on all matters of interest in the 25,000 entries. In 2010 the data sets were made freely available online and they can be downloaded from the UK Data Service (https://opendomesday.org/about/). The study documentation available on this website provides an invaluable guide to interpreting the database and understanding what was, and what was not, recorded in the Domesday Book, and how accurate it is. For our study, the data sets were imported into an Excel spreadsheet for analysis, with care being taken to remove duplicate entries. This has allowed a range of questions to be addressed in a way that has not been done before, *e.g.* 'Were the number of mills in Huntingdonshire more or less as you would expect for the county's amount of ploughland?' or 'Did proximity to a town increase the value of a mill?' However, it is important to note that the statistical analysis, *e.g.* the Excel-produced correlation coefficients in Table 4.3, page 55, use the figures recorded by the agents in the Domesday Book. They are therefore subject to the limitations described above and can only be an indicator to be used alongside other evidence. A correlation coefficient may give the impression of precision and certainty, but it requires careful interpretation.

The Hundred Rolls and Quo Warranto Pleas from the 1270s, the Huntingdonshire Justice Rolls 1286-88. These documents were written in Latin, and some extracts relating to Godmanchester and river navigation were translated by Fox in the early 19th century (Fox 1831). New translations have revised our insights into the activities that were taking place, and their consequences. However, the quality of the Latin in some of the original documents is variable, both in terms of its grammar and vocabulary, and this limits the interpretations that can be made.

Charters and Manorial Records of the Abbey of Ramsey. Founded in about 969 and dissolved in 1539, Ramsey Abbey had extensive landholdings in Huntingdonshire and further afield in East Anglia. It was ranked as the fourth wealthiest ecclesiastical body in England. Watermills at three sites on the Great Ouse were owned by Ramsey Abbey, and another site had close links. The surviving records of the Abbey's charters and (often fragmentary) manorial and court records give invaluable, although too frequently only scanty, details of the organisation and finances of medieval milling.

Petition to the Duchy of Lancaster, 1515 (TNA DL R3/23). An archive of material in the National Records Office represents the culmination of extensive disputes from the 15th century between the mill owners and those using the river for navigation and its floodplain for farming. The documents are written in English but require skilled transcription and interpretation. The vocabulary used to describe interventions such as sluices and weirs is inconsistent and often obscure, leaving the text open to alternative interpretations. Historians have long been aware of the final decrees from this and other 16th century court cases, but it would appear that few have examined the large body of testimonies and evidence and have instead relied on summaries contained in the decrees. For the 1515 case, the papers are not catalogued in chronological or sequential order but are arranged in alphabetical order of witness names. They are sandwiched between papers from a case of 1533 and, although the latter helpfully recite some of the 1515 outcomes, the Duchy papers require some untangling in order to follow the sequence of the 1515 legal case. The papers are numbered and we have provided these when we have referred to this source, but only the main reference (DL R3/23) is searchable in the National Archives catalogue.

Deeds of Covenant from the 1700s and 1800s (KBR2/BOX1/6, KBR2/BOX1/13). Disputes, and the need for agreement between competing uses of the river and its floodplain, have left an informative although incomplete trail of developments in the early modern period. These Deeds of Covenant are legal documents, written in English, but because they are only concerned with the interventions and channel modifications that caused a dispute, they give an incomplete record of control mechanisms and their impact.

The Appeal in the House of Lords. L T Simpson v The County of Huntingdonshire, 1904 (KBLC5/5 1,2,3,4 and KHAC1/1737). This complicated case concerning the Navigation and rights to levy tolls extended over almost ten years. The transcripts of the various hearings contain a vast amount of legal case notes, questioning and evidence with intense discussion of precedent and rights, ranging from the statements in the 13th century Hundred Rolls to the grievances of the 19th century.

Photographic and artistic images

A few artistic images were made of scenes along the river from the early 18th century through to the mid-19th century, but from *c.* 1880 these became abundant – first of the area between Huntingdon and St Ives, as we explain in Chapter 9, and later for the whole river. Photographic images, including postcards, proliferated from the same time and the watermills were a popular scene, with those at Houghton and Hemingford being very well documented both internally and externally.

CHAPTER TWO

The physical and historical background

The River Great Ouse rises at Syresham, near Brackley, in Northamptonshire and flows 240 km to The Wash near King's Lynn. It enters Cambridgeshire to the south of St Neots and flows northwards to Brampton, largely occupying a single channel (Fig. 2.1). Between Brampton and Earith the river runs eastwards, occupying several channels. Until the end of the 13th century, the river swung northwards at Earith in a single channel, forming the old county boundary between Huntingdonshire and Cambridgeshire (Summers 1973, 12). Since then, it has been diverted eastwards to Stretham, where it turns northwards to Ely, Downham Market and on to King's Lynn.

In this area the advantages of the physical environment for watermilling outweigh the disadvantages. The two main disadvantages are that firstly the Great Ouse's catchment is one of the driest in the country, which can result in very low river levels, particularly in the summer months. Secondly, its gradient is very gentle, *e.g.* the river falls only 12 m in the 75 km in which it flows across

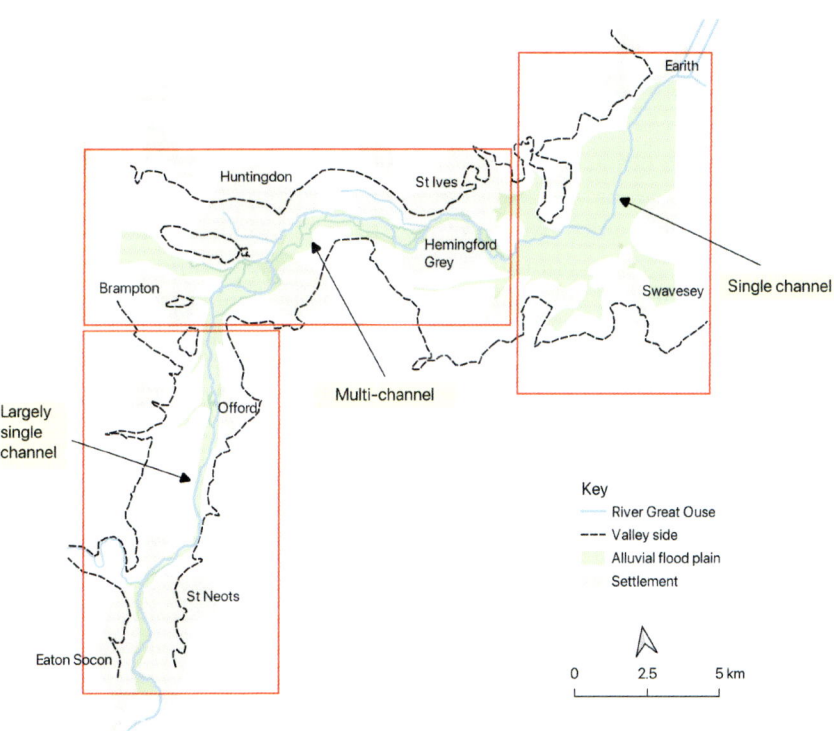

FIGURE 2.1. The River Great Ouse in Cambridgeshire: single and multi-channel sections

the county. The advantages are that the underlying rocks are mainly impermeable Jurassic clays and consequently, rain that is not intercepted or taken up by vegetation, or evaporated, finds its way into the river system. Also, at 8,380 square km this is the fourth largest water basin in England. As a result, the river has sufficient volume to generate considerable waterpower, *e.g.* downstream of Offord it has been estimated that there is a minimum discharge of a more than adequate 9.5 cumecs for 95% of the year (NRA Anglian 93). The careful management of water levels maximises this potential energy. Raising the height of a river by constructing dams, weirs or sluices increases the rate of flow immediately downstream. The force of a river is the product of its rate of flow and its volume, so even a small increase in height when there is a large volume of water, as there is on the Great Ouse, results in a significant increase in power.

The physical environment has conferred a particular advantage on the west–east stretch of the Great Ouse between Brampton and St Ives. The river's change of direction is the result of glacial diversion of drainage. In the Anglian glacial advance, approximately 475,000–425,000 years BP, the entire area was covered with a deposit of boulder clay. The subsequent Tottenhill glacial advance, approximately 160,000 years BP, pushed this material into a series of ridges and troughs, running west to east (Gibbard, West & Hughes 2018, 18). The River Great Ouse's northerly flow was obstructed by one of these ridges and it was forced eastwards until the ridge ran out near Earith. The trough created by the glacial advance is wider than the floodplain upstream; the average width of the alluvial section of the floodplain is 0.61 km between Brampton and Hemingford Grey, compared with 0.37 km between St Neots and Brampton (Fig. 2.1). This greater width has allowed the river to meander more freely across its floodplain.

In a lowland environment the resultant river pattern, with channels joining and re-joining, is characteristic of an 'anastomosing' or 'anabranching' system. The term anastomosing was first proposed by Whitcomb (1947, 64–68) to draw a distinction with braided river patterns. Anastomosing or anabranching rivers form in low energy environments with gentle gradients and fine sediment, *e.g.* sand and clay. Braided rivers have the same multi-channel pattern, but they form in high energy environments with steep gradients, a seasonal flow, such as that associated with snow melt, and a large load of coarse-grained sediment, *e.g.* sand, gravel and boulders. Makaske refined this definition and examined the causes of anastomosing river systems (2001, 189). He demonstrated that they are formed by avulsions – a diversion of the river's flow by an obstacle, *e.g.* a tree stump, or a lens of more resistant gravel. Of particular significance to watermilling landscapes is that the individual channels of an anastomosing river are highly stable and long-lasting, *i.e.* they offer a degree of permanence that makes their development economically viable. It also means that a newly cut channel will retain its form except in the most extreme flood event. Rhodes (2007, 135) identified that anastomosing or anabranching river patterns share characteristics with the rivers of lowland Britain. However, he urged caution in explaining these landscapes because they are currently a matter of research interest, concluding that, 'it is possible that the degree of human modification of these systems has been previously underestimated'. Lewin's study of lowland floodplains in England and Wales, in which he noted a strong association between 'historically anabranching' lowland river systems, *i.e.* systems that were anabranching in the past but no longer do so, and the development of watermilling in the medieval period, supports this view (2010, 268–277 and 285–286). He identified 17 sections of lowland river floodplain in England with these characteristics, including the Great Ouse between Huntingdon and St Ives. The combined length of these sections is 146.87 km, a small fraction of the length of our lowland rivers, emphasising that this stretch of our study area is a very particular environment.

However, although a multi-channel form is shown on the earliest map of this stretch of river, from 1515, our research shows that it is not a simple case of watermilling occupying a pre-existing landscape. Rather, watermilling adopted and adapted an anabranching system that may itself have been superimposed on the relict geomorphology of a high energy braided system at the end of the last glacial period, approximately 11,500 years ago, or even earlier (Rhodes 2007, 136). Documentary and landscape evidence shows that, prior to the 13th century, the river was largely confined to a single channel, with today's river pattern the result of human activity on an historically (*i.e.* previously) anabranching system. Four processes can be identified: modifying existing channels (*e.g.* increasing the depth of Hemingford Grey Backwater, pages 66–67); extending channels to connect with the main river (*e.g.* joining Cook's Stream to the main river, pages 68–70); excavating channels that follow the course of relict channels that perhaps only had water in them at the wettest time of the year (*e.g.* incorporating Portholme Brook into the watermilling landscape in the 18th century, pages 115–118); and digging new channels (*e.g.* the Abbot's *rivulus*, pages 64–66). Relict channels that only occasionally have water in them can still be found on the floodplain, *e.g.* Figure 2.2. These would have been easier to dig than a new channel and explains why 'artificial' channels may have a 'semi-natural' form.

Downstream of Hemingford Grey the river reverts to a single channel. Here, the valley floor is covered by river gravels for a stretch of 2 km, to St Ives Bridge, at which point alluvium again occupies the central portion of the floodplain. This is because the northward movement of the river between Hemingford Grey and St Ives has come up against the southward extension of a thin but resistant band of limestone, known as the St Ives or Elsworth rock. One consequence is the unusually steep slopes for this part of the Great Ouse valley, rising to a height of 25 m, that form How Hill, which runs from the village of Houghton to St Ives. The other consequence is that because the river's northward movement has been impeded, its available energy has been concentrated into a smaller area, making the deposition of alluvium less likely. Downstream of St Ives the river's gradient becomes gentler as it spills out into The Fens. Here, it has a wide alluvial floodplain but has lost its anabranching characteristics.

FIGURE 2.2. A relict channel with flood water near Buckden Mill, 2024

Before the construction of the Denver Sluice in 1651, a tidal influence was felt in St Ives, and occasionally further upstream (Summers 1973, 18). Even a weak tidal flow reduces the available power in a slow-moving river, and this helps to explain why only one watermill has been identified downstream of the former Huntingdonshire/Cambridgeshire County boundary, at Swavesey.

The physical environment of the River Great Ouse valley presents 'virtually no serious physical barriers to movement and communication' and 'It is not surprising therefore to find evidence of human occupation from an early date' (Green 2000, 15). A substantial number of artefacts have been recovered from the river gravels dating between 130,000 and 40,000 BP (Reynolds 2000, 42). The temperature recovered rapidly after 10,000 BP at the end of the last glacial period and by 7,000 BP the natural vegetation of oak, elm and hazel woodland on the heavier clay soils, and alder carr with willow on the margins of the floodplain, was established (Scaife 2000, 19–20). There is extensive evidence for Mesolithic, Neolithic, Bronze Age and Iron Age activity (West *et al.* 2024, Chapter 1).

However, the evidence suggests that it was during the Roman Period that the Great Ouse valley became important for grain production, which was ultimately to lead to its pre-eminence in watermilling. The excavations carried out in advance of the building of a new section of the A14 in Cambridgeshire showed evidence for an increase in the scale of arable cultivation during the Roman period, particularly at certain sites (West *et al.* 2024, Chapter 4). The main cereal crop found was spelt wheat. This is consistent with a national trend in the south and east of England during the early Roman period, which saw an increase in the cultivation of spelt wheat at the expense of emmer wheat. Spelt wheat can be grown in a wider range of soils than emmer wheat and this is 'understood as a move towards more extensive cultivation, with larger areas of land cultivated with lower inputs of labour and manure' (Lodwick 2017, 17–18). At Earith, only five miles downstream of St Ives, a 'port-village' from the Roman period has been excavated, with a canal-side granary (Evans 2013, Chapters 3 & 4), and it is probable that surplus wheat was taken downstream to this facility before export to the wider Roman empire. There is also archaeological evidence that Roman Godmanchester (*Durogivutum*) was a centre of agricultural activity.

The A14 excavations also provided evidence that the River Great Ouse valley was part of the transformation in arable practices in the 8th century that led to agricultural surpluses (West *et al.* 2024, Chapter 5). Free-threshing and bread wheat replaced spelt wheat (which is more difficult to process, requiring significant drying, often in an oven, before the grain can be removed from the husk). The mouldboard plough was adopted, which allowed heavier soils to be ploughed. There is also extensive evidence of ridge and furrow, a ploughing technique which improved drainage and enabled arable crops to be grown on land at risk of occasional flooding. Exactly when this was introduced is not known. However, some of the ridge and furrow in the study area dates from at least the end of the 11th century because its form has been preserved, for example, in the street pattern of St Ives (Burn-Murdoch 2009, 36–46). Circumstantial evidence – the agrarian reforms under the Danelaw, the involvement of the royal estates, and the establishment of watermilling from at least the 960s – suggests that it could be even earlier in date.

By the time of the Domesday Survey in 1086, Huntingdonshire was a prosperous county specialising in arable production, with an above average population density of 20–30 per square kilometre (Hodgen 1939, 275). Huntingdon was its only town, with a population of about 2,000 (Darby 1972, 375). The figures in Table 2.1 have many caveats and should be seen as indicators, rather than directly comparable statistics (see, for example, Darby 1972, 323–328), but broad comparisons are clear. The average value of Huntingdonshire's manors (£6.56) was greater than for all its neighbouring counties, sometimes significantly so. This figure was only a little lower than the value in 1066 (£7.13) and although this figure hides some significant variations between manors, it shows that overall Huntingdonshire avoided the steep decline in prosperity experienced by some counties. The average number of ploughlands and ploughs per manor were also greater when compared with all neighbouring counties. Ploughland is a good indication of the importance of arable farming, which in turn was dominated by grain production. The figures also hint at the county's potential with the average number of ploughs being lower than the average amount of ploughland – if all the land available for ploughing is being used these two figures should match but if the number of ploughs is lower it suggests that there is land available to be brought into arable production.

County	Average value per manor (£)	Average number of ploughlands per manor	Average number of ploughs
Huntingdonshire	6.56	8.3	7.35
Cambridgeshire	4.57	4.26	3.77
Norfolk	3.29	N/R	3.16*
Suffolk	2.4	N/R	4.1*
Essex	5.62	N/R	N/R
Hertfordshire	5.0	5.4	2.2
Bedfordshire	3.0	4.4	3.89
Northamptonshire	2.06	5.0	N/R
Lincolnshire	3.95	3.48	2.96

TABLE 2.1. Average value, ploughland and total number of ploughs per manor 1086

Source: Domesday Book Online (raw data), Palmer, J. and Slater, G. at opendomesday.org.

Ploughland: the amount of land which could be ploughed by an eight-person plough team in the course of a year.

N/R not recorded

* partially recorded

In conclusion, the physical and human geography of the River Great Ouse valley in the 10th and 11th centuries created the potential for the development of watermilling during the later Middle Ages and into the modern period.

Parish boundaries

Most parishes in England were established between 950 and 1150 as the area supporting a church and its minister through the payment of tithes (Winchester 2000, 13). Parish boundaries were defined in charters, not always precisely, but it was not until the late 18th century that most had been mapped (Pounds 2000, 78). The boundaries often followed physical features, especially watercourses (Firth and Firth 2023, 3). One explanation for a current boundary deviating from a river or stream is that the course of the waterway has changed. An example is on the River Ribble, near Rathmell, where the parish boundary follows the course of a former meander, known as The Crook, which has been 'cut off' by the main river to form an oxbow lake (Winchester 2000, 62–64). Another explanation is that the boundary has been changed because of a later development associated with the parish. Aston (1985, 42) noted a special relationship between watermill sites and parish boundaries: 'the association of boundaries with mills means that either that the mills were in existence when the boundaries were defined (thus indicating an increased number of Anglo-Saxon mill sites and a more extensive interference with river courses than we formerly thought) or that special arrangements were made to alter parish boundaries when new mills were built. Such changes should be documented, but few examples seem to be known.'

Along the River Great Ouse in Cambridgeshire, the parish boundaries generally follow the middle of the main channel. However, there are several places where they deviate – bisecting an island, or following a very minor water course,

FIGURE 2.3. A horizontal waterwheel, Orkney Dounby Click Mill (artist's impression)

FIGURE 2.4. A horizontal waterwheel, Orkney Dounby Click Mill, 2022

or crossing the river onto the neighbouring parish's land – before returning to the main river channel. As we investigated these, we concluded that, invariably, this deviation incorporated a significant parish asset, *e.g.* a ford, an osier bed, or a watermill and/or its associated leats and backwaters. Of these assets, the watermill and its related channels were by far the most frequent in these sites.

Moreover, in every case that we examined, the deviation was not because the river had changed course. This was such a reliable finding, that a boundary deviation became an immediate alert for the location of a watermill. This 'general principle' helped greatly with finding the location of long-lost watermills, and in explaining the development of channel engineering for watermilling in the medieval period. It was, of course, necessary to consider other possibilities for these deviations, but our analysis along the Cambridgeshire Great Ouse shows beyond reasonable doubt that the 'general principle' holds true. We are confident from a preliminary analysis that it applies along rivers in other lowland valleys and will help identify and understand the history and development of watermill sites. A series of examples is set out in the following chapters to illustrate this finding.

Watermill terminology

Rynne (2018, 2–6) details the two main types of watermill: horizontal-wheeled and vertical-wheeled. Horizontal-wheeled mills turn the upper millstone without gearing via a vertical drive-shaft, whereas in vertical-wheeled mills the axle is set horizontally, and gearing is required to turn the millstone. Horizontal-wheeled mills are smaller and easier to construct but they deliver less power. A small millpond is created and a leat dug to take the water to the mill. The water is directed onto the wheel via a large chute that used to be

FIGURE 2.5. The vertical undershot waterwheel at Houghton Mill, 2025

made from a hollowed-out tree-trunk. In England, the evidence from the small number of Anglo-Saxon watermills that have been found and excavated suggests that both horizontal and vertical watermills were constructed. An example is Tamworth where two generations of a horizontal-wheeled watermill have been excavated, covering a 200-year period from the early to the mid-9th century (Watts 2002, 77). However, they appear to have been more common in Ireland in the medieval period and they have remained in use into modern times in Scotland, Orkney (Figs 2.3 and 2.4) and Shetland. Vertical-wheeled mills are more difficult to construct but they deliver more power (Fig. 2.5). They can be undershot, with the water striking the paddles at the bottom of the wheel, overshot with the water falling onto the top of the wheel, or breast-shot with the water striking the middle of the wheel. Overshot wheels deliver the most power, but they can only be built where there is a difference in height of about

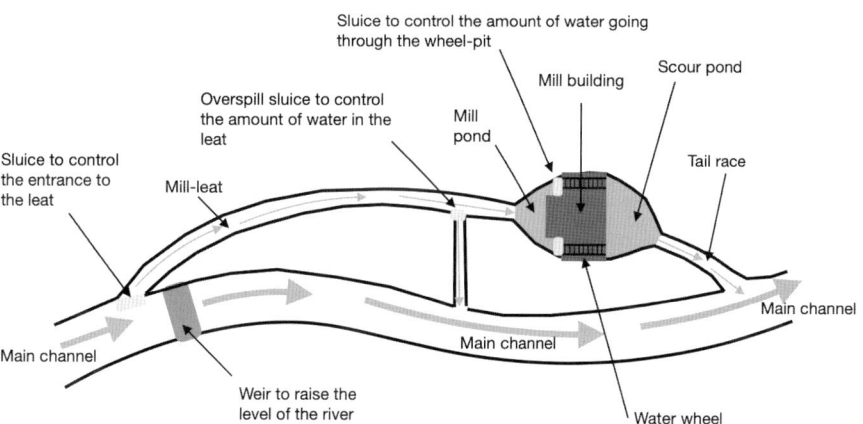

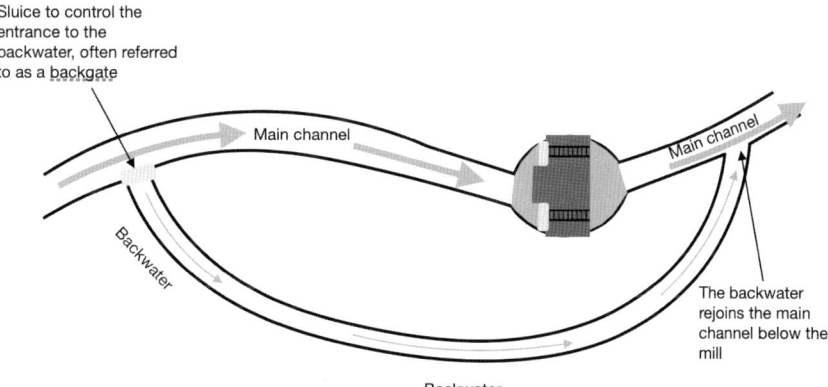

FIGURE 2.6. Watermill terminology

2 m between the upstream and downstream channels, or where this difference can be created, so they are generally only found in areas of steep relief. Undershot wheels deliver less power, but they can be built in low-lying areas. We can be confident that the watermills constructed on the Great Ouse would have had undershot wheels because of the valley's gentle gradient.

An essential pre-requisite for the successful operation of a watermill is control of the flow of the river or stream. This invariably requires channel modification and management which is achieved by digging leats (channels to and from the river) and ponds, and by constructing dams, weirs and sluices. These can be configured in several ways depending on the physical geography and the requirements of the mill; two possibilities are shown in Figure 2.6.

CHAPTER THREE

The first watermills: the Roman period to 1066

The earliest evidence of watermilling for grinding grain dates to the 3rd century BC in Byzantium and Alexandria, with the earliest written description, by a Roman engineer Vitruvius, in his book *de Architectura* of *c.* 25 BC (Watts 2002, 47–48). By the 2nd century AD the technology was highly sophisticated, as seen by the industrial mill complex in Barbegal in southern France; here the archaeological remains show a system of 16 overshot wheels aligned down a hillside in two parallels of eight. Such a system had the capacity to produce considerable amounts of flour – perhaps for a town but now thought for the production of non-perishable ships' biscuits ('hard tack') to provision Rome's Mediterranean fleet (Sürmelihindi 2018).

In England, there is archaeological evidence for Roman Period watermills at Haltwistle in Northumberland, Ickham in Kent (dating from *c.* AD 150) and six other possible sites, including Redlands Farm Villa at Stanwick on the River Nene (Watts 2002, 50–55). The Redlands Farm Villa was built on a sand island next to two water channels and during the first half of the 2nd century AD a rectangular building may have been a watermill, although no certain millstones were recovered (Allen *et al.* 2018). Stanwick is only a few miles from the River Great Ouse, so settlements, such as Roman Godmanchester (*Durovigutum*), would have been aware of this development.

Banfield (2023, 3) maps the location of twenty possible mill structures, with a greater number in the south of England, which could have been powered by humans, animals or water. Of the 29 millstones from the Roman Period found during the excavations for the 2017–2020 A14 road upgrade, 17 were from the Great Ouse valley near Brampton and Godmanchester. However, Shaffrey (2024, 22–23) concludes that it is likely that they came from animal-powered mills, although 'Larger watermills probably also existed in the region, and these remains should be searched for'. To date, therefore, there is no direct evidence of watermilling on the Great Ouse in the Roman Period, but Roman Godmanchester must be a prime place to search. Godmanchester was established as a military station (*Durogivutum*). Watermills have been identified at other military sites – Haltwistle and Chesters. There is evidence of channel engineering at Godmanchester that could be Roman in date (see below). The number of millstones excavated close by indicates a centralisation of flour production (Shaffrey 2024, 23). Excavations within the Roman settlement have shown that it was a significant centre of agricultural activity with evidence of multiple granaries and corn drying facilities (Haigh 1984, 8; Lyons 2019, 141–160).

There is a lack of direct evidence for continuity in the use of watermills in the immediate post-Roman Period, although Watts notes that 'if there was no continuity in the use of the watermill from the Roman Period, then it was fairly quickly re-established' (2017, 168). The earliest documentary evidence is from a charter issued by Aethelberht, king of Kent, in 762 (Watts 2002, 72). The earliest archaeological evidence of an Anglo-Saxon watermill is from Kingsbury, Old Windsor, on the River Thames. The remains have been interpreted as two vertical undershot waterwheels separated by a spillway channel (Watts 2017, 172). The mill was fed by a leat over 1 km in length, which took water from the River Thames. The preliminary date for the structure was 9th century, but it may have been earlier because dendrochronological dating of the base timbers indicates that they were felled at the end of the 7th century.

Documentary evidence records watermills from the 760s onwards (Watts 2017, 170–179). Little is known about the mill buildings from this period because only nine Anglo-Saxon sites have been identified by archaeological excavation. The evidence suggests that they were timber-framed with wooden cladding, and were thatched, and probably required major rebuilding every 20–30 years (Watts 2017, 183).

On the River Great Ouse, the first reference to watermilling is in the Chronicles of Ramsey Abbey (DeWindt 1976) where it is recorded that Houghton Mill was given by Earl Ailwin to Ramsey Abbey at its foundation in 969; therefore, watermilling must have begun (or recommenced) before that date. Hart (2000, Section 30) suggests that Huntingdonshire had become prosperous under the Eastern Danelaw (AD 870–917), with a revolution in land tenure, agrarian reform and the establishment of new trade routes. He concludes that, 'the overall picture at this period is one of innovation and bustling activity' and that 'because of their successful agrarian system, the Danelaw shires became wealthier than their English counterparts in Wessex and Mercia' (Hart 2000, 30). An increase in agricultural output at this time would have created a need for greater milling capacity, and this may have been met by constructing watermills. Certainly, it is difficult to explain how the Huntingdonshire Domesday mills could have achieved their comparatively high values without a considerable period of development before that time. Following King Edward the Elder's defeat of the Danish army at Huntingdon and Wistow in 917, large tracts of Danish-held areas came under royal authority. And, given that there was a watermill at Houghton in the 960s, it is highly likely that there would also have been watermills on the nearby royal estates of Brampton, Huntingdon and Godmanchester, where there would have been the required capital for investment. Raftis (1957, 5) agrees with the overall organisation and prosperity of pre-Domesday Huntingdonshire. Of the non-royal estates which were given to Ramsey Abbey: 'the accounts of the Ramsey foundation bear out very strongly this impression of a well-established agrarian economy in the

Huntingdonshire of the late 10th century.' The lands and estates that the Abbey received came 'clearly established, named, hidaged and sufficiently well-defined so that the transfers did not necessitate the elaborate descriptive detail of newly staked-out regions'.

In the Anglo-Saxon period watermills were a high-status asset. The mills and their water control systems were such a costly and sophisticated enterprise to build that they were located predominantly on the most important estates – those of the Crown or the major religious houses. These estates would have had the financial and human resources to maintain the mill and ensure its profitability. It is thus unsurprising that one of the earliest watermills for which there is archaeological evidence is on the site of what is thought to be a royal residence at Kingsbury, Old Windsor (see above). Gould *et al.* (2025) demonstrate the emergence of 'lordly estates' in the 10th century. This was part of a Europe-wide process with authority and status being structured around personal wealth and the demonstration of that to peers, rather than kinship. The authors suggest that although a watermill was potentially a profitable development, and especially so post-Conquest when 'suit of mill' – a requirement to use the estate's mill – became widespread, this was not necessarily the case (82). For example, at Wharram le Street and Wharram Percy there is evidence for the locations of five watermills along a 4 km stretch of stream. Two of these mills are only 100 m apart but the property of different owners. It is unlikely that there was sufficient power for both mills to operate at the same time, so sharing a mill would have made more economic sense. However, they argue that mills had a symbolic value to lordly centres, in addition to any economic value; the 'Installation of a watermill at a lordly centre would have constituted an ostentatious projection of innovation and wealth' (Gould *et al.* 2025, 84).

Bond (1979, 59–75) explains the very significant role the monastic estates played in the growth and development of watermills. Benedictine houses were often richly endowed, their landholdings stable, so they were in a good position to invest in expensive, but profitable, technology. In addition, the Benedictine rule recommended that each monastery should be self-contained, housing its own water supply and mill. Lucas (2014) agrees with this but argues convincingly, drawing on a wide range of primary and secondary sources, that ecclesiastical involvement in the development of the English milling trade was a complex process. He proposes that 'Monastic Innovation' was neither universal, nor ubiquitous, and involved only some of those houses with the capital to invest; and that ecclesiastical elites did not impose watermills on peasants and townspeople as a means of surplus extraction, *e.g.* up to half of all the milling being conducted throughout England in the late 11th century was within the domestic setting of the household using hand mills, or occasionally in larger settings using a horse mill. Thus, it was the religious houses with larger estates, and especially those established before the Conquest with 'suit of mill', who were the most involved in milling and the most active in exploiting their seigneurial privileges. This explains the importance of the Benedictines in watermilling, they being one of the oldest of the major religious orders. Lucas concludes that structures of ecclesiastical lordship and patterns of mill acquisition and innovation were shaped, not only by the size, wealth and distribution of a house's estates, but also by environmental and demographic factors. These included changing cultural attitudes and legal conventions; prevailing and emerging technical traditions; the personal relations of a house with its patrons, tenants, servants and neighbours; and the entrepreneurial and administrative flair of bishops, abbots, priors and other ecclesiastical officials.

The evidence in the landscape

The landscape offers indirect evidence for watermilling in this early period. Watermills from the 10th century were generally small, and would have been built on a leat coming off the main river, rather than on the main river itself (Watts 2002, 72–82). Using LiDAR, old maps and fieldwork, we have identified just such a leat at Houghton (see Fig. 5.1, page 65). This is almost certainly the original location of Houghton Mill, *i.e.* of the 960s or earlier. Documentary evidence confirms that it did not occupy its current site until the second half of the 13th century. We have identified other similar leats, at or near the location of Domesday watermills, and it is very likely that they were also the original location of watermills in the 9th–11th centuries, but unfortunately these sites do not have the supporting documentary evidence as at Houghton.

Whilst accepting the limitations of the landscape evidence described above, the complex arrangement of channels at Godmanchester merits closer examination because it may indicate an early origin, possibly Roman. The channels adjacent to the known site of Godmanchester Mill and the Causeway have been frequently explained as a combination of Danish defence works and a naval harbour, together with later channel engineering for watermills. Green (1977, 27) states that the three watermills at Godmanchester recorded in the Domesday Survey occupied separate sites which can be identified from the surviving positions of mill races and ponds (Fig. 3.1). He argues that to provide these arrangements it was necessary to build a channel from the main channel 'until it opened out to form a harbour under the walls of the town'. Based on the form of the harbour being similar to Danish harbour works elsewhere, he aligns these developments with the period of the Danelaw (870–917). To support this theory, he notes that a pond on Belle Isle, known locally as Gormon's Pond, could be a corruption of *Guthrum*, the name of the leader of the Danish army in East Anglia. Woodger (1990, 27–29) states that the three watermills at Godmanchester, together with the mills at Houghton, Brampton, Buckden/Offord Cluny and Eaton Socon were excavated by hand under Danish supervision, and also that the mills at Godmanchester were part of a defensive system. However, he cites no evidence. Nor does he explain his omission of the other mills on the Great Ouse at Eynesbury, Great Paxton, Huntingdon, Hartford, Wyton and Hemingford Grey, and his assertion that all the mills are on the north bank of the main channel is incorrect.

3. The first watermills: the Roman period to 1066

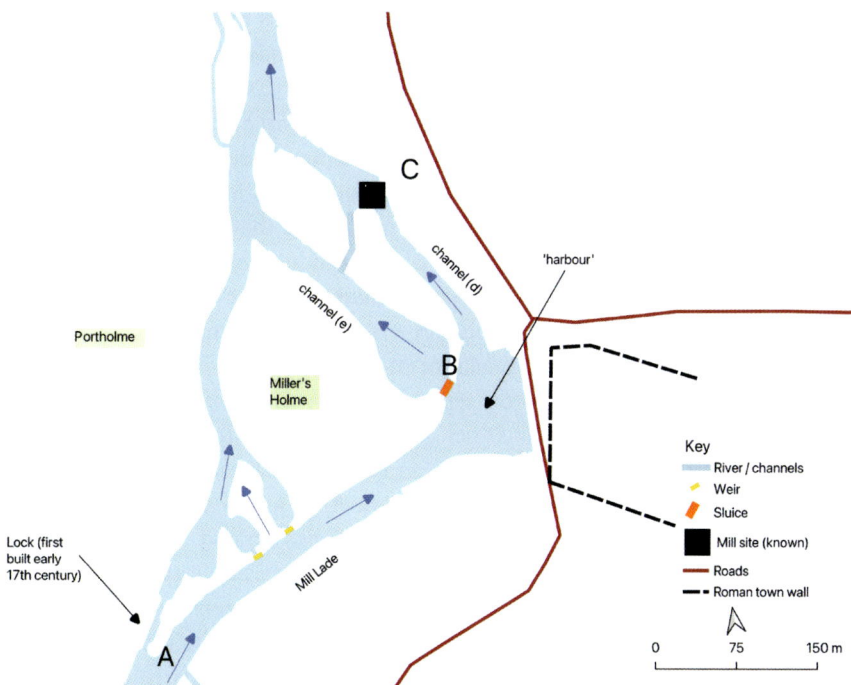

FIGURE 3.1.
Godmanchester: channels, ponds and possible watermill sites

The superficial geology and the channel bend dimensions on the floodplain support Green's view that the Mill Lade and the return channels are human-made. The main channel is the eastern reach of the Portholme meander, which follows the junction between the alluvial floodplain and the river terrace. The Mill Lade diverts from the natural course of the meander and, together with channel returns, creates a distinctly unnatural triangle in the river terrace. However, if the purpose had been to create a mill-leat and tail race for a mill, it would not have been necessary to cut a channel to meet the settlement and/or to create a harbour. A more straightforward explanation for Mill Lade is that it was originally cut to give the settlement, located on the ridge of drier river gravels, easy access to the main channel. This may have been constructed under the Danelaw, but form is unreliable as dating evidence and, with the 'harbour' being so close to the walls of the known Roman fort, it is equally probable that it dates from the Roman period.

The antiquary Camden (1610) gives '*Gormon*' as an alternative writing of '*Guthrum*', and '*Gormancester*' as an early name for Godmanchester, but this association does not prove that any 'harbour' was created at the time of the Danish occupation. The 'Danish theory' seems to have originated in an article by Goddard (1901, 326–337), followed by Allcroft (1908, 385–388), where they examined the 'docks and harbour' alongside the Great Ouse at Willington, Bedfordshire. Goddard concluded that 'in these Willington earthworks we have what is left of a Danish Waterburg which once gave shelter to a squadron of their ships while their fighting men with their brynjas and battle axes crossed over the river to the attack of Bedford. There was room for 25–30 ships with perhaps 2500 men' (Goddard 1901, 333–334). Farrar (1921, 125–137) continued to narrate graphic accounts of the Danes in this area, and Summers (1973, 24–27) considered the evidence for Danish military camps at several sites (including Willington) along the Great Ouse in Bedfordshire, and for the use of the river as a military highway. However, it was not until 2004 that archaeological examination of the Willington site dismissed theories of its Viking origins (Edmondson and Mudd 2004, 208–221). Dating evidence put the range of occupation between the 12th and mid-13th centuries and concluded that it formed part of a moated complex related to the Manor of Willington.

Green's siting of three mills on separate sites is problematic. Site A, where the Mill Lade leaves the main channel, is an unlikely one for a watermill. There is no leat or tail race and no other mill on the Great Ouse, or elsewhere to the authors' knowledge, found at such a location. Also, a mill at the southwestern end of Miller's Holme (a common name for islands created by channels associated with milling) would have been difficult to access, except by boat. Site B is a possible location with the water leaving the 'harbour' being controlled by a sluice, but access would have been even more difficult than for Site A. Site C is the most promising location: there is a mill-leat (narrower than the Mill Lade, *i.e.* offering greater control) and a tail race; there is easy access to Godmanchester's main street; and there is documentary evidence of a mill on this site from 1499. Given our argument that 'one mill = one wheel = one pair of stones' as the best interpretation for the Domesday record (see page 39), the most likely site for Godmanchester's three mills is Site C, *i.e.* at the time of the Conquest the three mills were housed in a single building, or in two or three separate but neighbouring buildings, on the same site.

The name 'Portholme', or the earlier 'Port mead' or 'the Port Holme', for the large meadow adjacent to Godmanchester (but in Brampton parish) has also been cited as possible evidence for a port, or harbour, at Godmanchester (Doody 2008, 10). This name is in use by 1550 (VCH l 1936, 12–20) but most substantial towns in medieval times were known as a 'port' from the Old English for a walled town, or market town (Blair 1994, 154), and this is a far more likely derivation of its name, *i.e.* it means 'the town's meadow'.

In summary, a probable sequence for the development of the channels at Godmanchester is:

- The Mill Lade was cut to give river access to the settlement of Godmanchester, creating a quayside, perhaps as early as Roman times;
- At least one of the return channels, (channel 'd' or 'e'), and possibly both, were cut at the same time;
- Site C was chosen as the site for the first watermill – date unknown but pre-1066 – with channel 'd' being constructed or adapted as the mill-leat and tail race, and channel 'e' being constructed or adapted as an 'overflow channel' to control the amount of water entering the mill-leat; and

- By 1086, three mills (pairs of stones) were located at Site C, which, from documentary evidence, was known to have had a mill from at least 1499.

However, in the absence of archaeological evidence, or pre-Conquest documentary evidence, the question as to when the Godmanchester mills were first built cannot be definitively answered.

Upstream of Brampton and downstream of St Ives the river was, and is, confined largely to a single channel, as has been discussed earlier, whereas the section between Brampton and St Ives is multi-channel. It is helpful to summarise what is known about this multi-channel section of the river at the commencement of watermilling, because our research has shown that the development of this multi-channel form is largely the result of the development of watermilling. Although a date cannot be put on the 'first watermill', it is reasonable to assume that, as an important grain-producing area, watermills would have been built at least at the same time as they are known to have become increasingly common in other parts of the country, in the 9th and 10th centuries. This would fit with the known watermill date for Houghton of AD 969. Therefore, an approximate date of AD 800 can be given for the 'pre-watermilling' landscape (Fig. 3.2).

Lee's Brook (a) has channel dimensions that suggest it is an artificial cut and/or a heavily modified relict channel (Fig. 3.3). Its course is largely straight, and it is steep-sided and relatively deep. It creates a more direct route from Godmanchester to settlements upstream, cutting off a great meander in the main river. It offers no advantage to the operation of Godmanchester's watermills. However, as late as the 1830s the weir at its western end was known as the 'Navigation Overfall' (R1/478). This suggests that in all probability it was dug so that river traffic from Godmanchester could avoid having to negotiate Brampton Mills. It can be dated back to at least the 13th century because the mills at Brampton used it, controversially, as a backwater. However, without direct evidence it is not possible to say whether it was part of the pre-watermilling landscape.

The channel dimensions of Bromholme Brook (b) indicate a natural watercourse that was part of the pre-watermilling landscape. However, its divergence from the main channel was heavily modified to create the tail race for Brampton mills at least by the time of the Domesday Survey.

Portholme Brook (c) is the western boundary of a Site of Special Scientific Interest. It has the appearance of an artificial channel, although part of its course may be taking advantage of a relict channel formed at the junction of the river alluvium of Portholme and the gravel terrace of Bromholme. It drains the ridge and furrow immediately to the west. This area of arable land and the watermills at Brampton probably developed in conjunction, so for this reason, Portholme Brook has not been included as a feature of the pre-watermilling landscape. However, it is mentioned here because it is known to have been adapted to supply water to Huntingdon Mill in the 18th century. It is now dry for most of the year, silted up and disused (Fig. 3.4).

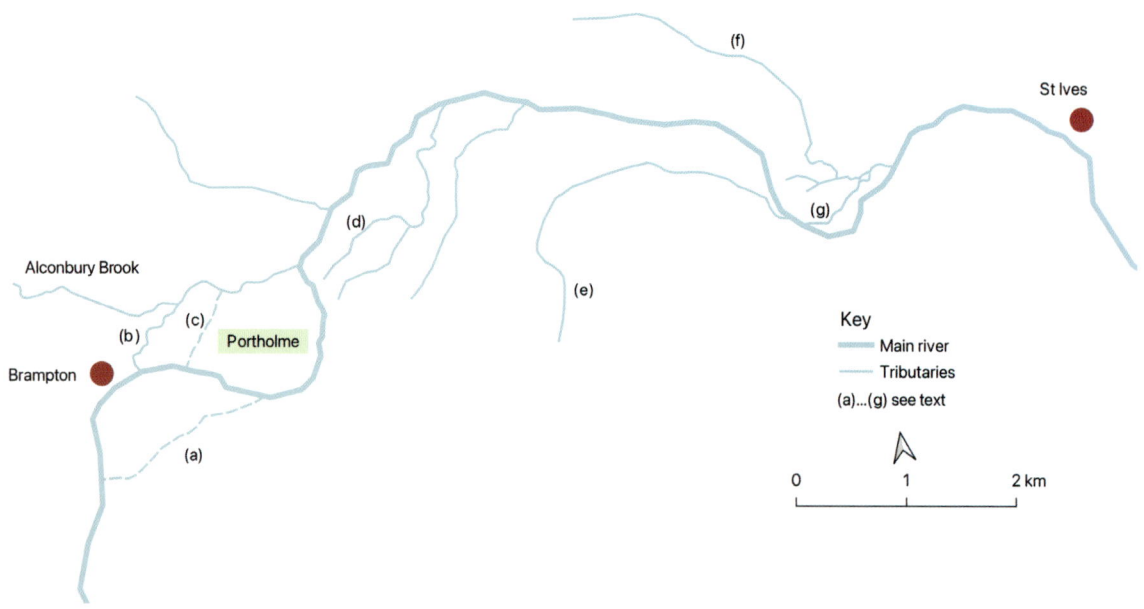

FIGURE 3.2. (above) The pre-watermilling landscape, Brampton to St Ives

FIGURE 3.3. Lee's Brook, 2023

FIGURE 3.4. Portholme Brook, October 2023

Cook's Stream (d) was not connected to the main river until the 13th century. Nor was there a connection between the main river at Houghton and what is now Hemingford Abbots Backwater until the 1270s, the latter being the downstream section of Godmanchester Drain (e). Back Brook (f) has the channel dimensions of a natural stream and was part of the pre-watermilling landscape. However, like Cook's Stream and Godmanchester Drain, it was separate from the main river until the expansion of watermilling in the 13th century, when it was adapted to act as the tail race for Houghton Mill. The channel dimensions of Hemingford Grey Backwater (g) indicate a natural origin. It was part of the pre-watermilling landscape, diverging from the main channel, because documentary evidence records that Reginald de Grey obstructed its entrance with a weir or sluice in the early 1270s, it previously having been navigable to river traffic.

In summary, today's multi-channel river form – largely the same as that shown on the earliest widely available maps from the Tudor period – did not exist in the pre-watermilling landscape. Subsequent chapters will detail how watermilling played a pre-eminent role in the development of the multi-channel landscape.

CHAPTER FOUR

A watermilling 'powerhouse': the Domesday Mills

Although there is considerable uncertainty about the number of pre-Conquest watermills, and when they were built, the Domesday Book shows that by 1086 Huntingdonshire was an exceptional county for milling. Ambler and Langdon (1994, 43) identified its 36 mills as having the highest average value of any county at £1 4s 5d compared with the national average of £0 11s 7d. Almost two thirds of Huntingdonshire's mills – 22 – were on the River Great Ouse, with an average value of £1 11s 9d. And of these, the 13 mills between Brampton and Hemingford Grey in the west–east multi-channel section of the river had an even greater average value of £1 18s 7d. (Huntingdon's watermill was located on Alconbury Brook, very close to the Great Ouse and part of the same river system, hence its inclusion in this analysis.) Although the Domesday Book only refers to them as 'mills', can we be sure that these were watermills? This is a legitimate question because of the lack of archaeological evidence and because a document from the late 10th century recording assignments of property to Thorney Abbey in the north of Cambridgeshire refers to payments made for mill oxen at Huntingdon and Yaxley (Watts 2002, 75). The Domesday mills were certainly not windmills because the earliest references to these in England date from 1185 (Rynne 2018, 12). It also seems implausible that animal mills (and hand mills) could have produced such high values. What allows certainty that they were watermills – at least for the 22 mills in manors bordering the Great Ouse – is the landscape evidence of channel engineering, *e.g.* mill-leats and tail races, which is presented below. The value and ownership of each of these Domesday mills is shown in Table 4.1.

Where two or more watermills are recorded in a town or village, it is not known if each watermill was a separate building on the same site, or on a different site, powered by one or more waterwheels; or whether the Domesday Book was referring to multiple sets of millstones in a single building. There is archaeological evidence of mills with multiple wheels from the late 7th century onwards in other parts of the country (Oosthuizen 2007, 13). Holt (1988, 131) puts forward the view that the medieval watermill was never adapted to drive more than one set of millstones: 'Every reeve's account recording the provision of stones for a new mill or the replacement of stones that were old or broken, confirms that. For where there was a demand for extra milling capacity, it was sometimes decided to build, what was in effect, a pair of mills each with its

Settlement	Number of Watermills	Total value £ s d	Tenant in chief 1086	Lord in 1086	Overlord in 1066
Hemingford Grey	2	£6	Aubrey de Vere	Ralph son of Osmund	Ramsey Abbey
Hemingford Abbots	1	10s 7d	Ramsey Abbey	Ramsey Abbey	Ramsey Abbey
Houghton	1	£1	Ramsey Abbey	Ramsey Abbey	Ramsey Abbey
Wyton	1	12s	Ramsey Abbey	Ramsey Abbey	Ramsey Abbey
Hartford	2	£4	King William	Ranulph brother of Ilger	King Edward
Huntingdon	1	£3	King William	King William	King Edward
Brampton	2	£5	King William	Ranulph brother of Ilger	King Edward
Godmanchester	3	£5	King William	King William	King Edward
Offord (Cluny)	2	£2 10s	Arnulf of Hesdin	Cluny Abbey	Bului
Buckden	1	£1 10s	Bishop of Lincoln	Bishop of Lincoln	Bishop of Lincoln
Paxton	3	£3 4s	Countess Judith	Countess Judith	King Edward
Eynesbury	2	£2 4s 12d	Countess Judith	Countess Judith	King Edward
Eynesbury	1	£1 2s 12d	Rohais wife of Richard	Rohais; St Neot's Abbey; William the Breton	King Edward
Swavesey (i)	1	£2	Count Alan of Brittany	Count Alan of Brittany	Edeva the Fair
Eaton Socon (ii)	2	£1 16s 5d	Eudo the Steward	Eudo the Steward	King Edward

i Cambridgeshire
ii Bedfordshire in 1086
Source: Domesday Book Online (raw data), Palmer, J. and Slater, G. at opendomesday.org.

TABLE 4.1. The value and ownership of watermills on the River Great Ouse in Huntingdonshire recorded in the Domesday Book

own mechanism and its own waterwheel but housed side by side in the same mill house'. Keith (2017) considers this question for Cambridgeshire, which records 130 mills in the Domesday Book, and concludes that this figure is wrong because the lack of feasible sites means that there could never have been more than 60 separate mills. He argues that there was insufficient power in Cambridgeshire's water courses for 130 mills. He further argues that, in many cases, the Domesday Book is recording the ownership of milling rights or sets of mill stones that were sometimes outside the boundaries of the manors in which they were recorded. This helps to explain the number of 'part mills' recorded in the Domesday Book, although in Cambridgeshire this accounts for only 11 of the 87 manors with recorded mills. In Huntingdonshire, as in Cambridgeshire, multiple mills were recorded in some manors, with a total of 36 mills in 23 manors. However, two of Keith's arguments do not apply here, *i.e.* discharge is significantly higher on Huntingdonshire's main rivers, the Great Ouse and the Nene, so there was sufficient power for the number of recorded mills, and no 'part mills' were recorded. Also, 'lost" mills have been located, as will be shown below. An alternative explanation for Keith's concern about the recording of the number of mills in the Domesday Book, in Cambridgeshire and elsewhere, is Holt's explanation quoted above, *i.e.* that additional capacity was achieved by adding wheels and sets of millstones either in the existing building, or in a new building fed by the same leat, or a channel taken from that leat. Keith's concern about the lack of power cannot be conclusively addressed but he accepts that we do not know the minimum power required for a viable mill, and it is likely that most millstones at this time were relatively small, *e.g.* Hodgen (1939, 262) suggests that their diameter may have been no more than 45–90 cm. We conclude that the Domesday Book was recording 'one mill = one waterwheel = one set of stones', not the number of mill sites.

The Domesday Book records 25 mills in 14 settlements that border the River Great Ouse in present-day Cambridgeshire. The absence of archaeological and documentary evidence means that even at the four locations where there are existing mill buildings – Houghton, Brampton, Buckden and Eaton Socon – there is no certainty of their Domesday sites. The evidence gathered suggests that Houghton definitely was, and that the other three probably were, at nearby sites. Only two of these mill buildings now have a waterwheel. Houghton mill was renovated by the National Trust to be a working mill and re-opened in 1983 (Howes 2020, 23–27). It has one functioning water wheel plus a hydro-turbine. Brampton mill has an ornamental water wheel incorporated into the restaurant that occupies the mill building. Four more of the Domesday locations were occupied by watermills through to the 19th and 20th centuries – Hemingford Grey, Huntingdon, Godmanchester and Paxton – and it is reasonable to assume that their Domesday mills were on or close to these known sites. The mills at Eynesbury, Offord Cluny, Hartford, Wyton, Hemingford Abbots and Swavesey have not previously been located but we have researched and present evidence, below, to show their locations, some with a greater degree of certainty than others (Fig. 4.1).

The distribution of these mills is explained mainly by the physical geography of the river valley. The south–north section of the river from Eaton Socon to Brampton has 11 mills at an average distance of one per 1.3 km, while the west–east section between Brampton and Hemingford Grey has 13 mills, at an average of one per 0.75 km. This is almost certainly because the wider floodplain between Brampton and Hemingford Grey, and its historically anastomosing form, offered advantages for channel construction and water management. The lack of mills below St Ives is due to the river's gradient becoming increasingly gentle as it emerges onto the Fens, reducing its power and making a watermill less viable. The river was influenced by the spring tides upstream as far as St Neots (Summers 1973, 18). Even a weak tidal flow would have reduced the available power in a such a slow-moving river. But, in addition to the physical geography, manorial ownership and economic factors help explain the distribution of mills as will be shown below.

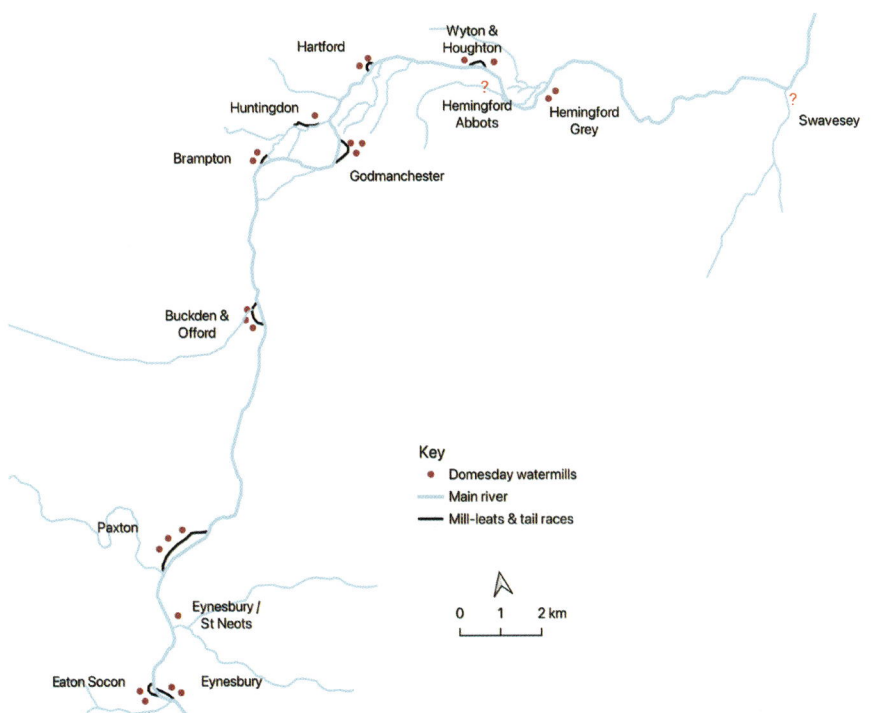

FIGURE 4.1. The Domesday Watermills on the River Great Ouse in Cambridgeshire

Locating the 'lost' watermills

A combination of LiDAR, aerial photographs, fieldwork, historical maps and documentary evidence have enabled suggested locations for the Domesday mills recorded in Eynesbury, Offord Cluny, Hartford, Wyton, Hemingford Abbots and Swavesey. These locations were all previously unidentified. Paxton has been included in this section because although there is a known mill site at Little Paxton, the location of the Domesday mills is uncertain.

Eynesbury

The Domesday Book records three mills in Eynesbury. Rohais (a Norman noblewoman and wife of Richard fitz Gilbert, one of the ten wealthiest landholders post-Conquest) was the tenant-in-chief for one of these, valued at £1 2s 12d. Countess Judith (a niece of William the Conqueror) was the tenant-in-chief for the other two, valued at £2 4s 12d. Rohais' mill is recorded as having two Lords (who held land from a tenant-in-chief, rather than directly from the king) – St Neots Priory and William the Breton. The association with St Neots Priory strongly suggests that this was the mill identified by Tebbutt (1966, 45–46) on the riverside just outside the Priory gatehouse. A lava millstone, 56 cm in diameter, was dredged from the river a short distance upstream when the present bridge was built, and it may have come from this mill. Locating Countess Judith's mills is more difficult. St Neots was part of Eynesbury in 1086 (Spoerry 2000, 148), so it is

4. A watermilling 'powerhouse': the Domesday Mills

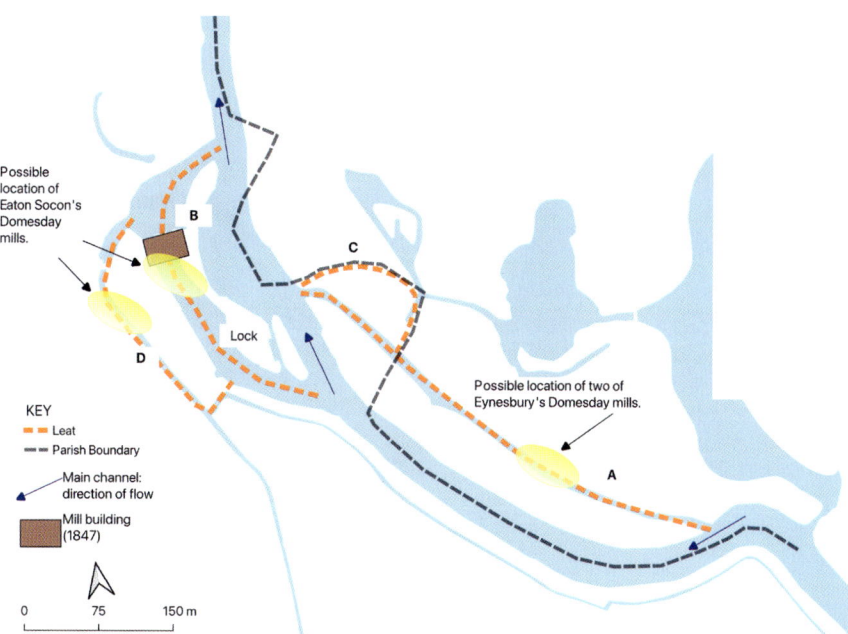

FIGURE 4.2. The possible location of the Domesday watermills at Eaton Socon and Eynesbury

necessary to consider a larger area than the current parish. The Paxton mills were given to St Neots Priory by Malcolm IV of Scotland in the mid-12th century, *i.e.* they were not part of the Eynesbury estate at the time of the Domesday survey, so they can be discounted. Hen Brook could have been adapted for watermilling but there is no evidence that it was. Brookside Mill was built on Hen Brook, but not until the 1850s and was steam powered. There is, however, landscape evidence for a watermill opposite the Eaton Socon mills. A weir controls water entering a cut channel that rejoins the main river near the lock. This channel is on Eynesbury land (Fig. 4.2, A). It would have been ideal as a leat for watermilling, and it is hard to think what other purpose it could have had. On the other hand, it is some distance from the settlement, and there is no supporting archaeological or documentary evidence to explain its origins. Ownership of these mills passed to the Earls of Winchester who, in turn, granted them to the Abbot of Sawtry in the mid-13th century (VCH e 1932, 272–280). They changed hands again: in 1279 the Abbot paid scutage (a fee) to the Countess of Derby. Then, beyond that date there are no references. It is possible that their relative isolation meant that they were abandoned when milling capacity was concentrated at fewer sites in the 14th–16th centuries. And as for the location of these mills, the leat opposite Eaton Socon seems to point to the most likely site.

Paxton

In 1086, Great and Little Paxton were one estate called *Pachtoun*. There appears to be only one possible site for a watermill in today's parish of Great Paxton. At the bottom of River Lane there is an island that creates a mill-leat and

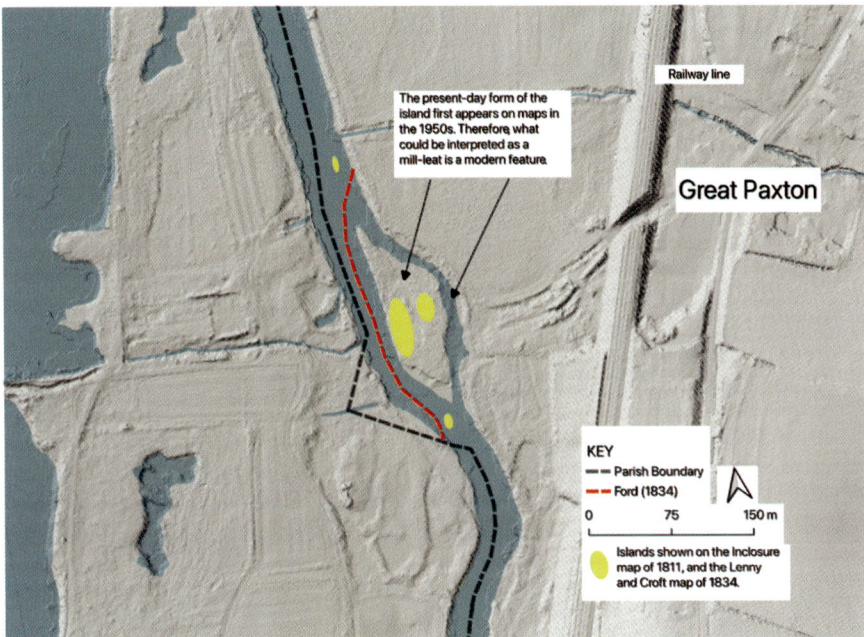

FIGURE 4.3. LiDAR map of the River Great Ouse at Great Paxton

tail race configuration (Fig. 4.3). However, historical maps show a different landscape to that of today. Two main islands with two small islands are shown on the 1811 Inclosure map (KHP64/26/1) and the 1834 map (R1/478). Only one of these small islands is on the 1886 OS map (Huntingdonshire XXV.4). On the 1834 map the location of Wray House Ford is shown, with the parish boundary deviating onto Southoe land (as it still does), which indicates that the ford was the responsibility of Great Paxton. All these details combine to make it an extremely unlikely site for a watermill. However, there remains the need to explain the record in the Hundred Rolls for 1279 (Illingworth 1818 ii, 687) that the Abbot of Sawtry held a watermill in Great Paxton, a gift from the King of Scotland (Malcolm IV). Given the modifications noted above to the Great Paxton stretch of the river, it cannot be ruled out that similar, now obscured, changes in the 11th–13th centuries enabled a watermill to be located here.

Little Paxton is the more probable location for the Paxton watermills in 1086. In 1279 there were five watermills here (Illingworth 1818 ii, 673), and watermilling continued into the 20th century (Howes 2020, 32). The 1834 map (R1/478) shows several islands upstream of the site of the paper mill that was built in 1799 and operated through to 1988. These can be seen on the LiDAR, and they are now combined as one island, reclaimed for housing (Fig. 4.4). These islands are, in all probability, the result of cutting a leat from the main river at its confluence with the River Kym, 1.5 km in length. A complex series of channels, weirs and sluices has altered the natural flow of the river and the

4. A watermilling 'powerhouse': the Domesday Mills

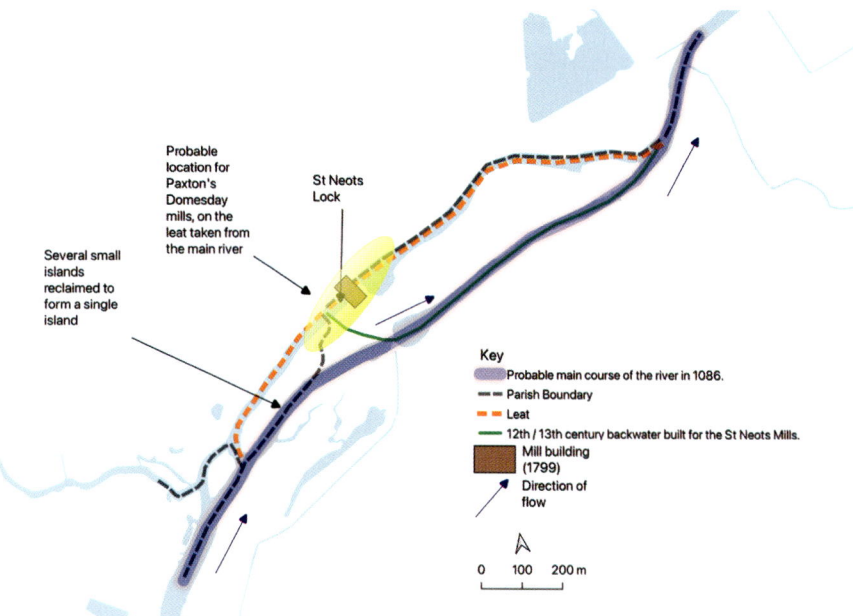

FIGURE 4.4. The probable location of Paxton's Domesday watermills

main channel was re-purposed as a backwater in the 12th and 13th centuries. King Malcolm gave three of the five mills to the Abbot of Sawtry and the other two to the Priory of St Neots. It is very likely that the mills he gave to the Priory were on, or near to, the site of the Paper Mill – it was called the *St Neots* Paper Mill, and the St Neots parish boundary deviates to encompass the site. The leat draws a considerable amount of water from the main river and could have supported the other mills (or pairs of stones) mentioned in the 13th century documentation.

Offord Cluny

Offord Cluny and Buckden are settlements on opposite sides of the River Great Ouse between Brampton and Paxton. The Domesday Book records two mills at Offord, valued at £2 10s, with Arnulf of Hesdin as Tenant-in-Chief and Cluny Abbey as Lord. There was one mill at Buckden, valued at £1 10s, with the Bishop of Lincoln as the Tenant-in-Chief and Lord. Two blocks of the Buckden mill building constructed in 1867 survive as part of a residential development. The mill building is constructed across a leat controlled by weirs and is likely to have been on this site since the lock was first built in 1618. However, this may not have been its Domesday site because there is a cut channel to the west of the mill (Fig. 4.5) that bears all the hallmarks of a mill-leat. The building straddles the parish boundary and is sometimes referred to as 'Offord and Buckden Mill', but this is misleading. The Gordon map (1730) shows a mill on the Buckden side of the river. The Offord Inclosure Award

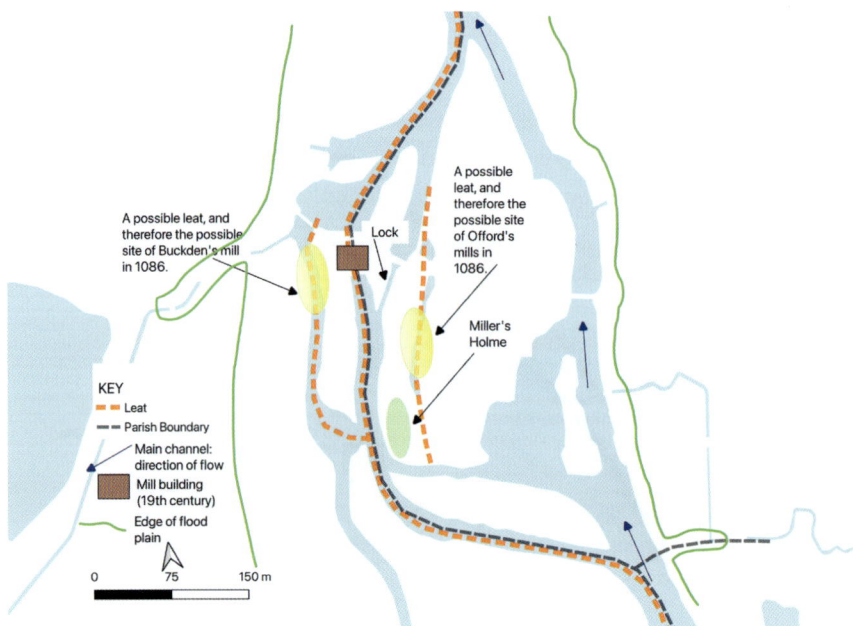

FIGURE 4.5. The possible location of the Domesday watermills at Buckden and Offord

of 1813 includes directions that 'nothing done was to prejudice Buckden mills' (VCH d 1932, 260–269) and the 1886 OS map labelled the site as Buckden Corn Mills (Huntingdonshire XXI.12). This gives certainty about the location of the Buckden mill but uncertainty about the location of the Offord Domesday mills. A short distance south of Offord, the river divides into a complex series of (now) heavily modified channels, controlled by a series of weirs and a sluice. The main river follows the eastern channel. There is no obvious reason for the river branching to the west at a sharp angle (Fig. 4.5), so the eastern channel was probably the main channel before the watermills were first built. This would make the western channel a leat – but why would Offord construct a leat on the Buckden side of the river? The most likely explanation is that the land between the main river and the edge of the floodplain on the Offord side is too constricted a site. The deviation in the parish boundary supports this argument – it does not mark a former course of the main river, but defines the land Offord needed to manage its leat. It is known that before 1305 Cluny Abbey had acquired 'two mills and the site of a mill' (VCH h 1932, 319–322) (presumably two pairs of stones in one building, or two small buildings next to each other, see page 39), so it is reasonable to assume that there was one Domesday site. Both the Inclosure Award map (KDMC/343) and the Lenny and Croft map (R1/478) identify Miller's Holme. The LiDAR reveals a channel crossing Miller's Holme, still visible in the landscape (Fig. 4.6), and this could be the line of the original mill-leat. The available evidence strongly suggests that the location of the Offord mills was a little to the south and east of the known Buckden mill site, on Offord Common.

4. A watermilling 'powerhouse': the Domesday Mills

FIGURE 4.6. The relict channel crossing Miller's Holme, Offord Common, 2024

Hartford

Two watermills at Hartford with a combined value of £4 are recorded in the Domesday Book. The first direct evidence for their location is the 1515 Petition to the Duchy of Lancaster (TNA DL R3/23, 009):

> Also after, as the said Commissioners came rowing in the said highstream, they came to a certain place where a isle is grown with elm trees which has divided the highstream there and upon the northside thereof the Priory of Huntingdon had a mill. And there also is a certain dam or bank made in the said highstream, which does obstruct and is much hurtful for boats and other vessels which come and conduct merchandise to pass and re-pass from the said town of Huntingdon to [King's] Lynn and other places and out to the sea.

The map illustrating the Petition (Fig. 4.7, i) shows this location with the symbol for a watermill to the west of Hartford parish church on the north bank of the river opposite two islands; it looks to straddle the channel between the north bank and the island. The 'dam or bank' is the black blob between the two islands. The Jefferys map of 1768 (KHAC4/4347, see Fig. 4.7, ii) shows the two islands, but no watermill. Today, these two islands are part of the north bank of the river, but the LiDAR (Fig. 4.7, iii) identifies their original extent, and therefore allows us to locate the site of the Hartford watermills with a high degree of certainty. Further evidence is on the Jefferys map, with it showing what was probably a service road, now built over, connecting the High Street to the approximate site of the watermills.

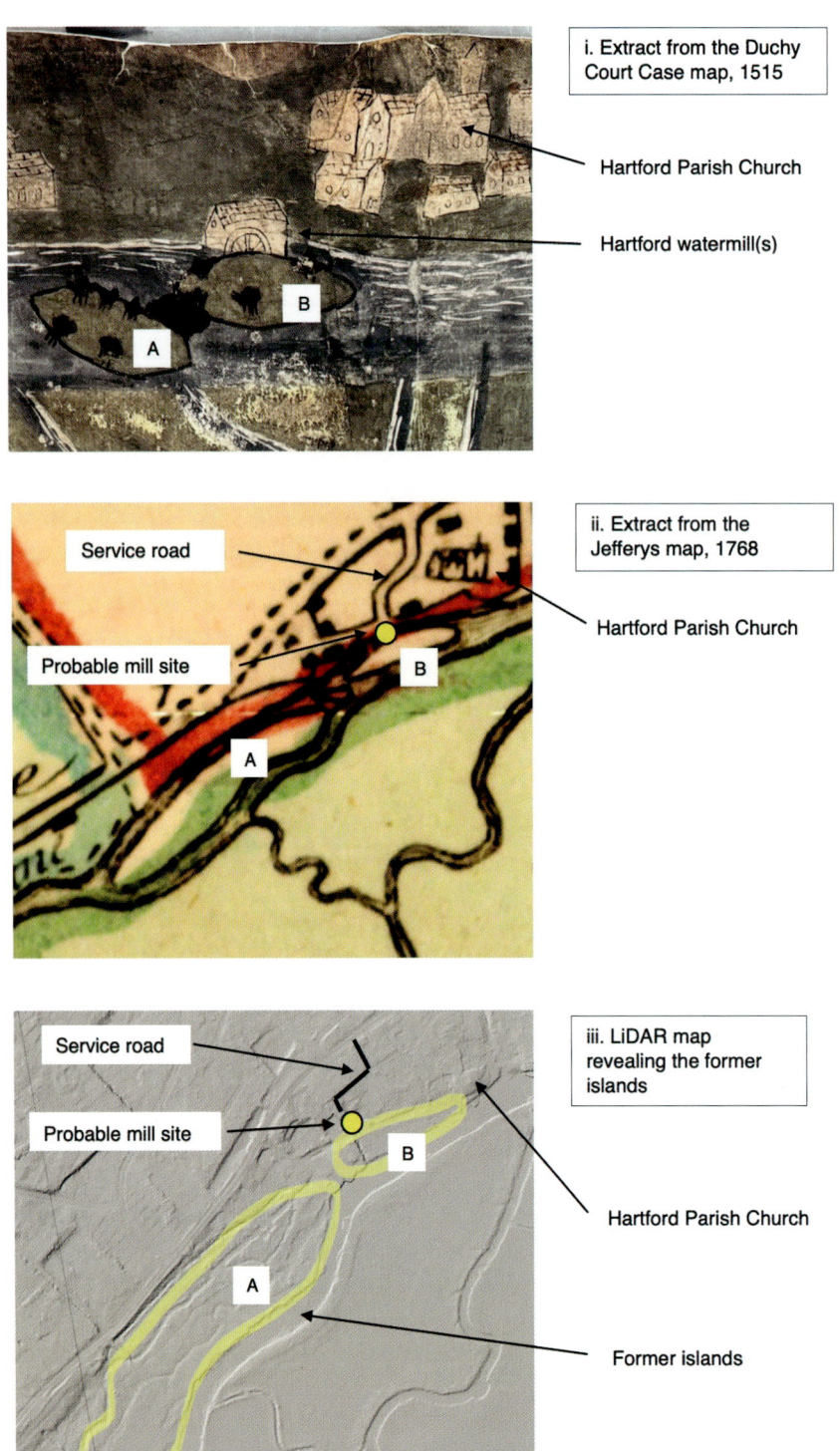

FIGURE 4.7. Locating Hartford Mills

Wyton

A watermill at Wyton was valued at 12s in the Domesday Book – a relatively low value for this stretch of the river, although still above the national average of 11s 7d. There is then no further firm documentary evidence of this mill – although it may be one of the three mills recorded in Houghton cum Wyton in the Hundred Rolls of 1279. But it is impossible to be certain because the adjoining villages of Wyton and Houghton, have been *de facto* a single unit since they were given to Ramsey Abbey in the 960s by Earl Alfwold (Ailwyn) (VCH g 1932, 178–181). The parish of Wyton has a short stretch of river frontage and there is no obvious site for a watermill in the current landscape. However, the Jefferys map (Fig. 4.8, i) shows an island, now bisected by the parish boundary. The LiDAR identifies this island (Fig. 4.8, ii) and fieldwork shows that the channel around the north side of this island is still present, partly underground. The water drops down from the main river into this channel and would have provided sufficient energy to power a small undershot waterwheel. Therefore, a possible site for the 'missing' watermill at Wyton would be along this channel to the west of the parish boundary. The island itself may have been created by the building of a leat and tail race for the watermill; either dug as a completely new channel, or a heavily adapted relict channel.

Hemingford Abbots

At Hemingford Abbots, the Domesday Book records a watermill valued at 10s 7d. The 1515 Duchy Court Case map shows a mill on the south bank of the river, opposite Houghton, in the parish of Hemingford Abbots (see Fig. 6.1, page 91). The court documents describe this as a fulling mill belonging to Ramsey Abbey. The *Liber Gersumarum* of Ramsey Abbey (DeWindt 1976) records a fulling mill at Houghton in 1406–07, which is probably the same mill as described in the 1515 papers. However, this could not have been the site of the Hemingford Abbots Domesday mill, because the course of the river was modified in the second half of the 13th century, with the fulling mill being constructed on one of the new channels (see pages 64–66). It could have been near this site but there is no evidence of a leat. It is also a mile from the village settlement, so a location near Hemingford Abbots Manor Farm and Granary is an alternative possibility. A mill here would have been closer to where the grain was stored and would have had the advantage of being away from the main river channel, making water control easier (Fig. 4.9). But the LiDAR shows no evidence of a site near the village, although this could be because the landscape has been heavily modified by the construction of flood defences, most recently in the early 21st century. Grain may also have been transported from Hemingford Abbots Manor Farm to the Houghton mill site. There is documentary evidence of this happening in 1297 when a complaint was recorded in the Court Rolls of the Abbey of Ramsey and the Honor of Clare (Ault 1928, 220) that the tenants of Hemingford Abbots:

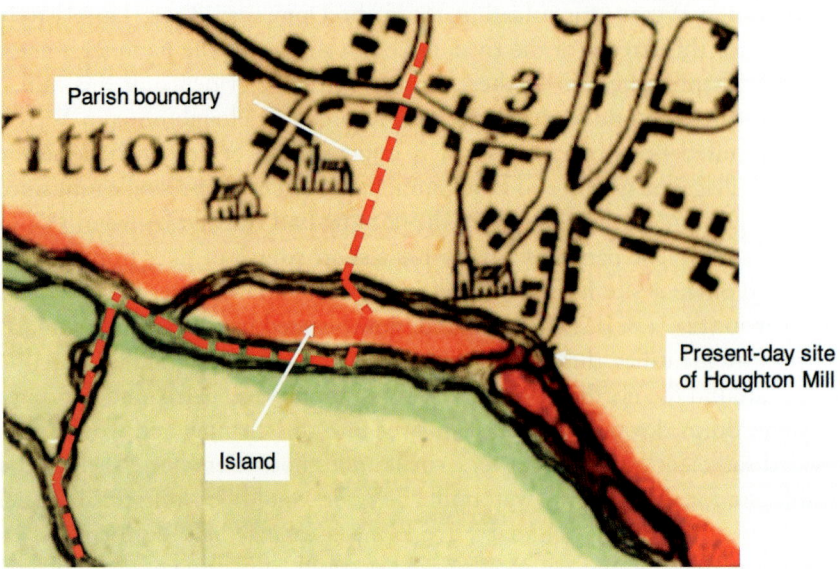

i. Extract from Jefferys map, 1768, showing the Wyton / Houghton Island

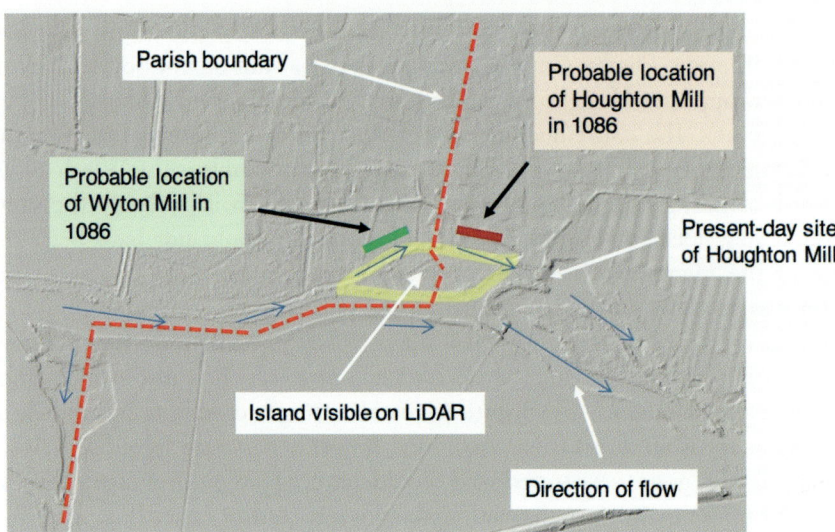

ii. LiDAR showing probable locations of Wyton and Houghton Mills in 1068

FIGURE 4.8. Locating Wyton Mill

'allege that Richard the miller … grinds the villagers' grain badly unless they pay a toll to his assistants and because he does not send the mill's boat for their grain to be fetched as he was accustomed to do, to the detriment of the lord. Wherefore it is decreed that Richard must amend his ways henceforth and that he should send across the boat for the corn to be fetched'. However, without new evidence the site of the Hemingford Abbots Domesday watermill remains conjectural.

4. A watermilling 'powerhouse': the Domesday Mills 49

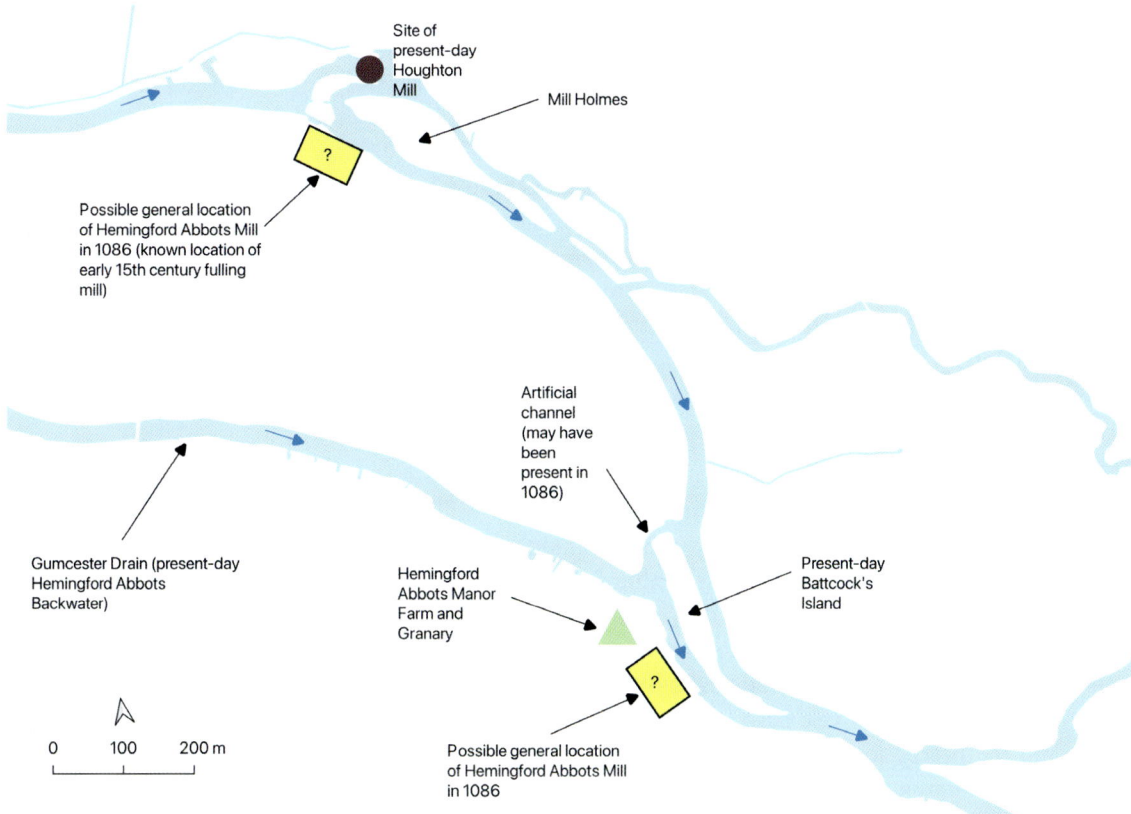

FIGURE 4.9. Possible sites for Hemingford Abbots watermill

Swavesey

The Domesday Book records a mill with the value of £2 at Swavesey owned by Count Alan of Brittany. In 1066 it had been owned by Edeva (Edith the Fair), the (probable) first wife of King Harold. This was a valuable mill and likely reflects its monopoly position, with 'suit of mill' being enforced by Edith and Alan across their considerable land holdings in the area. However, there is no archaeological, documentary or landscape evidence for a mill on this section of the River Great Ouse. Swavesey village is nearly a mile from the river so the watermill may have been nearer the settlement on, or near, one of the minor streams that drain north towards the main river. However, these have been heavily modified, removing any landscape evidence. Analysis of earthworks has revealed a long, linear pond on the site of Swavesey Priory (CHER 02420) but there is nothing to suggest that it was associated with milling activity. There is a channel from the river to the Priory, but this linked to a dock and is clearly associated with the movement of goods. A watermill is referenced in 1368, and again in 1457. Its value declined by two thirds during this period and there is no definite record of a watermill after this date. There is a possible record of a watermill in 1476 – 'a mill house was in the lord's hands on the rectory manor' – although it could equally be a reference to a windmill (VCH n 1989, 386–392). It does, though, raise the possibility that there was a watermill on the stream running through the rectory manor, or a leat taken from it. This possible location is shown on Figure 4.1.

What impact did the Domesday watermills have on the landscape?

The 'lost' Domesday watermills at Eynesbury, Paxton, Offord Cluny/Buckden, Hartford and Wyton were located on leats taken from the main river. These created islands, which are still present in the landscape, or identifiable on LiDAR images. At the sites where there has been continuity of water milling through to the 19th and 20th centuries, the nature of the Domesday landscape can be difficult to interpret because the mills have been continually re-developed. However, some reasonable assumptions can be made.

Eaton Socon

The Domesday Book records that Eaton Socon had two mills with a value of £1 16s 5d, with Eudo the Steward, a high-ranking Norman nobleman, the Tenant-in-Chief. Although then in Bedfordshire, this location has been included in the study area because it is opposite the possible mill location in Eynesbury, and therefore part of the same river landscape. The mill building seen today, now a pub and restaurant, was built in 1847. It is located on a leat taken from the main river (see page 41, Fig. 4.2, B). The level of water reaching it, and the nearby lock, is controlled by a weir. A deviation in the parish boundary, with Eaton Socon taking land from the Eynesbury side of the river, follows a small, curved channel, shown on maps up to the 1940s (C) but now largely infilled because of floodplain modification. This deviation must have been to give Eaton Socon control over water levels reaching the mill and the lock, two of its important assets. But the lock was first constructed in the 17th century, so the leat and/or the curved channel may not have been part of the 1086 landscape. However, immediately to the west of the current mill site is a watercourse flowing into the mill pond (D). It is no longer connected to the main river, but there was a connection as late as 1884 (Bedfordshire IX.9), and it is reasonable to consider that this could have been the original mill-leat and tail race. On balance, the Domesday mills were on a leat taken from the main river, probably the smaller western channel, but possibly the larger leat, the site of the 1847 mill building.

Brampton

At Brampton, the Mill Stream branches off the main channel and takes water to the current mill site (Fig. 4.10). Given that this is the probable site of the two mills in 1086, it seems likely that this was the leat constructed to supply the Domesday mills. Bromholme Brook acts as the tail race for Brampton mill. Its sinuous course and channel dimensions suggest it is a natural channel, not an artificial cut; however, it has been heavily modified to carry water away effectively from the scour pond.

4. A watermilling 'powerhouse': the Domesday Mills 51

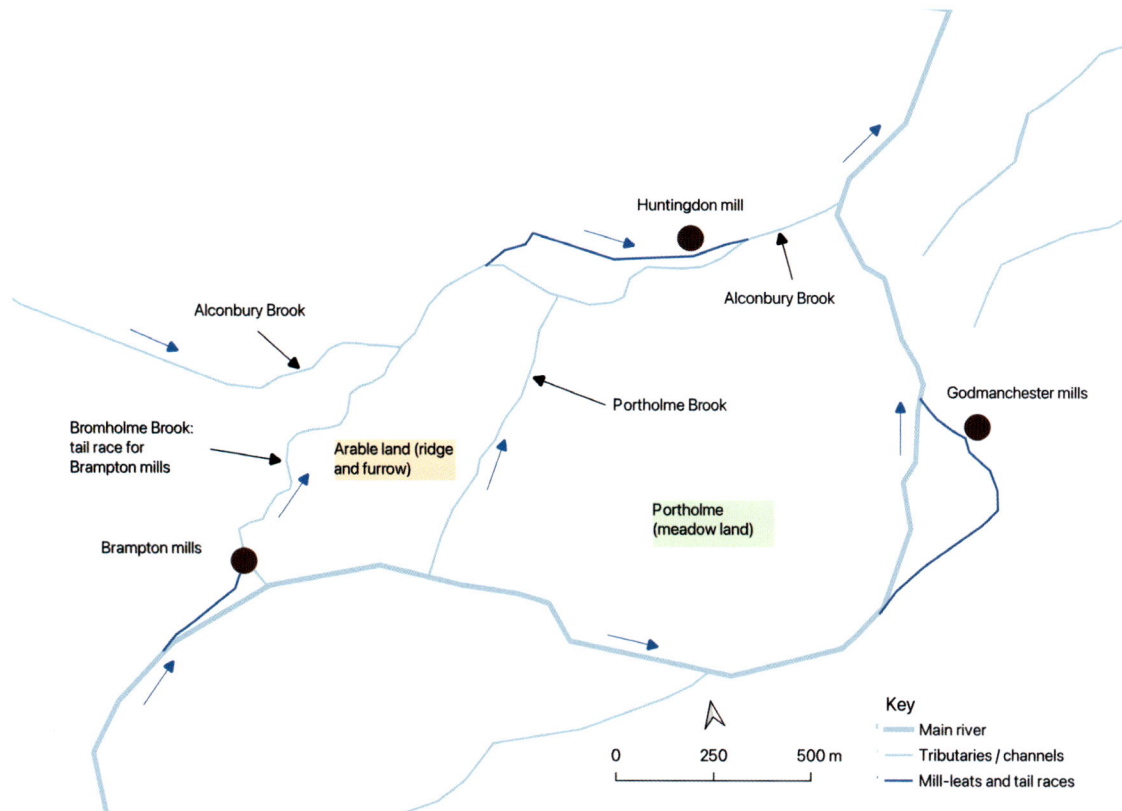

FIGURE 4.10. Brampton, Huntingdon and Godmanchester Mills, AD 1086: mill-leats and tail races

Huntingdon

At Huntingdon, a mill-leat leaves the main river 520 m upstream of the mill site, a relatively long distance especially in comparison with the tail race, which is less than 100 m (Fig. 4.10). This was constructed to maintain a height differential between the leat and the main river of about a metre. It is highly likely that this was the leat supplying the Domesday watermill because it offers such a significant advantage over any other option.

Godmanchester

The Huntingdon pattern is repeated at Godmanchester (Fig. 4.10), with water being taken away from the main channel and then returned downstream. As has been mentioned, water control at this location may have a very long history so the leat and tail race were almost certainly in existence in 1066.

Houghton

The area around Houghton mill was significantly re-developed in the later Middle Ages and so in 1086 it could not have been located at its current site. It is almost certain that the Domesday mill was located on the leat identified on the LiDAR map, down-channel of the Wyton mill (see Fig 4.8). The Wyton and Houghton mills were of relatively low value in 1086 (12s and £1 respectively) and it is conceivable that this channel could have generated sufficient power to run both mills. There is evidence from other parts of the country that there were many ways of configuring mill-leats and tail races to exploit the energy available (Tann 1965, 65). Given that both mills were owned by Ramsey Abbey, it is possible that there was a single mill with one or two pairs of stones and that the Domesday Book was dividing the value between the two manors. 'Shared ownership' is quite common in the Domesday Book, with at least 369 'part mills' recorded, although in this instance its purpose would have been to apportion ownership between the two parishes.

Hemingford Grey

Hemingford Grey's two mills, at £3 each, were the most valuable of all the mills on the River Great Ouse in 1086. But there have been so many modifications to the site, particularly to create the lock, that it is impossible to identify a leat or tail race from 1086. However, it is hard to imagine how its mills could have attained such value without channel engineering to control flow, so it is almost certain that there would have been a leat and/or tail race of some configuration.

Battcock's Island

The small, undoubtedly artificial, channel that creates Battcock's Island (see Fig. 4.9) may date from this time. It could have been cut to create an island for growing osiers (willow). There are several such islands along the river, known as 'holts' and in 1515 it was called 'Abel Holt' (TNA DLR3/23, 022). However, a more likely explanation is that it was cut to create a more direct route, by boat, from the village of Hemingford Abbots to Houghton. It reduces the length of the journey from 1.5 km to 1 km and this would have been a significant advantage, especially if the Hemingford Abbots mill had been located on the south bank of the river opposite Houghton.

In conclusion, the impact of water milling on the landscape in 1086 was limited to a relatively small area around the mill sites, including mill-leats, tail races and ponds; all controlled by dams, weirs and sluices. Some still survive, others exist only as relict features. Overall, the plan of the river system would have looked very similar to the pre-milling plan, with its multi-channel form significantly less developed in 1086 than today.

Why were these mills so valuable?

This is an obvious question and has been asked by many historians but, to date, it has not been satisfactorily answered. The Huntingdonshire Domesday mill values are extraordinarily high. Huntingdonshire's climate and soils can be ruled out as being particularly advantageous; although good for grain production, the same conditions are found in many other parts of central, eastern and southern England. For example, nationally there was a strong positive correlation (0.72) between the size of a county and the amount of ploughland (Tables 4.2 and 4.3). Huntingdonshire fitted with the expected pattern – it was the third smallest county and had the seventh smallest amount of ploughland, *i.e.* it had a little more ploughland than might be expected, but not exceptionally so. Hackney (2020) suggests that having fewer, but perhaps larger, busier mills to serve the population over a large area where conditions were not conducive for their establishment could have been the reason for their high value at Domesday. However, there was a strong positive correlation (0.7) between the number of households and the number of mills, *i.e.* Huntingdonshire had the number of mills that would be expected for the number of households, not fewer (see Table 4.2). As has been shown, the physical geography of the River Great Ouse valley was conducive to watermilling, especially in the west–east section from Brampton to Hemingford Grey. To illustrate this further, the River Great Ouse in Huntingdonshire has more mill sites per kilometre (one every 3.3 km) than the Nene in Northamptonshire (one every 4 km). In response to Hackney's article, Keith (2020) suggests that demand from urban areas affected mill values, an effect also noted by Holt (1988, 12). An analysis of the mills within a six-mile radius of Bedford, Northampton, Huntingdon

TABLE 4.2. Domesday Book, key statistics

County name	Number of households (i)	Total ploughland (ii)	Total number of mills (iii)	Total value of mills in pounds (iv)	Average value of mills in pounds (v)
Bedfordshire	3501	1579	102	76	0.74
Berkshire	6182	1286.625	164	107	0.65
Buckinghamshire	5162	2295.5	135	68	0.5
Cambridgeshire	4885	1701	130	89	0.68
Cheshire	271	1083.83	25	2	0.08
Cornwall	10856	2573	6	3	0.5
Derbyshire	2971	748.74	70	17	0.24
Devon	17439	7916	97	29	0.3
Dorset	7505	2224.25	282	113	0.4
Essex	14347	5203	237	not recorded	n/a
Gloucestershire	8659	3271.28	266	86	0.32
Hampshire	9987	2768	340	170	0.5
Herefordshire	4866	1251.15	108	43	0.4
Hertfordshire	4549	1728	132	65	0.49
Huntingdonshire	2507	1119.75	36	44	1.22
Kent	13011	2218.75	360	181	0.5
Leicestershire	6562	1591	129	30	0.23
Lincolnshire	22021	5018.935	433	158	0.36

(Continued)

County name	Number of households (i)	Total ploughland (ii)	Total number of mills (iii)	Total value of mills in pounds (iv)	Average value of mills in pounds (v)
Middlesex	2221	676.25	34	26	0.76
Norfolk	28087	4230.89	506	not recorded	n/a
Northamptonshire	8030	2828	262	105	0.4
Nottinghamshire	5639	1189.625	128	60	0.47
Oxfordshire	6489	2550.25	195	146	0.75
Rutland	851	140	7	3	0.43
Shropshire	4952	2739.875	94	19	0.2
Somerset	6267	4793.25	380	130	0.34
Staffordshire	3072	1362.25	67	14	0.21
Suffolk	20101	3980	235	not recorded	n/a
Surrey	4313	1018.375	119	91	0.76
Sussex	10015	2780.5	165	72	0.44
Warwickshire	6438	2175.5	125	55	0.44
Wiltshire	10268	3460.25	429	272	0.63
Worcestershire	4536	460.125	114	46	0.4
Yorkshire	7780	5724.75	117.5	37.81	0.32

TABLE 4.2. Domesday Book, key statistics (Continued)

Source: Domesday Book Online (raw data), Palmer, J. and Slater, G. at opendomesday.org.

i) The sum of householders recorded in the survey for that county.
ii) An area which could be ploughed by an eight-oxen team during the agricultural year, approx. 120 acres.
iii) Rounded to the nearest whole number.
iv) The Somerset figure excludes a significant transcription error in the Domesday records
v) Essex, Norfolk and Suffolk are excluded from any calculations involving mill value, which was not recorded in the Domesday Survey.

N.B. London, Winchester, Bristol, Tamworth, Northumberland, Durham and much of north-west England were not covered by the Domesday Book.

and Cambridge supports this argument. Table 4.4 shows that the average value of mills within a six-mile radius of the four towns was 30% higher than their respective county average. But this factor, although significant, cannot alone explain the 110% difference between the value of the mills on the River Great Ouse and the national average.

Ambler and Langdon suggest that the domination of Huntingdonshire by large ecclesiastical estates may be an additional factor and the evidence for this is strong (1994, 44). The role of the Church has already been noted, and especially the importance of the Benedictine order. All the religious institutions who held land along this stretch of the River Great Ouse at the time of the Conquest were Benedictine, and Figure 4.11 shows that in 1086 Huntingdonshire had the third highest concentration of ploughland held by the Church (44% of the county's total). It is significant that Middlesex, with the second highest concentration of ploughland, and Surrey, with the fifth highest concentration, had the equal

TABLE 4.3. Correlation coefficients, Domesday mills

Total number of watermills (Huntingdonshire 1086)	36	
Average number of watermills per site	1.565217391	
Average value of watermills per site	458.4782609	
Average value of each watermill (pence)	293	
Average number of households per settlement with a watermill	57.26086957	
Average area of ploughland per settlement with a watermill	19.38636364	
Correlation between number of watermills and number of households	0.341936367	Weak positive.
Correlation between number of watermills and ploughland	0.581599516	A moderate positive correlation.
Correlation between number of watermills and number of households in settlements with a watermill	-0.04180254	Weak negative.
Correlation between number of watermills and ploughland in settlements with a watermill	0.718865546	A strong positive correlation.
Correlation between number of watermills and number of households in settlements on the Ouse with a watermill	-0.14676904	Weak negative.
Correlation between number of watermills and ploughland in settlements on the Ouse with a watermill	0.804202245	A strong positive correlation.
Correlation between number of watermills and number of households in settlements on the middle section of the Ouse with a watermill	-0.19009685	Weak negative.
Correlation between number of watermills and ploughland in settlements on the middle section of the Ouse with a watermill	0.796521279	A strong positive correlation.
Correlation between number of watermills and number of households in settlements on the southern section of the Ouse with a watermill	0.487653299	Weak positive.
Correlation between number of watermills and ploughland in settlements on the southern section of the Ouse with a watermill	0.762972376	A strong positive correlation.
Correlation between value of mills and ploughland on the Ouse	0.291836426	Weak positive.
Correlation between value of mills and ploughland on the middle section of the Ouse	0.403636083	Weak positive.
Correlation between value of mills and ploughland on the southern section of the Ouse	0.548340316	A moderate positive correlation.
Correlation between number of households and total number of mills.	0.7	A strong positive correlation.
Correlation between number of households and total value of mills.	0.26	Weak positive.
Correlation between number of mills and total value of mills.	0.72	A strong positive correlation.

Source: Domesday Book Online (raw data), Palmer, J. & Slater, G. at opendomesday.org. Authors' calculations.

TABLE 4.4. Mill values within a six-mile radius of selected towns

Town	County average value of mills (£)	Average value of mills in a 6-mile radius of the town (£)	Percentage difference between 6-mile radius and county average values
Bedford	0.75	0.95	27%
Northampton	0.4	0.57	33%
Huntingdon	1.22	1.82	49.00%
Cambridge	0.73	0.83	13.70%

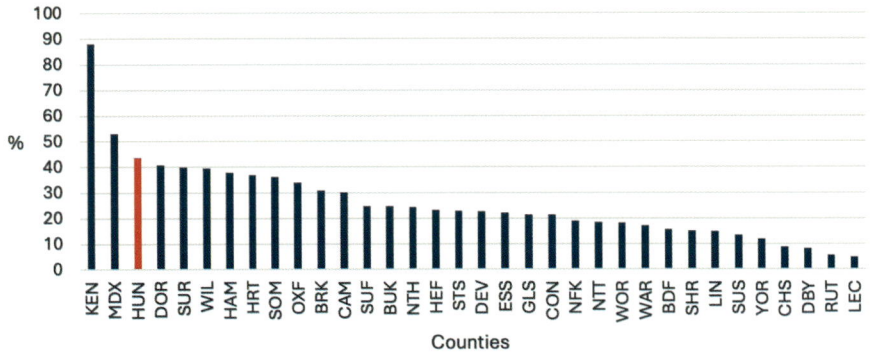

FIGURE 4.11. Percentage of land held by religious institutions, 1086

second highest average value of mills. The largest religious institution in Huntingdonshire was Ramsey Abbey and it held 25% of the county's ploughland. Ramsey was one of the richest abbeys nationally in 1086. By rigorously enforcing 'suit of mill' – its right to compel tenants to use its mills – it has been described as 'arguably both avaricious and authoritarian' by Lucas (2014, 309).

Ramsey Abbey may also have been transporting its grain upstream by boat to Hemingford Grey and Houghton, rather than risk financial loss by building any new mills in the more difficult physical conditions downstream. (It has previously been noted that Hemingford Grey is the lowest point on the river that enabled relatively straightforward channel engineering). Until 1066, Ramsey Abbey was the Overlord of Hemingford Grey and thus it would have been sensible to develop its milling capacity here. By 1086, ownership of Hemingford Grey manor had passed to Aubrey de Vere, albeit in a controversial action, with Ramsey Abbey continuing to claim ownership. But De Vere's ploughland holding was far too small to serve the two most valuable mills on the river, and so, to maintain their value, he would have needed grain from elsewhere. Therefore, it is logical to consider that a relationship with Ramsey Abbey continued, particularly as Ramsey Abbey held the neighbouring estate of St Ives with nearly 30 ploughlands and no mill. Table 4.5 lists all the ploughlands and mills owned by Ramsey Abbey in neighbouring counties, and Figure 4.12 shows their distribution. There were significant landholdings in Bedfordshire and Cambridgeshire. In Bedfordshire, Ramsey Abbey had sited mills to support its ploughland in the south of the county (at Pegsdon and Barton-in-the-Clay). At Little Barford, in the north-east of Bedfordshire, on the border with Huntingdonshire and Cambridgeshire, it had a mill valued at £0 12s 0d (*i.e.* in line with the national average of £0 11s 7d) in an estate with only five ploughlands. This suggests that it was providing milling capacity for estates elsewhere, probably for those in the south of Huntingdonshire, or to the south-west of Cambridgeshire. In Cambridgeshire, Ramsey Abbey had a sizeable holding of 80.5 ploughlands, but here it had only two mills, both at Burwell, and relatively small in value at £0 6s 7d. These would probably have been able to serve the 16 ploughlands in Burwell, but not the Abbey's other Cambridgeshire ploughlands. So, was Ramsey Abbey transporting grain along the Great Ouse from its Cambridgeshire estates to its

TABLE 4.5. Ramsey Abbey estates in Huntingdonshire's neighbouring counties

County	Ploughland	Number of mills	Mill value (£)
Bedfordshire	62	4	2.08
Hertfordshire	20	0	0
Cambridgeshire	80.5	2	0.33
Lincolnshire	9.25	0	0
Northamptonshire	20	3	2.2

N.B. Ploughlands are not recorded in Norfolk, Suffolk or Essex, and Ramsey Abbey had no land holdings in Rutland.

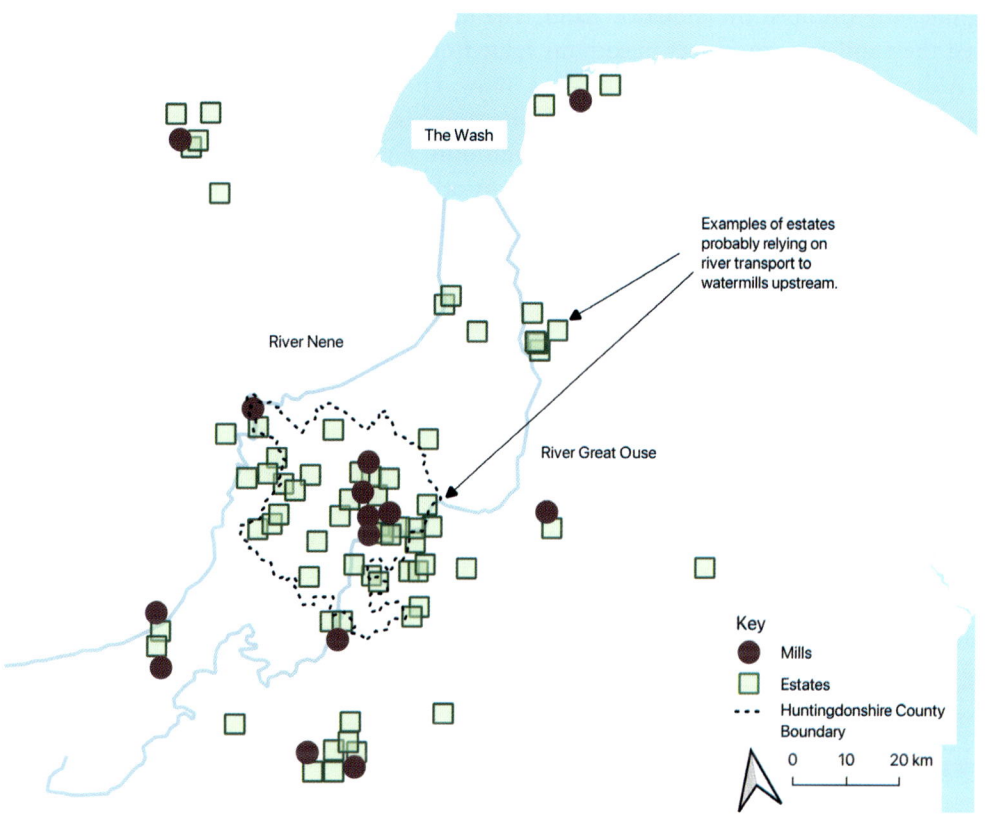

FIGURE 4.12. The estates and mills belonging to Ramsey Abbey in 1086

mills in Huntingdonshire? And is this evidence of a planned centralisation of milling capacity which would thus make the Huntingdonshire mills especially valuable? There is documentary evidence of grain being transported upstream from Holywell to Houghton in the 13th century (see page 73) – but in the absence of 11th century documentary evidence, the answer remains 'probably'.

Evidence from the Domesday Book shows that, in relation to Huntingdonshire's mills, royal ownership was more significant than monastic ownership. The history of these royal estates in Huntingdonshire may well be a significant factor in their milling prosperity and importance in 1086. The royal estates had the resources and authority necessary for major investment and would likely have capitalised on the situation. For the mills along the Great Ouse between St Ives and Brampton the Lord of the western group – comprising Godmanchester, Brampton, Hartford and Huntingdon – in 1066 was King Edward. The Lord of the eastern group – comprising Wyton, Houghton, Hemingford Abbots and Hemingford Grey – was Ramsey Abbey. By 1086 the royal sites had transferred to King William, and these were the most valuable (aggregate value £17). Ramsey Abbey owned Houghton, Wyton and Hemingford Abbots (aggregate value £2 2s 7d). Hemingford Grey (value £6) had transferred to Aubrey de Vere, one of King William's barons. At this time, the value of the royal hand significantly trumped the monastic hand. The royal estates would surely have used their authority to extract maximum value from their milling capacity.

Although the statistics of Domesday show Huntingdonshire with the number of mills to be expected for both the number of households and the amount of ploughland, it does have a significantly higher percentage of two and three-mill locations, compared with the 33 other counties in the Domesday Book. Huntingdonshire records 30% compared with 19% for two-mill sites, and 13% compared with 5% for three-mill sites. It would be reasonable to suggest that the grouping of mills – regardless of whether the Domesday Book was recording wheels and stones in the same building or a nearby building – allowed for shared resources of water engineering and milling equipment, and the rationalisation of transport, labour, management and maintenance. These economies of scale would surely have helped reduce both capital and running costs and thus increase value. The reason for this higher percentage of two and three-mill clusters is likely to be a combination of two factors: the lack of suitable watercourses for mills other than on the two main rivers of the Great Ouse and Nene, and the control exerted by the royal estates, particularly around the main urban site of Huntingdon. And it is also to be noted that the average value of these Huntingdonshire multiple mill sites is greater than that of their

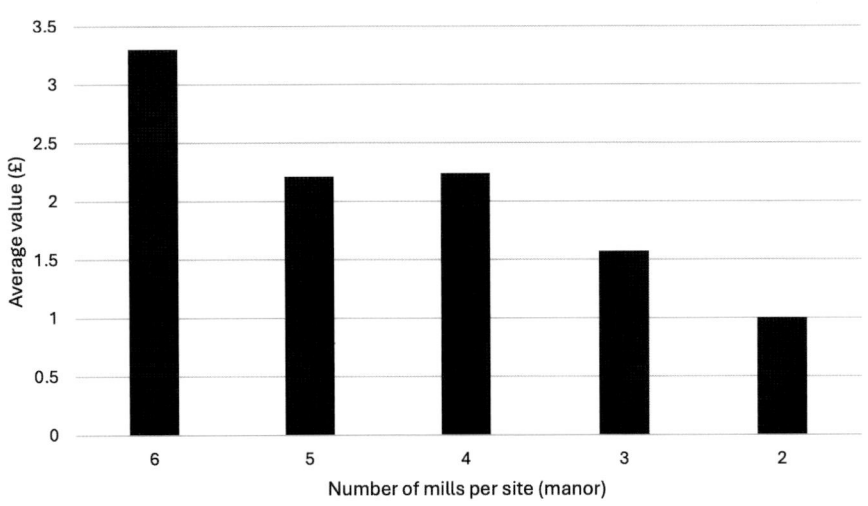

FIGURE 4.13. Average value of multiple mill sites (England, 1086)

national equivalents. Three-mill sites are valued at £4 2s 0d in Huntingdonshire compared with £1 10s nationally. Two-mill sites in Huntingdonshire are valued at £3 1s 7d compared with £1 nationally. But 'concentration' alone cannot explain the value of Huntingdonshire's mills.

In summary, there is no single or simple explanation as to the high value of Huntingdonshire's Domesday mills. Instead, there is an accumulation of evidence and suggestions. This unique set of circumstances lifts Huntingdonshire to the top of the Domesday 'league table' of mill values:

1. The county had a very favourable natural environment. Its climate and soils were good for grain production, and sections of its main river valleys, particularly from Brampton to St Ives, were ideal for water channel engineering.
2. This favourable natural environment was successfully exploited from at least the period of the Danelaw in 870–917. Subsequent decades of successful royal control of the Huntingdon area led to greater strategic organisation, rationalisation, and business sophistication of the estates than elsewhere.
3. Huntingdon, located on the River Great Ouse, was an important town and affected mill values positively.
4. Ramsey Abbey's efficient control of its estates within and beyond Huntingdonshire, with the possible imports of grain to Huntingdonshire mills, made the Huntingdonshire mills economically secure.
5. The combination and domination of royal and ecclesiastical political power ensured that there was no piecemeal development by minor owners. The watermills were commercial enterprises in the hands of a few large owners who controlled the whole county.
6. The Great Ouse in Huntingdonshire had a greater concentration of mills than elsewhere, partly because of its geography and partly because of the degree of centralised control, which was made easier in a relatively small county. Thus, Huntingdonshire benefited from the economic efficiency of groups of mills more than elsewhere.

CHAPTER FIVE

The Age of Backwaters: 1086–1350

The growth and development of watermilling along the River Great Ouse in Cambridgeshire aligns with most national developments during this period. There were two major innovations in the use and technology of mills. In the late 12th century the introduction of fulling mills for processing cloth was the first time watermills were used other than to mill grain (Watts 2016, 236). A waterwheel powered notched, wooden hammers to beat newly woven cloth, thickening it and felting its fibres. This resulted in a cloth for outer garments that would be thicker and more resilient to wind and rain. Fulling mills were concentrated in the north and west of the country where steeper gradients enabled the construction of powerful overshot waterwheels, and where the local type of wool required heavy pounding (Pelham 1944, 52–53). However, they were also built on lowland rivers where there was a demand and/or an economic opportunity. Windmill technology had been introduced from the mid to late 12th century (Rynne 2018, 12). Windmills were located mainly in the Midlands and the East of England where supplies of running water were less available. The 4,000 or so windmills that were built never rivalled the quantity of nearly 6,000 mills – almost all watermills – that had been recorded in the Domesday Survey. By the end of the 13th century that figure had increased to an estimated total of at least 9,000 watermills (White 2012, 52).

The Hundred Rolls survey of 1278–79 records that 48 windmills had been built in Huntingdonshire (Illingworth 1818 ii, 600–625). Notably, the seven lowest value watermills of Domesday – Broughton, Catworth, Kimbolton, Leighton, Spaldwick, Upton and Wistow, all on minor streams, were replaced by windmills during this period. Unfortunately, the Hundred Rolls do not give a complete record of the County's watermills but, from the figures available, Holt (1988, 109) estimates there was an increase of 30% capacity since Domesday, all on the Rivers Great Ouse and Nene. Along the Great Ouse, new mills are recorded at Eaton Socon (one), Paxton/St Neots (two), Brampton (one, a fulling mill) and Hemingford Grey (one). Three mills are recorded at Houghton cum Wyton so one of these was certainly a new mill (and was possibly a fulling mill, as later documentation may show). Also, a reorganisation is noted in this joint parish: the separate mill recorded at Domesday for Wyton 1279 is not mentioned. And there may have been a watermill at St Ives. The value of these mills increased during this period, *e.g.* as early as 1135, the value of the mills in the two Ramsey Abbey manors of Hemingford Abbots and Houghton cum Wyton was triple that of Domesday (Raftis 1957, 64–65), although how much this was due to a rise in corn prices or improvements in milling efficiency cannot be estimated. Demand was stimulated by a growing national population, from about two million in 1086 to perhaps six million in 1300 (White 2012, 6–7) with a similar two to threefold increase estimated for Huntingdonshire (Walters 1973, 101–112).

About 130 years after Domesday, a new manorial dynamic emerged in Huntingdonshire following a decline in the extent and strength of the Crown's holdings. This was to be of great significance to the development of watermilling. The mills at Eynesbury and Paxton had passed to Sawtry Abbey and St Neots Priory by the middle of the 12th century. By 1147 the manor of Hartford was granted to the Priory of St Mary in Huntingdon. The manor of Brampton remained with the Crown until 1194 but from then on had a complicated succession of owners. In 1205 the borough of Huntingdon, and in 1213 that of Godmanchester, were granted independence by Royal Charter – in return for an annual fee. The new Freemen of these two towns would become increasingly active in defence of their 'rights' against their powerful neighbouring manorial lords – both ecclesiastical and aristocratic (Langdon 2004, 18). At Huntingdon the tithes of the mill were given to the Priory of Huntingdon, although whether the Priory had any control over the operation of the mill, or simply received the tithes, is not clear. Lastly, there was change in Hemingford Grey; John de Grey (Earl of Kent) took over the manor in 1256 and was succeeded by his son Reginald de Grey in 1266. One other notable development along the River Great Ouse was the St Ives Easter Fair. Ramsey Abbey received a Charter for the Fair in 1110. By the mid to late 12th century St Ives Fair had become one of the four largest in England, extending to almost six weeks' duration and handling a wide international trade. Ramsey Abbey was at its high point of political and economic power.

Houghton Mill and Hemingford Abbots Backwater

The first record of changes to the river appears in a *Quo Warranto* Plea of 1274 (Illingworth 1818 i, 297). In this the inhabitants of Huntingdon attested that navigation to Huntingdon from the port of [King's] Lynn was impeded by the actions of three mill owners – Reginald de Grey, the Abbot of Ramsey and the Prior of Huntingdon. The Huntingdon Eyre records that these actions were taken before 1272 (DeWindt and DeWindt 1981, 411) and with Reginald de Grey becoming Lord of the Manor in 1266 this gives a specific date for the beginning of a major series of modifications to the river. This date aligns with the economic and manorial developments described above, and with similar disputes on other rivers (Bond 2007, 155). The complaint was that the mill owners were obstructing navigation to towns upstream, depriving them of trade and the income from tolls. Within the very short testimonies, two important points are made – which the complainants felt were fundamental. Firstly, that ships were 'accustomed and had right to navigate' and that 'it was the high river of our Lord the King' (Fox 1831, 190). However, whilst it was considered illegal to block a tidal river which was a highway under the protection of the Crown, it was less clear, and thus open to dispute, about blockages on a non-tidal river (Summers 1973, 27–28). And so, despite evidence of hitherto continuous navigation of the river upstream to Huntingdon and beyond, the removal of the obstructions was not enforced. The riparian owners (who were the mill owners) saw the river above St Ives as their property. Thus, the attorney for the Abbot of Ramsey, when asked if the removal of the dams etc 'would be to the injury of the said Abbot', said that 'it would' (Fox 1831, 194). Ault (1928, 109–110) writes that the abbots [of Ramsey] 'enjoyed grants of immunity from royal and other seigneurial influence' and that Ramsey Abbey was thus 'a singularly privileged institution in the 13th century'. It is not surprising that the Abbot's influence, combined with the political sway of de Grey and the ecclesiastical authority of the Prior of Huntingdon, meant that Huntingdon's complaint failed. The disputes would continue for well over 300 years.

But what changes were being made to the river? The *Quo Warranto* Pleas are in Latin, and local histories have generally relied on Robert Fox's 1831 translation. Only three Latin terms – *stagnum*, *exclusa* and *rivulus* – are used to describe the full range of possible water control mechanisms, including weirs, sluices, dams, leats, millponds and embankments. However, these terms can be translated differently. For example, Fox opts to translate *stagnum* using the generic English 'obstruction': ships are 'prevented by an obstruction in the river, formed by Reginald de Grey'; later, they are 'hindered by the obstructions of Reginald de Grey' (Fox 1831, 188 and 193). However, the use of 'obstruction' impedes understanding of the precise features of the River Great Ouse *stagna* (the plural of *stagnum*). In the same way that the word 'dam' can refer to a multitude of structures, from a vast reservoir contained in a flooded valley, to a barrier of logs and branches constructed by beavers, so the medieval *stagnum* could denote artificial constructs of different size and shape. Notably, the term was used variously to refer to natural standing pools of water (the usage closest to its classical origins), but also to the dams or embankments that rose above those millponds, which blocked and diverted the river to create pools of (relatively) still water, which acted, in Langdon's words, 'as a store of hydraulic energy' (Langdon 2004, 76). The water accumulated and retained by and in the *stagnum* would then be diverted through a mill-race to power a waterwheel during hours of operation.

Contemporaneous sources illustrate the different uses of the term. Records from Ramsey Abbey of *inquisitiones* ('judicial inquiries') held in December 1255 in the Parish of Shillington, Bedfordshire, indicate concerns surrounding the communal upkeep of the millpond at Pekesdene (Pegsdon, see Fig. 4.12). A series of judicial orders gives instructions, either that named individuals will help to clean out the *stagnum molendini*, or that other persons must be found to do so. The action involved implies a body of standing water that must be kept free of debris; the descriptive genitive *molendini* (Latin *molendinum* = 'mill') confirms this *stagnum* is attached to the mill (Hart and Lyons Vol I 1884–93, 468, 470, 472). The alternative use of *stagnum* to refer specifically to a dam or embankment is likewise illustrated by a record produced a century earlier, concerning the Cistercian abbey at Sallay (Sawley, in modern-day Lancashire). It is recorded that one Henry de Lacy allowed the monks 'to strengthen their *stagnum*', which lay above his land, 'for the purpose of constructing a fishery and a mill' (McNulty 2013, 127). Evidently, this *stagnum* was a dam and retaining embankment, the strengthening of which had the dual purpose of diverting the river to create a larger pool of slow-moving water suitable for a fishery and of controlling the diverted flow through a mill-race, to power a waterwheel slightly further downstream. It is these dual uses of the term *stagnum* that must be borne in mind when considering the watermills on the River Great Ouse: *stagnum* denotes either an artificial pool of relatively still water closely connected to the operation of a mill, or the dam structure that has been built into and across the river itself. In many cases, the term *stagnum* is used to refer to the retainer (the dam) and what is retained (the water) as a single unit that acts as the 'power source' for the associated mill. In our interpretation of the Latin texts, *stagnum*, *exclusa* and *rivulus* are left untranslated in order to highlight the different water control mechanisms.

The key to understanding what exactly was happening, is the reference in the 1274 Plea: 'the Abbot of Ramsey and his agents manufactured a certain small *rivulus*. This *rivulus* draws in the greater part of the waters from their ancient course, with the result that ships cannot navigate by the one channel or the other, to the great injury of the town of Huntingdon and the whole neighbourhood' (Illingworth 1818i, 297). The context makes it clear that *rivulus* is describing a small channel – a leat – that is taking water out of the main river. The only reason for constructing such a leat would have been to control the amount of water flowing through Houghton Mill. It therefore must have been upstream of the mill site. A watercourse 500 m upstream of Houghton Mill fits this description. It leaves the river at a right angle, is straight, small (300 m in length), and defines the parish boundary. It discharges into what was then 'Gumcester Drain', a stream rising a short distance away on Godmanchester Common and entering the main river at the eastern end of Battcock's Island in Hemingford Abbots. By constructing this leat, the Abbot created a backwater to cope with excess flow. The entrance to the backwater, located in the present landscape at Four Gates Pit Sluice, would have been controlled by a weir, or possibly a sluice, and it would have been set at a height that prevented too much water from reaching the mill. And for the first time, the main river was connected to what is now the Hemingford Abbots Backwater (formerly Gumcester Drain), a significant step in the development of its multi-channel form (Figs 5.1 and 5.2).

Why was it necessary to go to such lengths to control the level of water when Houghton Mill had been in existence for at least 300 years? The 'Abbot's Leat' helps answer this question and understand other significant changes that were happening at this location. Letters patent of 1524 (TNA R3/23, 022) record that the Abbot had constructed 'a great frame of woodwork with seven floodgates'

5. The Age of Backwaters: 1086–1350   65

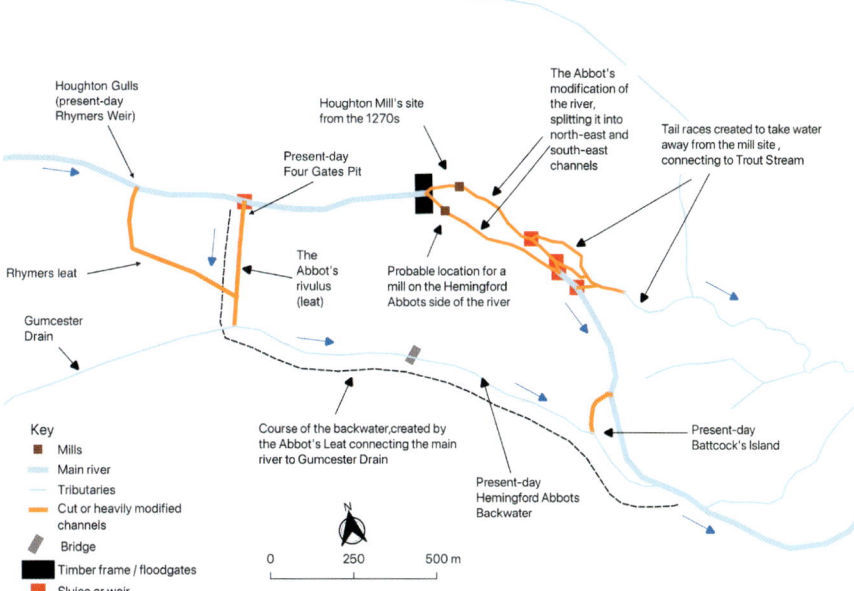

FIGURE 5.1. Houghton Mill Backwater and the Abbot's *rivulus* (leat)

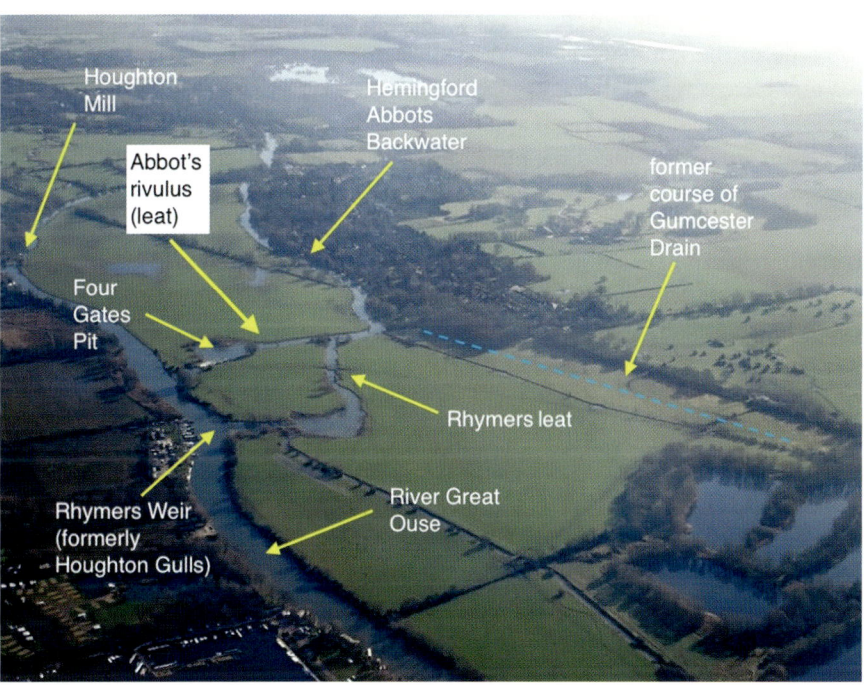

FIGURE 5.2. The Abbot's *rivulus* (leat) today

at Houghton to divide the main channel into two streams. One flowed north-eastwards to his corn mills and one south-eastwards to a fulling mill. Unfortunately, the document does not date when the Abbot did this, but it must have been before 1407 because there is a reference to a fulling mill at Houghton in the *Liber Gersumarum* of Ramsey Abbey in 1407 (DeWindt 1976). Diverting the main river and building new mills, dams and millponds, would have required a greater degree of water control, making the construction of a backwater essential. It is highly probable that these changes happened at the same time as the Abbot's Leat was constructed, in the third quarter of the 13th century. This sequence of events would explain the disappearance of the mill at Wyton from the records by the end of the 13th century, because the works on the main river would have left it on a relict channel. Houghton Mill was re-located on the north-east channel, where it is today. Therefore, the scour pool and tail races below Houghton Mill would have been created at the same time – all in all, a significant re-shaping of the landscape which increased the river's multi-channel form.

Hemingford Grey Backwater

The evidence shows something very similar happening at Hemingford Grey. The *Quo Warranto* Plea of 1274 named Reginald de Grey's *stagnum* as an obstruction to navigation. More detail is found in the Hundred Rolls of 1279–80 (Illingworth 1818 ii, 601): 'They also report that the Lord Reginald de Grey undertook to construct the *stagnum* on the upper bank belonging to the Lord the King between Hemingford and Huntingdon by diverting the watercourse for the use of his mill at Hemingford, such that small boats and ships that were accustomed to come to the borough of the Lord the King recently do not come, for this reason'. Here is a very different meaning of *stagnum* to Langdon's translation of 'millpond' (Langdon 2004, 26) and one which is much closer to Fox's translation of 'obstruction'. Looking at the physical geography of this section of the river, the *stagnum* must have been a weir, or sluice, at the entrance to what is still known as the Hemingford Grey Backwater (the present-day Six Gates Pit), because this is the only place where water could have been diverted to the Hemingford Grey Mills (Fig. 5.3). *Stagnum* is being used to describe an obstruction to a naturally occurring side channel (see below), although it is easy to understand why the term was chosen, because the function of the *stagnum* was to increase the amount of water in the main channel on which the Hemingford Grey watermills were sited.

An obstruction (whether a weir or sluice) at this location would have proved a barrier to river traffic that had previously used this side channel to avoid the mills sited on the main channel. The northern parish boundary follows the course of this channel, and Oosthuizen (1993, 7) writes 'that this makes it likely that this [the Backwater] was once the main course of the [Great] Ouse'. However, the form of today's main river and the backwater contradicts this theory. Both are just as would be expected from their channel bend dimensions, and there is no sign on the LiDAR or on the ground of the backwater having previously occupied a larger channel. This is typical of historically anabranching rivers, with channels maintaining their form for many hundreds of years and small streams occupying relict channels. A more straightforward interpretation of the parish boundary is that it originally ran eastwards along the main channel, but that de Grey changed (presumably by negotiation and purchase from his neighbour the Abbot of Ramsey) the boundary of his manor because control over the backwater was essential to his milling operation. The *stagnum* increased

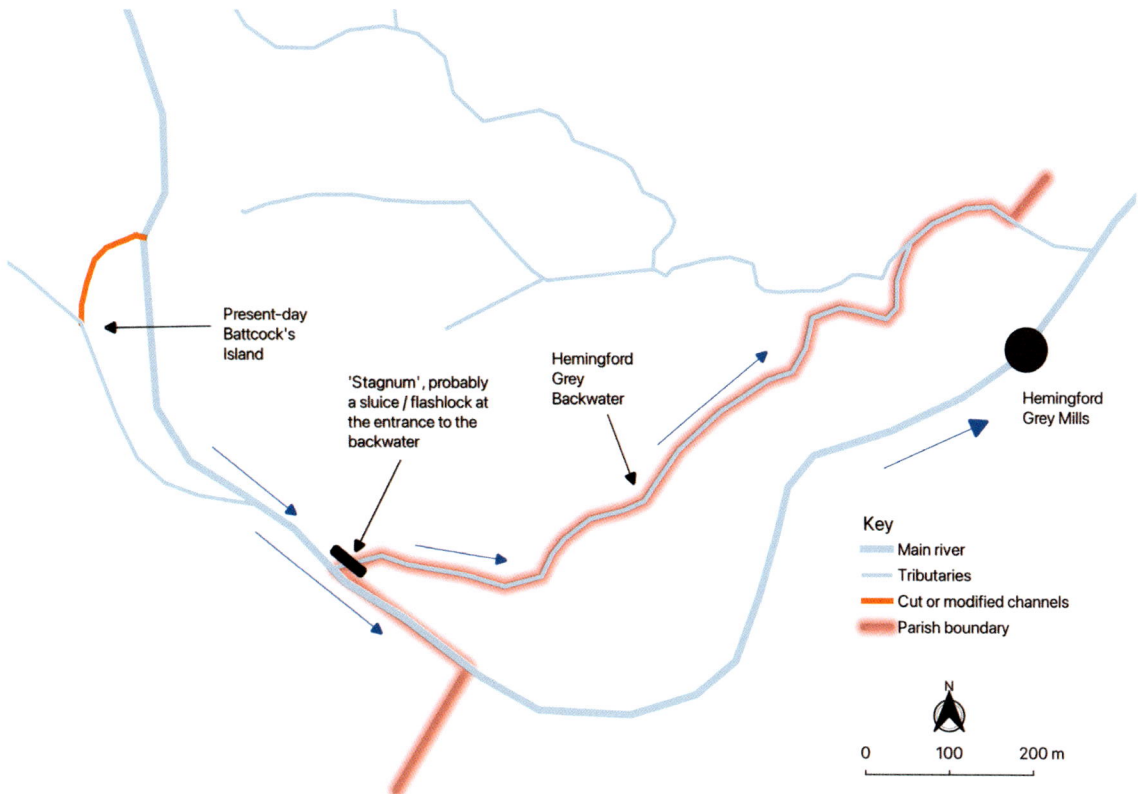

FIGURE 5.3. Hemingford Grey Mills Backwater

the level of water in the main river, and therefore the power reaching de Grey's mills. At the same time, it provided a safety valve to protect the mills. If, on occasion, the water level became too high, it could spill over into the backwater and re-join the main channel below the mills. It is reasonable to conclude that de Grey would only have undertaken such an extensive amount of engineering to enable expansion of his milling capacity. The Huntingdonshire Eyre of 1279 supports this assertion (DeWindt and DeWindt 1981, 487):

> Re the purprestures [illegal encroachments on someone else's land], etc., they report that the water of the Ouse is blocked by a … mill belonging to Reginald de Grey in Hemingford, such that ships are unable to pass through just as they used to do, and because of which the villa at Huntingdon, which is a villa of the lord the King, is deteriorating, to the injury of the whole neighbourhood.

Two Backwaters at Hartford

Along with the Abbot of Ramsey and Reginald de Grey, the Prior of Huntingdon is cited in the *Quo Warranto* Plea of 1274 as obstructing the river with *exclusae*. Fox (1831, 188) translates this as 'dams'. However, the *Rotuli hundredorum* of 1276 (Illingworth 1812, 198) records that the Borough of Huntingdon described these obstructions as 'fit for purpose whenever navigators require them', *i.e.* they were not a permanent barrier, so 'water gates' or 'sluices' is a more appropriate meaning. It is probable that they were 'flashes', removable panels, to allow water

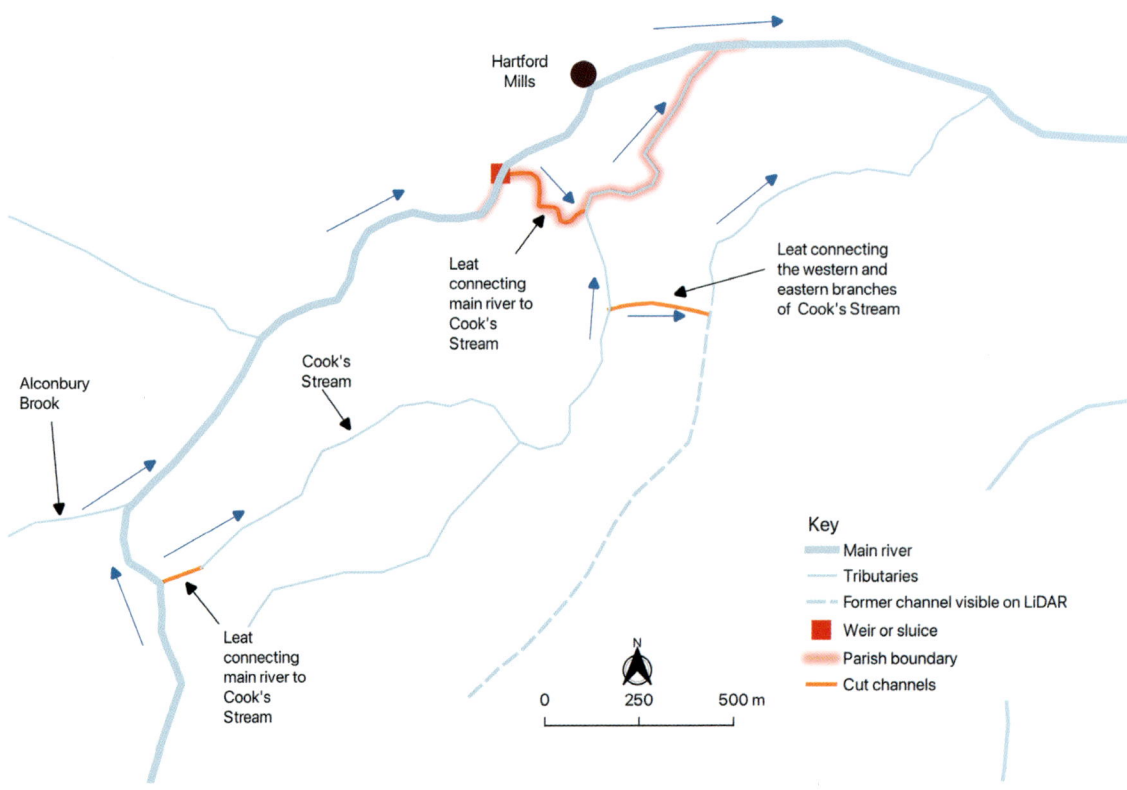

FIGURE 5.4. Hartford Mills Backwater

transport (Langdon 2004, 75). As at Houghton and Hemingford Grey, there is evidence of backwater construction, but because it did not affect navigation it was not part of the complaint. Upstream of the site of the mills is a sluice controlling the entrance to a sinuous channel that takes water away from the main river, discharging into Cook's Stream, which in turn discharges into the main river below the mills (Fig. 5.4). The most straightforward explanation of this configuration is that it was created as a backwater to give the Prior control over the amount of water reaching his mills. That the Hartford parish boundary diverts from the main channel of the river to follow the sinuous channel and then continues along Cook's Stream south of the river on Godmanchester land, supports this explanation, *i.e.* it is another example of a parish boundary being changed to ensure control over an important asset.

The landscape evidence suggests that Hartford Mills used Cook's Stream as a second, more significant, backwater. Cook's Stream has the bend dimensions of a natural channel for most of its length. However, it leaves the main river at a very unnatural right angle for no apparent reason. Also, it is the only one of the streams flowing eastwards from Godmanchester, which is connected to the main river (Fig. 5.4). Documentary evidence supports this connection being the result of deliberate modifications on the low-lying land ('the reed medewe') between Godmanchester and Huntingdon. An inquest in 1276 recorded that the Prior of Huntingdon was responsible for the perpetual maintenance of a

5. *The Age of Backwaters: 1086–1350* 69

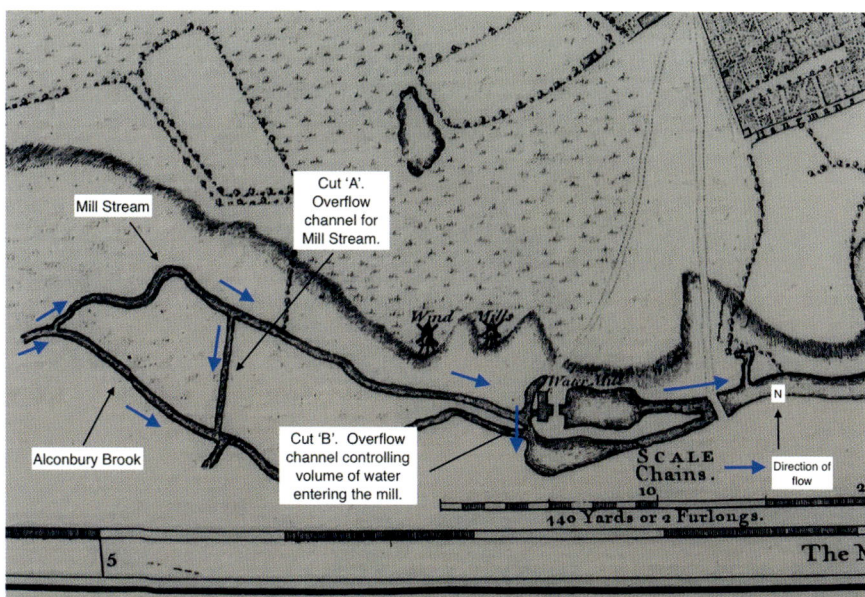

FIGURE 5.5. 'Plan of the town of Huntingdon' 1768 by Thomas Jefferys, showing the Huntingdon Mill Overflow Channels

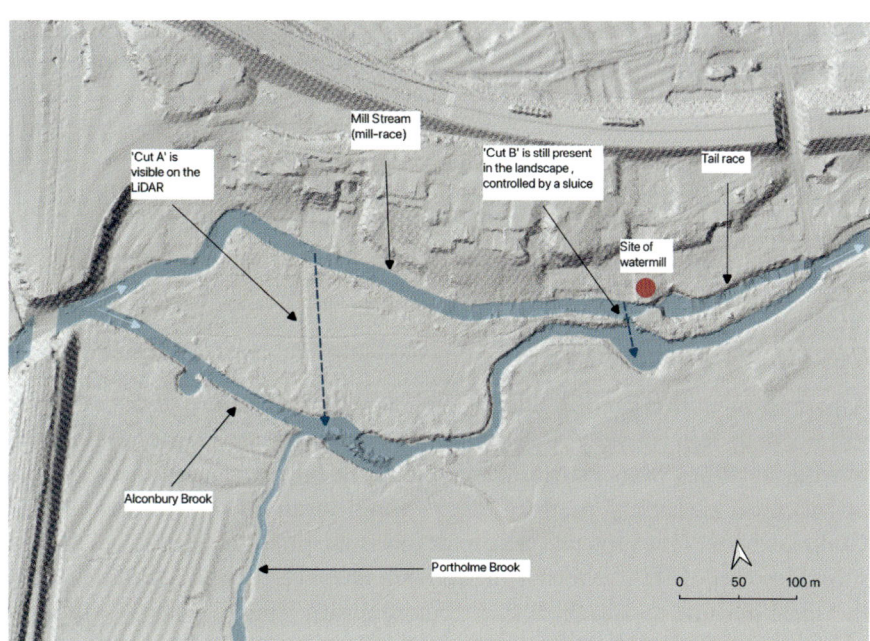

FIGURE 5.6. Huntingdon Mill LiDAR, 2023

causeway between Godmanchester and Huntingdon (Fox 1831, 362–368). Flood gates were built into one of the causeway's arches, and from this it can be concluded that, by this date, the stream had been connected to the main river. The flood gates allowed the Prior of Huntingdon to control the level of water in the main river, to the benefit of his mills at Hartford. The 1276 inquest set

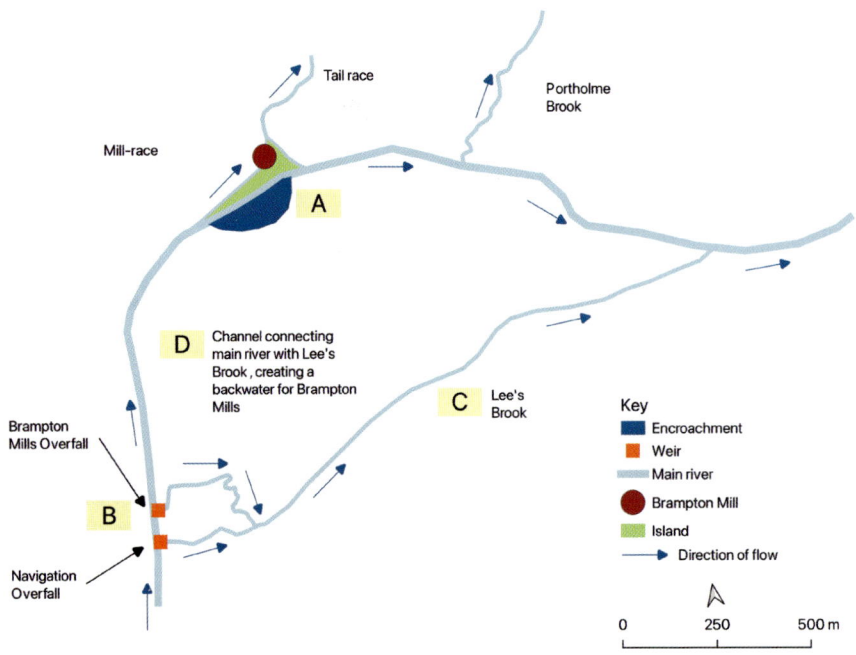

FIGURE 5.7. The impact of Brampton Mills on the Landscape in the 13th century

out the Prior's responsibilities to draw the flood gates if Godmanchester land was endangered by floods. The stream was later named after one Robert Cook who fell from the causeway in 1637 and, in thanks for his narrow escape from drowning, donated funds towards the bridges' future repair, but the stream's association with the milling developments of the 13th century is indicated in alternative names still in use, *e.g.* 'Back River' (Green 1977, 41) and 'Cook's Backwater' (Perrins 2023, 6).

Backwaters at Huntingdon and Godmanchester

A pattern of mill expansion and the creation of backwaters to act as 'safety valves' can be seen emerging at Hemingford, Houghton and Hartford. However, moving upstream from Hartford, there is no documentary or other evidence of backwater construction at the first two mill locations of Huntingdon and Godmanchester. The probable reason for this is the physical constraints of those sites. However, there is evidence of 'overspill channels' that would have served the same purpose as a backwater. At Huntingdon, Jefferys' 'Plan of the town of Huntingdon' of 1768 (Dunn 1977) shows a cut connecting Mill Stream with Alconbury Brook and a smaller cut immediately upstream of the mill site (Fig. 5.5). Both would have served as 'safety valves' for the mill-leat, using Alconbury Brook as a backwater. They could have been constructed during this period, but there is no direct evidence that they were. The cut linking Mill Stream with Alconbury Brook was not shown on the first large-scale OS map in 1886, and therefore was presumably no longer in use, but it can be seen on the LiDAR (see Fig. 5.6). At Godmanchester, one or more of the channels that connect

Mill Lade with the main river (see Fig. 3.1) may have been cut at this time to control the amount of water reaching the mills, but there is no documentary or archaeological evidence to support this suggestion.

Brampton's backwater

At Brampton a fulling mill was recorded in 1278 in addition to the two grain mills of the Domesday survey (Illingworth 1818 ii, 607). The site had expanded since 1086 and would have required more water. In the Huntingdon Eyre of 1286 (DeWindt and DeWindt 1981, 487), a complaint brought by the Borough of Godmanchester, alleged that the bailiffs of John of Hastings, the owner of the Brampton mills, had constructed 'unlawful' dams, weirs and sluices that were causing flooding and the degradation of Godmanchester land. The complaint stated that a 'certain *stagnum* newly constructed at the mill house' caused a 'purpresture, six pertica [c100 feet] in length and three feet in width'. The landscape evidence suggests that *stagnum* is used here quite conventionally, to refer to a mill pond created by building a dam, raising the river banks, and/or deepening the channel bed, at or very near the mill house. The complaint continues, 'And similarly … those men … have constructed a certain *stagnum* across a stretch of the Ouse (which is common property), twenty feet in length and twenty feet in width, and as a result of the construction of that *stagnum*, Godmanchester meadow is flooded and degraded'. That this *stagnum* has been placed 'across' [*extransverso*] suggests a construction spanning the river's width. This, and its dimensions, indicates a *stagnum* of a different type to the one located at the mill house itself. It would have been a blockage in the river, but rather than a dam (which would be a complete obstruction of the flow), it indicates what would be recognised today as a weir. The Sheriff ordered that these features 'be cleared away and demolished'. However, a channel making an obvious encroachment onto Godmanchester land, close to the mill site, and fitting the 13th century description, can still be seen. This is probably the larger of the two 'purprestures' (Fig. 5.7).

The Borough of Godmanchester's fourth complaint was that 'those bailiffs have constructed a certain sluice at Brampton in a certain place far away from where it should be and where it was before, whereby, on account of the watercourse being thus diverted, the greater part of the meadow is abstracted' (DeWindt and DeWindt 1981, 487). The probable location of this sluice is revealed by comparing LiDAR, historical maps and field observations. Upstream of the mill there is a blocked-up weir at the entrance to a sinuous channel (B on Fig. 5.7, page 70). On the Lenny & Croft map of 1834 (R1/478) it is labelled 'Brampton Mills Overfall'. It takes water from the main river to Lee's Brook (C on Fig. 5.7), suggesting that Brampton Mills exploited Lee's Brook, on Godmanchester land, as its backwater. The channel's sinuous course, which can be tracked on the ground (D on Fig. 5.7), is hard to explain but it could have been following field boundaries and/or relict channels. This sluice and channel are – as the complaint states – a long way from where a backwater for Brampton Mill might be expected to be. However, it makes sense from a milling perspective – why go to the expense and trouble of constructing a new backwater when there is a suitable channel ready to be adapted and connected?

Backwaters on the river south of Brampton

There is no backwater at the location of the Buckden and Offord mills, but almost any of the complex network of channels, controlled by weirs, as shown on the historical maps could have been used to manage the level of water in the mill-leats. However, at Little Paxton, where the floodplain is wider, there is a repeat of the pattern seen on the Brampton to Hemingford Grey stretch. In the middle of the 12th century, King Malcolm of Scotland, who was the lord of Little Paxton, gave two mills to the Priory of St Neots (Illingworth 1818 ii, 673). It is reasonable to assume that these were at or near the site of the St Neots Paper Mill that closed in 1988. One compelling piece of evidence is the deviation in the parish boundary. It is one of the clearest examples of a boundary being modified to include important assets, *i.e.* the Priory's two mills, plus a backwater, which was necessary to manage the level of water in the mill-leat (Fig. 4.4, page 43). The backwater may have been the original main course of the river, but the Lenny and Croft map (1834) is unequivocal as to its continuing purpose, clearly labelling it 'Back Water'. Along this stretch of the river there is a rare contemporary account of the importance of water control for medieval watermills. Dugdale (1693, 479) records that 'In 1324, there were three water mills belonging to the Priory at St. Neots, but in 1370 they had been destroyed in a great flood and were of no value'. The location of the Eaton Socon/Eynesbury mills is, like Buckden/Offord, a constricted site. The complex arrangement of channels and weirs indicates the importance of controlling water levels. However, the only possible backwater is the small, curved channel (C on Fig. 4.2, page 41), indicated by a deviation in the parish boundary, but this may have been associated with the lock, rather than the mill.

Was there a watermill at St Ives?

There is no mill recorded at St Ives in the Domesday Book. Given the size of St Ives' agricultural capacity – in the top 8% of the county – it seems surprising that it was not self-sufficient in milling its own grain. Although, as discussed earlier, the physical geography of this section of the river is less conducive to watermilling, but it does not rule it out completely. There is no archaeological evidence for a watermill at St Ives in any period, but there is some limited documentary evidence from the 13th century through to the Dissolution of the Monasteries in the 1530s, and also some landscape evidence, that, together, suggests there might have been a watermill here in the later Middle Ages.

The first reference is to a windmill, not a watermill. A Charter of Abbot Ranulph of Ramsey Abbey, who was elected in 1231 and died in 1253, records the granting of a windmill to the Prior of St Ives: 'the windmill outside the village of St Ives, which mill William of Timeworthe sold to us, along with its site and produce' (Hart and Lyons 1884–93, vol. ii 225–226). The next reference is in 1252, when an inquisition into the returns from Ramsey Abbey's lands in Holywell (Hart and Lyons 1884–93, vol. i 302) concluded that: 'Each and every person must also remember that they ought (*de jure*) to do suit of mill at Houghton, which they have not done after the construction of the Prior's mills at St Ives'. Here, two mills are mentioned, so the Prior must have acquired or perhaps built another grain mill, or mills, in addition to his windmill gifted in the Charter, although it is not specified whether they were wind, water or animal-powered. And clearly, Ramsey Abbey was determined not to lose any milling business from its Holywell tenants who appear to have been recently 'poached' by the Priory for its new mills. The Holywell grain was thus ordered to by-pass St Ives and be taken to Houghton as before, presumably by river. One more brief reference explains that shortly before 1440 the Prior exchanged land in Bury for a building at St Ives 'near the Priory and the Prior's mill' (VCH i 1932, 210–223). Again, no information is given as to the type of mill or its specific location. However, it is believed that it may have been in the vicinity of the Priory Barn (parts of the walls of which remain) where grain would have been stored, which is very close to the river.

After the Dissolution of the Monasteries in 1539 the Slepe and the Priory estates were taken by the Crown and then passed to new owners who kept them largely intact. The 'List of the lands of dissolved Religious Houses' (PRO 1967, 242) records that there were 'two mills within the site of the Priory of St Ives'. What type of mills is not specified, and no further records relating to mills on the Priory estate have surfaced. However, there are clues on the first detailed maps of St Ives, drawn by Edmund Pettis (Pettis's Ancient History of St. Ives, 1728 and 1732), and in the present-day landscape. On his 1728 map Pettis labels a field at the junction of the present-day Needingworth Road and St Audrey Lane 'Mill Hill'. On the 1732 map he draws a small circle with a dot in the middle in the north-east corner of this field (Fig. 5.8). It is highly likely that he is using this symbol to show a windmill, but there is no indication if it is a working windmill, or disused. An identical symbol is used on the 1728 map on common land on Somersham Heath (Fig. 5.9) to show another windmill site. Either of these locations could be the site of the windmill recorded in the documentary evidence, above, as they fit with the description that it was '*extra villam Sancti Ivonis*', i.e. beyond the houses/residences of St Ives.

On both maps Pettis shows the stream known today as the 'Old River' or the 'Chubb or Chub Stream' but he calls this 'Priory Dike' (Fig. 5.10). The shape and form of the Old River resemble the leats seen elsewhere on the river associated with medieval watermills, which led Burn-Murdoch (2009, 37) to conclude that 'it was probably dug to provide water to power the Priory's watermill'. The cut probably took advantage of relict channels on the meadow, and this would explain its non-linear (but not completely natural) form. It

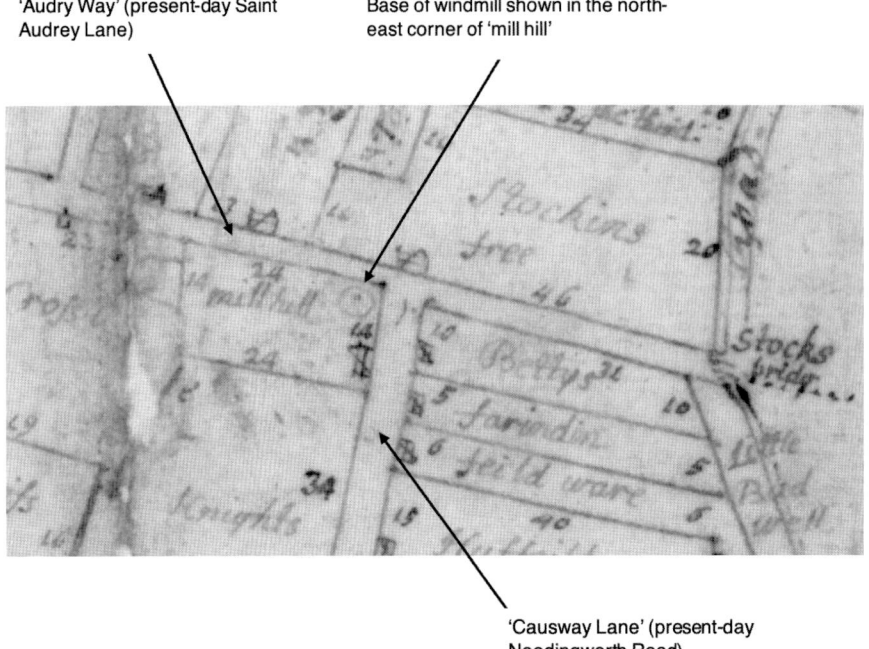

FIGURE 5.8. Map of St Ives by Edmund Pettis 1732, showing 'Mill Hill' windmill

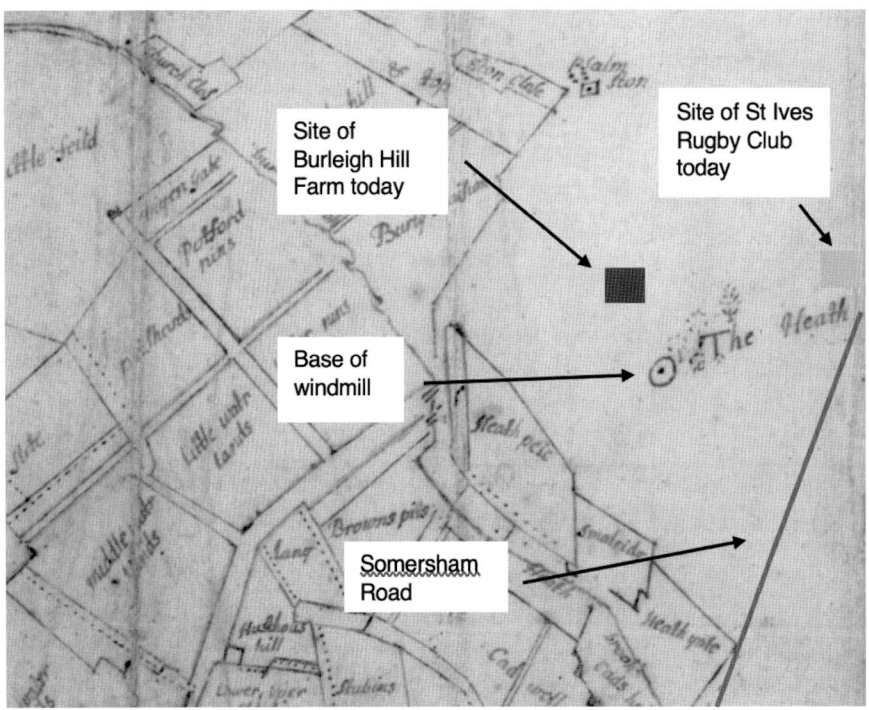

FIGURE 5.9. Map of St Ives by Edmund Pettis 1728, showing 'Burleigh Hill' windmill

5. *The Age of Backwaters: 1086–1350*   75

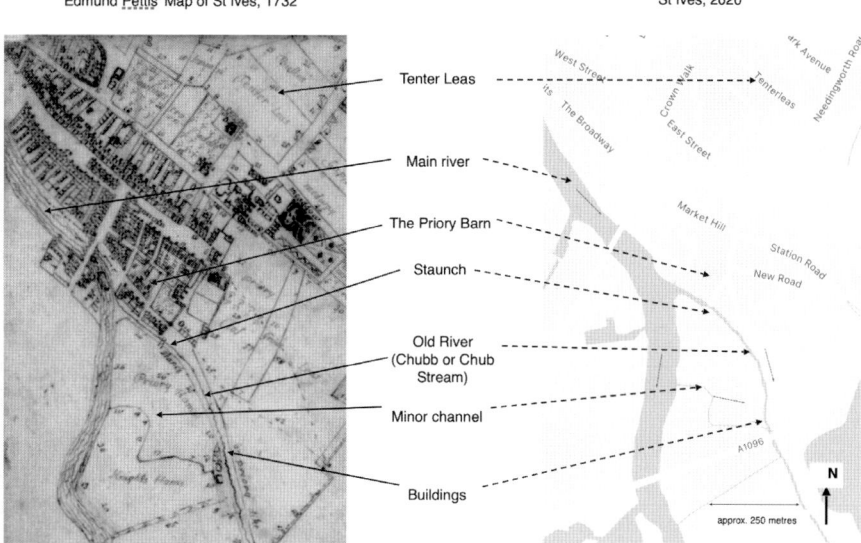

FIGURE 5.10. Map of St Ives by Edmund Pettis 1732, next to a map of St Ives 2020

is also possible that it was originally dug to give the Priory easy access to the main river and/or to act as a drainage channel, and that it was subsequently adapted for watermilling, if a watermill ever existed. Another minor channel from the main river flows into the Old River. Pettis drew it with a markedly sinuous form – and it looks the same today. It is identical to the short, sinuous streams at Hartford and Brampton, both associated with channel engineering for a watermill. On Pettis' 1732 map there are two buildings close to where this minor channel joins the Old River. These are not shown on the 1728 map, but that does not mean that they were not there, and it is possible that they were associated with milling activity.

Pettis labelled a field 400 m north of the former Priory as 'Tenter Leas', which describes a field equipped with racks for the stretching of cloth. This strongly suggests that there was a fulling mill relatively nearby to produce such felted cloth – and in medieval times this would have been a watermill. With fulling mills recorded at Brampton and Houghton in the 13th to 15th centuries, the industry was established in the area. However, there is only conjecture as to whether the Priory built a watermill as a fulling mill or converted an earlier grain mill, or if it built a watermill at all.

There is one further occurrence of the word 'mill' on the Pettis maps. One of St Ives' three large open fields is called 'Mill alis King's brook feild', *i.e.* Mill or King's brook field. At the southern end of this field, on land opposite the junction of what is now Pig Lane and Saint Audrey Lane, is a parcel of land labelled 'mill fours' near 'Bugel moor brook' (Fig. 5.11). Was this the site of a windmill, or could there have been a watermill on Bugel Moor Brook? There is no symbol for a windmill and initially it is hard to imagine that a watermill could have been built on such a small water course. However, prior to the

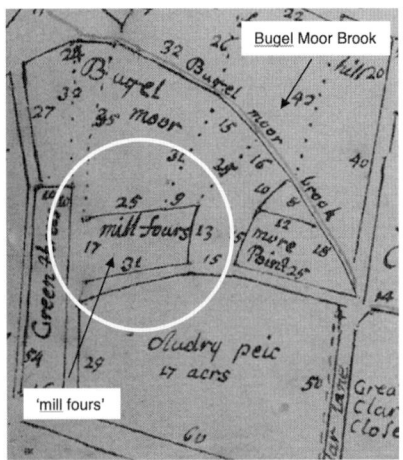 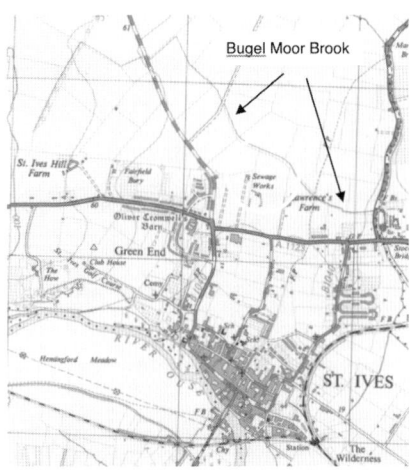

FIGURE 5.11. Map of St Ives by Edmund Pettis 1728, showing 'Mill fours' and 'Bugel moor brook' alongside the 1949 OS map

post-1950 development in St Ives this was a more significant stream, which can be seen on the 1949 OS map (Huntingdonshire 52/37). Today much of its course is underground but then, and especially if it was fed by field drains, it might have been able to power a small watermill. Alternatively, it could have been the site of a small animal-powered mill.

To summarise, although there was no watermill in St Ives in 1086, documentary evidence records at least two (grain) mills between the 13th to 15th centuries, at least one of which was a windmill. Pettis' maps provide place-name evidence for a watermill involved in cloth production. The landscape evidence strongly suggests a watermill on the Old River. The most likely site is between the present-day weir and the minor channel. The group of buildings identified on Pettis' map near to the confluence of the Old River and the minor channel might have been associated with milling, but without a successful archaeological excavation here – or new documentary and/or cartographic evidence being discovered – there is no conclusive proof. Although unlikely, there might have been a watermill north of Saint Audrey Lane on Bugel Moor Brook. On balance, St Ives probably did have a watermill, but there is no conclusive proof.

What impact did the Age of Backwaters have on the landscape?

As can be seen from the above, a clear pattern of development emerges in the second half of the 13th century. Economic development and population growth led to the mill owners expanding capacity and introducing new technologies, such as fulling mills. This all required an increase in water power and so the mills were re-located, either onto the main river, or onto bigger, new channels. In turn, the increase in channel size and the quantity of water necessitated improvements in the control of the water, and hence the construction of new weirs, dams, sluices, mill-leats, tail races, overspill channels and backwaters. The different types of *stagna* used to do this help explain the characteristics of this stretch of river. (The same application will probably help with understanding the development of other lowland river landscapes.) Where backwaters could be constructed, they were: at Hemingford Grey, Houghton, Hartford, Brampton, Little Paxton and possibly Eaton Socon. At the other locations channels were modified to manage an increased flow of water. The impact of these developments on the landscape was profound and continues to the present-day; most of the backwaters formed in the 13th century are still present in the landscape. The construction of the backwaters for Houghton and Hartford mills has had a big influence on the development of the multi-channel form of the river between Brampton and Hemingford Grey. Relicts of land encroachment can still be seen, *e.g.* on Godmanchester's West Meadow. Islands were created, *e.g.* Millers Holme at Houghton. Tail races to discharge the water going through the mills were enlarged and/or cut. Parish boundaries were modified to encompass these assets and although some were 'tidied up' by the Boundary Commission in 1974, many remain. This sequence of development is so consistent that it can be used to understand the landscape history of watermilling locations on other lowland rivers, and the development of features, such as parish boundaries, which will be discussed further in Chapter 10.

CHAPTER SIX

River Wars: 1515 – matters come to a head

The late 13th century litigation regarding the Huntingdonshire mills, as described in the previous chapter, was solely concerned with the rights of navigation. In 1215, Clause 33 of Magna Carta established the free passage of ships and boats on rivers, and this principle was confirmed by Edward I in 1297 in the 'Great Charter of the Liberties of England' (Henderson 1896). But conflicts of interest over the use of rivers persisted – especially where barriers and mechanisms for fisheries and milling impeded the passage of shipping. A commission of 1287 investigated the complaint by the men of Huntingdon that: 'the water of the great river, between the said borough and the town of St Ives, is so diminished by reason of watercourses therefrom and obstructions in the said stream, that ships and boats laden with merchandise can no longer pass as they were wont' (The Protection of Public Rights of Navigation 2015, 14). In *c.* 1300, the Prior and monks of St Neots requested that the navigation of the Great Ouse be re-opened (TNA SC/8/171/8518) – presumably for trade and communication with their mother house in Normandy. They stated that although they were sited on the river and owned nine mills, they were 96 leagues from the sea.

However, in the early and mid-14th century there appears to be no record of navigation disputes in Huntingdonshire. This could be because documentary evidence has not survived. But more likely it reflects the severe national socio-economic downturn caused by climatic deterioration in the first half of the 14th century, plus the ravages of the Black Death from 1348, which caused prices and population to fall (Rippon 2001, 16). Cold weather and torrential rains in the summer of 1315, followed by spring rains in 1316, resulted in the worst year for cereal crops throughout the entire Middle Ages (Fagan 2000, 39). The 1340s were particularly cold and wet, with the most prominent narrowing of tree rings in 1348 (Campbell 2016, 10). The Black Death, a pandemic of bubonic plague, spread from Europe across Britain between June 1348 and December 1349, with further outbreaks in 1361, 1368–1369, 1375 and then sporadically for the next 300 years (Bos *et al.* 2011, 506–510). Lewis (2016, 785–786) notes a broad consensus among historians that in England the post-Black Death population fluctuated for the next two centuries somewhere around 30–55% below its previous level. Her test-pit data for Eastern England (which included Houghton cum Wyton in its sample) points to a decline, averaging about 45%.

14th and 15th century navigation disputes

As the economy began, slowly, to recover after the Black Death, litigation regarding navigation on the Great Ouse, and on rivers elsewhere, resumed in earnest in the third quarter of the 14th century. Across England, rivers continued to be blocked by both fishing weirs and mill weirs, as many had been in the late 13th century. A statute of 25 Edward III in 1350, followed by a very similar statute (The Protection of Public Rights of Navigation 2015, 5) in 1371, stated that:

> because the common passage of ships and boats in the great rivers of England were often disturbed by the levying of wears, mills, stanks [ponds], stakes and kiddles [sticks or posts with nets, used to trap fish], which were levied and set up in the time of the King's Grandfather in great damage of the people, it was accorded and established that all the said wears, mills, stanks, stakes and kiddles set up in the Time and aforesaid and after, in ... should be cut and wholly pulled down without repairing.

In 1370, following complaints by merchants from the counties of Leicester, Derby, Northampton, Bedford and Huntingdon, a commission investigated the loss of navigation on the Great Ouse caused by the mills between St Ives and Huntingdon (Maxwell Lyte 1914, 35). As with the earlier commission of 1287 (Maxwell Lyte, 1895), the findings and any actions are not known. In 1376 a further petition was made to Parliament (VCH f 1932, 309–314) citing the economic damage to Huntingdon due to obstructions in the river from mills. And lastly, in 1398, commissions to 'execute the statutes of 25 Edward III and 45 Edward III' (The Protection of Public Rights of Navigation 2015, 19) were set up in all the major counties of England, including Huntingdonshire. After that there are no further records about the Huntingdonshire mills and navigation for over a hundred years until the early 16th century.

The combination of the late 13th and late 14th century complaints about obstruction to navigation could indicate that the mill owners had managed to defeat the legal challenges and that there had been no waterborne trade above St Ives for more than a century. But this is not quite what was happening. Despite the disputes, the late 13th century alterations to the river to facilitate the expansion of mills at Hemingford Grey, Houghton and Hartford, had remained *in situ* and become established. And it would seem that some form of compromise between the mill operations and the navigation had been reached. Many of the complaints had been that the ships could not pass 'as they were wont to do' or 'as they were accustomed': phrases that explain that previously the ships had unimpeded passage, but also which imply that some passage still existed, albeit in a different form. What was happening was that the navigation was largely sectional between mill dams. It was described as very unsatisfactory, labour-intensive and expensive (TNA DL3/23, 010 and 011). Boatmen could unload their cargoes at appointed sites called 'the drawing place', haul their boats and goods around the mill dams and then reload at the other side. ('It requires the help and labour of diverse persons and is much chargeable, but if the boats and vessels might keep [to] the high stream one person or two might do all the same business') (TNA DL3/23, 010). Or, the better option, if granted, was for the miller to open one of the mill sluice gates to allow the boats through-passage by water. This action, functioning as a 'flash lock', released a 'flash' – a large head of dammed-up water for the boats to ride over. Such an amount of water took some time to replace, and therefore its release and use was unpopular with the millers. For both operations the millers charged a toll. Thus, since 1274, when they had expanded their mills and constructed dams, leats and weirs, the mill owners at Hemingford, Houghton and Hartford, had taken, and maintained, complete control of the river. It should be added that millers south of Godmanchester may well have been acting similarly, but for that there is no documentary evidence.

15th century disputes over flooding

Another series of long-running disputes began in the 15th century. This time not about navigation but the flooding of agricultural land, allegedly caused by the height of the mill dams. The disputes were entirely local, predominantly between the Borough of Godmanchester and the mill owners of Hartford (the Prior of Huntingdon) and Houghton (the Abbot of Ramsey) (KG/A/3/8, KG/A/1/12, KG/A16/1). The Borough of Huntingdon and the owner of Hemingford Grey mill (the Earl of Kent) were also involved, but not in the forefront of action. The arguments were bitter and protracted, spilling over from court proceedings into riot, civil disobedience and destruction of property.

Litigation would again appear to be a bellwether for an increase in milling activity and/or investment. This was obviously the case in 1274, as has been explained earlier. The same then occurred at the end of the 14th and in the early 15th century but was more complicated. Local rental agreements illustrate the general stagnation in corn prices and arable farming after the Black Death. The Houghton corn watermill had a rental of £6-13-4d in 1399 and £7-6-8d in 1405, and windmill rents at Warboys, Wistow and Holywell ranged from £1 to £2 – all at least 30% reduced from their pre-Black Death values (Raftis 1922, 280). However, in 1399 it was recorded that a Hemingford Abbots mill (adjacent to the Houghton Mill site) was a fulling mill. William Smyth and Stephen Fuller took on the lease for 10 years at an annual rent of 20 marks (£13-8/-). It is not known exactly when it changed from being a corn mill, or was built anew, but it was likely to have been during this period of downturn in arable farming. (There were relatively few fulling mills at this time in the east of England: in Huntingdonshire, one on the Great Ouse at Brampton with another at Elton on the River Nene (Holt 1988, 157).) Constructing or fitting out a fulling mill would have required substantial capital expenditure, but its initial high rental in comparison to that of the adjacent corn mill indicates its higher revenues. In 1406 Thomas Styward had it for seven years at an increased rent of 24 marks (£16). The 20% increase in rental within seven years suggests that it was a successful venture, and that the Abbot's strategy to diversify from corn to cloth had paid off.

As explained in Chapter 2, fulling mills were more generally sited on faster flowing rivers where steeper gradients allowed for powerful overshot water wheels to drive the heavy hammers that pounded the cloth. The topography of the Houghton site with a slow-moving river and very little gradient would only allow for an undershot wheel. Therefore, the only way to increase the speed and power of water to the mill wheel was to raise the height of the Houghton mill dams. Inevitably any alteration in river levels caused a knock-on effect which upset operations at the neighbouring mills. Those upstream at Hartford were particularly affected; an increased height in their tail races prevented their mill wheels from working, and so to counter this their dams needed to be raised; the mills downstream at Hemingford Grey were affected, to a lesser extent, but they too would raise their mill dams. This caused disputes and litigation for over a century – not between the mill owners, but in actions brought by the Godmanchester farmers whose fields between the mills were flooded because the river levels were held up.

The bailiffs of Godmanchester take action

The geography and topography of the parishes between Hemingford Grey and Huntingdon made large areas of Godmanchester lands, on the floodplain south of the river, vulnerable to flooding from the main river channel. (This is a marginal landscape with little tolerance for rises in river levels before water will flow over the floodplain.) Only a few acres of Hartford – those south of the river and contained by the short backwater for its mill – were liable to flood. But large meadows at Houghton and Hemingford Abbots, on both sides of the river in the floodplain, would have been quickly affected by high water levels, and likewise at Hemingford Grey. Any rise in water levels in the backwaters would have similar impacts – but perhaps more acute for Godmanchester lands due to the complexity of the geography of two of these channels. The long backwater for Hartford Mill – Cook's Stream – was wholly within Godmanchester parish. The Hemingford Abbots Backwater for Houghton Mill had commandeered the Gumcester Drain which drained the fields and meadows of Godmanchester. In Houghton and Hemingford Abbots, the tenants of the Abbot of Ramsey, and similarly the tenants of the Earl of Kent in Hemingford Grey, were not in a position to complain about flooding caused by their own manorial lords. But the Godmanchester men, as Freemen of their Borough, could and did complain strongly about their lands being flooded, being determined to protect their own interests for which they paid an annual fee-farm rent to the King.

The Court of the Duchy of Lancaster

The 15th century disputes about flooding of Godmanchester lands caused by the height of mill dams were all heard in the Court of the Duchy of Lancaster, and this would continue into the 16th century. Godmanchester and Huntingdon were part of the Earldom of Leicester; in 1265 Henry III gave the manors to his second son Edmund when he conferred on him the titles of Earl of Leicester and Lancaster. In 1351 the title was elevated to Duke of Lancaster by Edward III and the Lancaster estate was made a County Palatine. As part of this special status the Duke received devolved royal powers which included controls in the law courts within the area of the Duchy. The Duchy possessions were essentially a private royal estate and Henry IV ensured that they did not merge with other Crown lands but were administered and inherited separately. The Duchy court dealt with issues relating primarily to land held by the Crown in right of the Duchy. During the navigational and flooding disputes, petitions from the bailiffs of Godmanchester and Huntingdon frequently mention that should they be unsuccessful in their claims, the towns might be unable to pay their fee-farm rents to the Duke of Lancaster – who was also the King. The annual fee-farm rent of Godmanchester had been set at £120 with its charter in 1212, and that of Huntingdon at £40 in 1205. In 1252 – possibly as part of an agreement due to the navigation above St Ives being impeded by the Abbot of Ramsey and others – Huntingdon agreed to an annual rent increase of £20 in exchange for rights to the tolls on goods coming into St Ives during its six-week Easter Fair. In 1260 this arrangement provided Huntingdon with an income of £100, however the complete demise of the Fair in the early to mid-14th century, due to competition elsewhere and certainly compounded by the Black Death, left Huntingdon disadvantaged with its increased annual rent of £60 and much diminished income. The ability to pay the rent remained a concern even into the 17th century when it was then paid to the Earl of Sandwich, no longer the Duchy. A byelaw of 1680 stipulated that the townsfolk had to grind their corn at the Town water mills or face a fine of 10s as the mill was the borough's main source of revenue for the payment of their 'great fee-farm rent' (VCH k 1932, 121–139).

A series of court cases

The full picture of the causes of the flooding of Godmanchester land is not detailed until a major commission held in the Court of the Duchy of Lancaster in 1515 (TNA DL3/23). But a series of 15th century disputes charts the progression and intensity of events leading up to that commission. In 1415 the bailiffs of Godmanchester achieved a decree in the Duchy Court against the Prior of Huntingdon (KG/A/3/8). Commissioners were appointed 'to view the premises at Hartford, and the level and course of the water, and to assign a floodgate or *lawesyard*, conveniently to turn the course of the water to the said mills in such place, and of such reasonable height, length, breadth as they might see fit, doing least hurt to the parties, and the said tenants and other inhabitants adjoining'. In an agreement signed by both parties, the Court was to oversee and supervise the proper operation of the floodgates.

The word '*lawesyard*' was used frequently in the Duchy Court documents for over 100 years from 1415. This word has not been found in any dictionary and the OED does not list it. Was it a term specific to the Huntingdon area? It is an intriguing puzzle. However, as there is no explanation of its definition in any of the documents, clearly all parties must have been cognisant of it and understood meaning and context. Each reference in the Duchy Court documents (at Hartford, the Abbot's Leat and the Hemingford Grey Backwater) describes a wooden construction (a yard) across the river which acted as a floodgate with adjustable settings. The structure probably functioned like a sluice, staunch or flash lock as has been described earlier in this chapter. And the *lawesyard* ordered to be built at Hartford in 1415 would seem to be similar in function to the *exclusae* at Hartford of 1274 (as described in Chapter 5) to be 'fit for purpose whenever navigators require them'.

The situation at Hartford was seemingly unresolved and in 1426 the gates were broken open again (KG/A/1/12). When this was repeated in 1467 the Duchy Court renewed its supervision order, and included Houghton Mill as well as Hartford; 'if any default now or hereafter happen to be in the setting of the said *excluses* or *damminges*, that then such defaults at all times shall be reformed by the oversight of the Council of the said Duchy for the time being, and not by the said Bailiffs'. Interestingly, at this point the Court awarded the bailiffs and inhabitants of Godmanchester toll-free passage in the river (Fox 1831, 197). Was this recompense in recognition of the continuing damage done to their fields by flooding caused by the mills? Letters Patent were signed by all parties in 1470.

The 1467 order (which is recorded later in the 1515 evidence and depositions) included the 'Houghton gulls' (see Fig. 6.1, page 91). These were five channels or outlets from the main river, cut by the Godmanchester men on Godmanchester land on the southern bank of the river. Their function was to lower the level of the river by releasing water, and channel it into the Abbot's Leat to flow from there into the Gumcester Drain. The 1467 order allowed these emergency outlets to remain, but their use was to be supervised by the Court, and their maintenance paid by the Abbot.

Despite the Court orders, matters deteriorated again, and in 1500 the Duchy Court heard how 'the inhabitants of the town of Godmanchester of late assembled themselves in riotous manner and riotous with force of arms that is to say with bows, bills, swords, bucklers and other weapons contrary to the peace and laws of our Sovereign Lord the King with great violence and might took and carried away the floodgates of the Mills of Houghton' (KG/A16/1). Predictably the Court found against the men of Godmanchester because they had contravened the 1467 supervision to which they had signed their agreement. The Godmanchester men were duly ordered to repair and reinstate the Houghton gates and watercourses and make their peace with the Abbot. In 1502, most probably after further action by the Godmanchester men, the Court, recognising its own limitations in supervising the floodgates, ordered that independent parties should position the height of the Hartford gates – and if there were disagreements, 'then Humphrey Coningsby Sergeant at Law and Robert Brudenell shall set such order and directions therein as by their wisdom shall be most indifferent in the premises etc' (KG/A16/1).

A new petition

Having failed in 1500 to effect any change to the mill dams by law or by violence, the bailiffs of Godmanchester joined forces with the bailiffs of Huntingdon and returned to the law, with a combined petition of complaint to the Duchy Court in late 1513/early 1514 (TNA DL3/23, 004) about both flooding and lack of navigation. They complained, again, that the mill dams at Houghton and Hemingford Grey were too high. Arable lands were flooded, hay crops were frequently swept away from the meadows, and the Godmanchester and Huntingdon mills were unable to work. Boats carrying grain and other merchandise were impeded and often had to wait two days for water levels to drop. The bailiffs warned of the 'utter undoing' and the 'decay' of the towns of Huntingdon and Godmanchester unless the dams be taken down.

The Duchy Court set up a commission on 30th March 1514, asking Sir John Mordaunt, Sir Thomas Bonham (Receiver General of the Duchy), Sir William Walwyn (Auditor of the Duchy) and John Corner to investigate, visit the towns, examine witnesses and report back at Michaelmas.

The Abbot's tale

The Abbot of Ramsey was the first to give evidence to the commission as he replied to the Huntingdon and Godmanchester complaint. He claimed that he respected the 1467 decree, making sure that water levels at his dams at Houghton did not exceed the height of a watermark set up by that decree. He had obeyed the ruling that he should maintain the Houghton gulls. But he complained that the Godmanchester men continued to disregard the law and were again using violence. They had broken open the Houghton gulls in three consecutive months, each time more deeply, and at one point causing the river level to drop three feet. In an effort to retain the water released through the Houghton gulls, so as to keep the river level at a sufficient height to drive his mills, he had built a dam within his own manor. This dam was on the Gumcester Drain just above the Hemingford Abbots bridge. But the Godmanchester men had subsequently broken this dam, as well as the dam at the Houghton–Hemingford Abbots mill site. The Abbot sought recompense of £24 for a lost season's work at his mills.

An interim order, an extension to the commission and its questions

There was considerable frustration and anger on both sides of the dispute. The situation was similar to that of 1500 and was rapidly getting out of control. Events had overtaken the extent of the commission, so in Spring 1515 the Court made an interim order lasting until All Saints' Day (1st November). The Abbot could repair the Houghton gulls to allow his mills to operate. He had to ensure that none of his dams caused flooding to Godmanchester land. But if the dams did cause flooding, then it would be lawful for the Godmanchester men to open the floodgates 'without any let, vexation or hindrance from the Abbot'. This was a surprising new direction by the Court. All parties signed the agreement.

Within months the Godmanchester and Huntingdon bailiffs returned to the Duchy Court with a new complaint. They said that since the Feast Day of St Philip and Jacob (May 3rd) the Abbot had defied the interim order and had rebuilt his dam on the Gumcester Drain, making it wider and higher. The Godmanchester lands were flooded as a result. The bailiffs asked if they could peacefully remove the dam. (It was taken down, but it is not known whether peacefully or not). The Court then amended the terms of the commission to include examination of the dam at the fulling mill site, the dam on Gumcester Drain, and the other dams at the Houghton mill site. They first listed three and then added another 13 detailed questions to be asked of the witnesses:

1. *In primis*. Whether there be any bank or dam of earth made and set up across one side stream coming or descending out and from the water of Ouse at and before a fulling mill of the said Abbot within his said Lordship of Hemingford Abbot, and if any such be, for what purpose and intent it was made and whether it be the let of the watercourse and what hurt growth thereby, to whom and to what value.

2. Whether there be plain south from the said fulling mill any common sewer or drain which hath used to hold its course under a bridge at Hemingford Abbots townsend or not, and whether divers fields arable, a pasture called the East pasture with divers other pastures and meadows of the Town of Godmanchester has been accustomed to be drained time out of mind by the said sewer, or not, and to what intent the Abbot has now lately caused a great dam of timber and earth a little from the said bridge to be made across the said sewer or drain, and whether by reason of the said dam the said fields, pastures and meadows have been divers times surrounded and hurt, and what loss and damage the King's tenants of Godmanchester have taken and sustained thereby and to what value.

3. Whether that across the high and middle course of the water of Ouse be set certain floodgates between the said fulling mill and other corn mills of the said Abbot in his manor of Houghton to the entire letting and impediment of a common passage some time used to be had with boats and other vessels from the said towns of Huntingdon and Godmanchester to the haven town of Lyn, to the common wealth of all the country there about and nigh to the said towns or not.

4. Whether by the blocking of the [river/navigable] passage the common wealth of these parts and specifically the towns of Huntingdon and Godmanchester are thereby greatly decayed or not?

5. Whether because of the floodgates built at the fulling mill, the waters of the Ouse are stopped and blocked from their course or not?

6. Whether because of the two dams made at Hemingford Bridge and the fulling mill and also because of the floodgate, all the waters of the [Gumcester] Drain as well as of the River Ouse are caused wholly and entirely either to go through the corn mill of the Abbot or else to return backwards again?

7. Whether by the purprestures of dams and floodgates the water is compelled and forced to return backwards and surround the meadows, pastures and part of the arable lands of Godmanchester many times and for the most part of the year or not?

8. How many acres of land, meadow and pasture and meadow belonging to the town of Godmanchester, as a consequence of these purprestures and nuisances have the [mis]fortune many times a year to be surrounded and overflown with water? And what hurt [damage] the king's tenants have and sustain yearly and to what value?

9. Whether by reason of the purprestures any hurt, damage or nuisance is done to any other of the King's subjects or to any other townships other than Huntingdon and Godmanchester, or not?

10. Whether the frame and timber work of the floodgate has been renewed since it was first built, or not, and if it has been, then how often, and whether at any time of the renewal of the frame has it been pitched and set higher than it was originally, and if it has been, then how much higher, and whether the frame has been estreated [been subject to a fine] at any time or not?

11. Whether any of the mills on the River Ouse or on any side stream of the river have been at any time sited and built higher – in their ground work [ie foundations] since they were first built or not, and if so which [mills] these are, who owns them, and to what height and how long since this was done?

12. Whether there are any new mills built and made since the 7th year of the reign of King Edward IV [1467] and then how many, where and who owns them?

13. To enquire of all other manner of nuisances and purprestures made on any other part of the Ouse between Huntingdon and St Neots such as dams, lawesyards, banks, walls and blockages which as well as hindering, stop or entirely impede the passage of boats, flood the lands, meadows and pastures of Huntingdon, Godmanchester and other places

14. Whether any lawesyard on the River is clearly blocked and dammed up so that no water can pass through as it has been accustomed to do previously or not?

15. Whether the middle course of the River Ouse is blocked in any more places between Huntingdon and St Ives other than at the Abbot's mill at Houghton at the floodgate which stops and impedes the passage, or not. If it be so, where is it and by whom?

16. Whether all the transport as has been used to be made by the River Ouse from Lynn to Huntingdon can now only be made to St Ives, 3 miles from Huntingdon, a town of the Abbot, and to his great and singular profit yearly and to the great and endless decay of the towns of Huntingdon and Godmanchester, or not? (TNA DL3/23, 008)

The commissioners visit and examine the witnesses

The commissioners Sir Thomas Bonham and Sir William Walwyn were in Godmanchester, Huntingdon, Hartford, Houghton, Hemingford Abbots and Hemingford Grey for three days from 30th July to 1st August 1515. They were accompanied by 'many of the most discreet, sage and honest and of the eldest of the King's towns of Huntingdon and Godmanchester'. In a very thorough tour where 'they took 3 or 4 boats together' (TNA DL3/23, 009) they visited all the sites of mills, dams, floodgates, drains and gulls. They saw the 'drawing-place' around the mills where boats were unloaded and reloaded. The Hemingford Abbots fulling mill at the Houghton site was in disrepair and they noted that the water for its dam was diverted to the dams of the adjacent corn mills. They saw the ruin of the Abbot's 'Great Dam' on the Gumcester Drain and heard how he had employed over 40 men to build up the banks of the Hemingford Abbots Meadow to prevent his own land from flooding. At Abel Holt they saw a large new construction belonging to the Earl of Kent and heard how he had piled earth and timber on top of the *lawesyard* that was there previously. (In doing so he had changed a variable floodgate into a solid dam.) The Earl had done this in order to bring more water power to his mills at Hemingford Grey – recently expanded from three mills to four. The commissioners were told that this dam caused water levels in the tail race from the Houghton mills to rise to such an extent that those mills needed more power for the free running of their mill wheels, which could only be achieved by raising the water level upstream, exacerbating the flood risk. The complexity of the overall situation was evident.

Witnesses were questioned. Their depositions varied noticeably. The tenants of the Abbot of Ramsey at Houghton and Hemingford Abbots frequently appeared to have poor, often contradictory, memories about dams and floods. But they did offer some detailed information. Robert Fuller of Houghton noted that the drawing place had been raised more than two feet. He also said that if the dam at Abel Holt had remained at its previous level 'then the water must pass there so that the Abbot's mills might then go and grind with much lower water than they do now' (TNA DL3/23, 015). The Godmanchester and Huntingdon witnesses were very forthcoming and gave graphic evidence. John Pelle, bailiff of Brampton, described the costs of the loss of hay from Portholme meadow. Thomas Hall, who wrote his deposition 'in his own hand', described how he went 'wet-shoed in the meadow which before that was dry'. William Dalton reckoned that over 400 acres of meadow and arable land was flooded. Another witness explained how the 'great, mighty, strong, broad and high dam' across Gumcester Drain had caused floods such that where 'he being upon a horse in the said cornfield, rode in water to the horse's belly' (TNA DL3/23, 018).

The Decree

The Decree of the Court was produced in 1515 (KPGMD/2913/Z/9/B). It did not address all the original complaints – in particular, it did not mention navigation. For all the other complaints, it responded only to the complaints most pertinent to Huntingdon and Godmanchester. First, the Court decreed that there should be no blockages made on the Gumcester Drain. Next, a timber *lawesyard* 24 feet (7.32 m) wide was to be built by the Abbot, and at his cost, at the entrance to the Abbot's Leat. The structure would be sited across this channel, which marked the boundary of the parishes of Godmanchester and Hemingford Abbots, thus giving both parties legal access to the *lawesyard*. The decree ruled that all future maintenance of the *lawesyard* would be shared between the Abbot and Godmanchester. Finally, the height and settings of the *lawesyard* were to ensure no flooding of Godmanchester lands, and, equally, that river levels would be sufficient to allow the Abbot's mills to operate. If the Abbot did not open the gates as soon as necessary, then the Godmanchester men had the right to do so directly. The decree had followed the ground-breaking ruling of the interim order some months earlier. So perhaps it came as no surprise when it was delivered? The decree and agreement were signed by all parties.

The 1515 evidence and decree reveal that the need for greater water power for the fulling mill at the Houghton site was most probably the cause of much of the 15th century complaint and litigation about flooding. The fulling mill had affected Hartford mill causing it to raise its dams. And the combination of raised dams at both Houghton and Hartford mill sites had inevitably caused flooding on Godmanchester land. The situation was not relieved when the fulling mill fell out of use ('in decay') because coincidentally the Earl of Kent had expanded his mills down-stream at Hemingford Grey and had raised and reinforced his dams to gain more water power. The Abbot channelled the water of the fulling mill dam into his corn mill dams to counteract the high water forced into his Houghton mill tail race by the Earl's dam. When the Godmanchester men broke open the gulls to release water into the Gumcester Drain, the Abbot then dammed Gumcester Drain.

Interestingly the commissioners made no ruling about the actions of the Earl of Kent. Perhaps they felt that the height of his dam was a matter to be sorted between him and the Abbot. The Court had done its work in sorting out the direct causes of the main problem which affected its own tenants, primarily the Borough of Godmanchester and, next, Huntingdon. The Court's ruling was a very sweet victory for Godmanchester, and for nearly the next four centuries the Borough frequently and assiduously availed of its right to control the floodgates along the river whenever they feared the town's lands might be threatened by flooding.

The 1515 map and landscape impact

At the end of their visit, the Commissioners requested ('desired') that the bailiffs of Godmanchester have a *platte* [map or plan] made of the whole area for 'the intent that it may the more certainly and specially be known and understood by the chancellor and council of the Duchy' (TNA DL3/23, 011). The result (TNA MPCC 1/9) is a remarkable piece of cartography, and the earliest surviving large-scale map of the area (Fig. 6.1). It is a topological map, with scale and direction significantly distorted. Quite large, it measures approximately 1.2 by 0.6 m. It represents an area of approximately 32 square km, from Huntingdon and Godmanchester in the west, to St Ives in the east. There are several annotations, only a few of which are now clear enough to be read. Some parts of the map are faded and/or damaged but overall, its condition is good. The map's creator is unknown but was clearly skilled in surveying and map-making. For example, the relative locations of the intricate channels on the river's floodplain, which are challenging to plot today, even with the advantage of aerial photography, are shown with a high degree of accuracy. Pictorial symbols, and colour, are used with great effect to emphasise key features. The map is vitally important to the understanding, not only of the 1515 dispute, but also to the development of the multi-channel form of the river between Huntingdon and Hemingford Grey. It allows understanding of the landscape prior to 1515 and presents a moment in time showing what was there, and what was not. When interpreting the map, it is important to note that it was produced by the Godmanchester complainants and is inevitably presenting their view of the case. However, the cartographer was obviously careful to include all the places seen on the Commissioners' 'site visit' and mentioned in the depositions.

FIGURE 6.1. (opposite) 'Huntyngdon & Godmanchester'. Plan of the River Ouse and waterways between Huntingdon and St Ives bridge, c. 1515

What is shown on the map?

The main focus of the dispute is presented in the centre of the map, and it is drawn to the largest scale; this is the area of flooded meadow (A) caused by the dam built by the Abbot across Gumcester Drain (B). A sailing ship, possibly of sea-going size, is shown on the river, near Huntingdon (C). It is stranded between Huntingdon Bridge and mill dams at Hartford and has presumably been drawn to emphasise how the actions of the mill owners had brought an end to ship-borne transport and trade between King's Lynn, the coast and Huntingdon. The road over Huntingdon Bridge (Ermine Street) and the routeway onto the meadow (J) is shown with a line of open circles, possibly representing horseshoes or hoof prints. The arches on the Godmanchester causeway are shown, with the connection of Cook's Stream's to the main river clearly illustrated (D). Hartford Mill is located, with the disputed dam between the two islands (E). The 'Houghton Gulls' (channels) are prominent (F), discharging into Gumcester Drain. They are upstream of the Abbot's Leat (G) and the map makes it easy to understand why they were dug – if the Abbot was keeping the river level too high with his 'great frame of timber' (H) at the Houghton and Hemingford Abbots mills, the 'gulls' acted as a safety valve by taking water away and preventing overflow from the river onto Godmanchester Eastside Common. The ridge and furrow of Godmanchester's arable land stands out clearly (I). The significance of the meadow as land for seasonal grazing is emphasised by the legend on the road: 'driftway to the East Pasture'. This links directly to today's name, 'Cow Lane' (J). The Hemingford Abbots bridge across

FIGURE 6.2. (opposite) LiDAR: Huntingdon to St Ives, 2024

6. River Wars: 1515 – matters come to a head   91

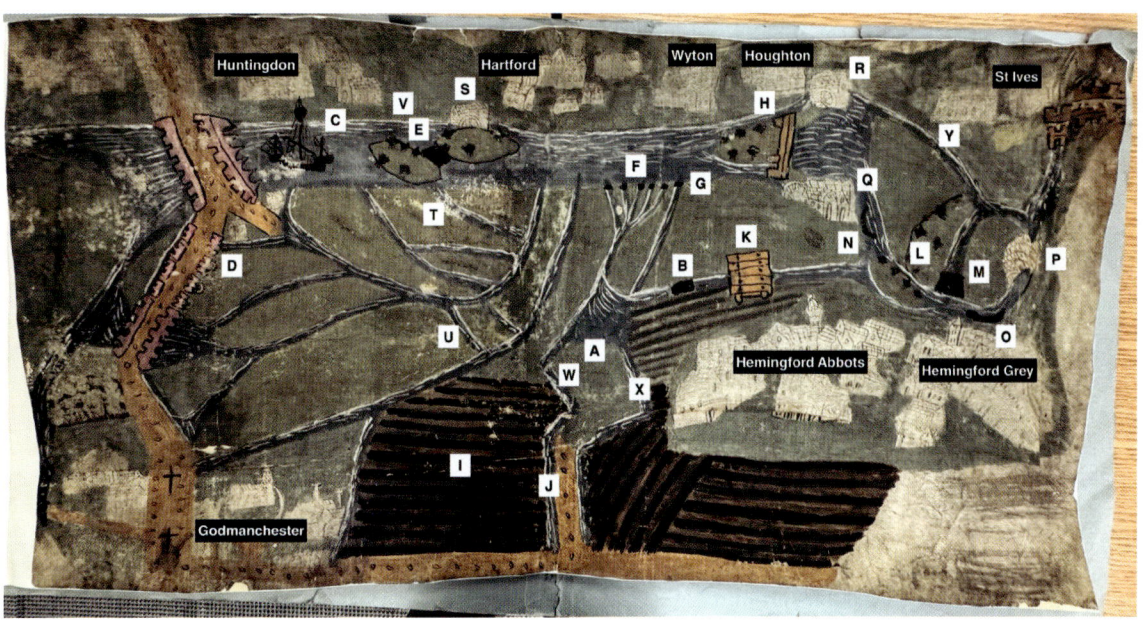

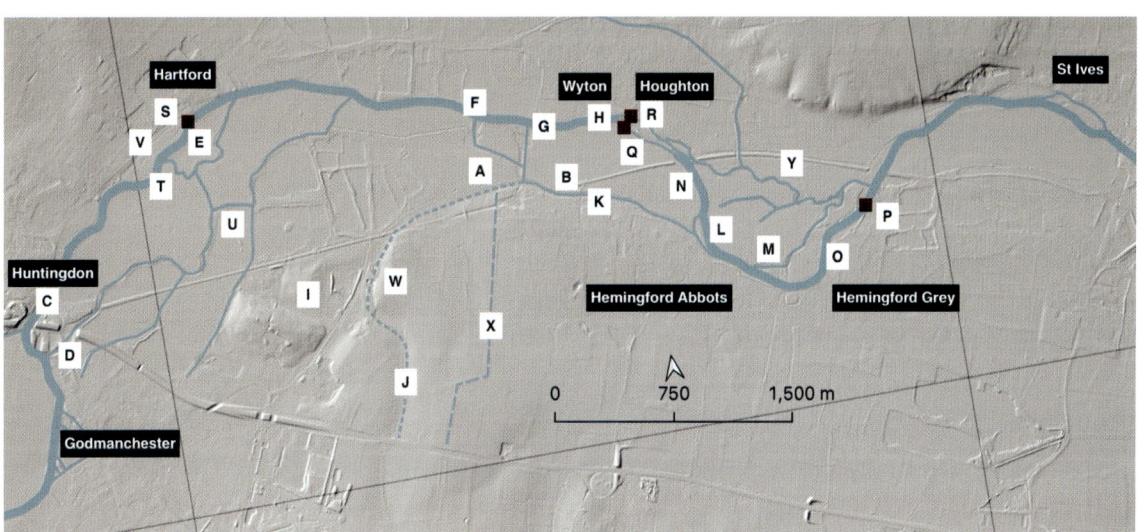

Gumcester Drain (K) is drawn prominently as it was a key reference point for the Commissioners for the location of the dam built by the Abbot.

The distance between Houghton Mills and Hemingford Grey Mills is intentionally reduced, because this was not the primary area of argument about flooding. However, this area was important to the secondary argument about navigation. The bailiffs of Huntingdon and Godmanchester had complained that the Earl of Kent's dams at Hemingford Grey Mills contributed to the 'great damage, nuisance and utter undoing of the King's towns' by obstructing river traffic (TNA DL3/23, 004). The Commissioners investigated this complaint on their visit to 'A place called Abel holt' – shown with a symbol representing osiers (L), occupying the present-day Battcock's Island and part of Houghton Meadow. (A holt was a plantation of osiers which were used for making baskets, hurdles and fish traps.) The Commissioners recorded that the Earl of Kent had recently 'built a dam of bank with timber and earth, much more high than it was before when the said *lawesyard* was there by more than a yard of height' (TNA DL3/23, 010 and 011). This was at the entrance to Hemingford Grey Backwater (M), the site of the present-day Six Gates Pit. All the solid dams at the gulls, mills and backwaters are shown on the map as black blobs. The dam at the Hemingford Grey Backwater is the biggest of them all. It is significant to note that across this obstruction is the label *aqua de ouze* (River Ouse), indicating that this was the river channel vessels were now being prevented from using. This is potentially confusing – why would vessels have been using a channel that had been obstructed as long ago as the 1270s to create a backwater? The answer lies in the description of the *lawesyard* as consisting of 'timber and planks', *i.e.* a kind of 'flash lock' that could be drawn up and opened to let vessels through. This would explain how small river traffic had been permitted to bypass Hemingford Grey Mill (which completely blocked the main channel) in the preceding 240 years, and how the Earl's recent actions of changing the *lawesyard* into a dam (a weir in this context), had curtailed all navigation around the mills. Two symbols, (N) and (O), are drawn on this section of the river; black, slightly curved, elongated shapes. They are almost certainly barges – open, clinker-built wooden boats, with a shallow draught so as to be able to use the smaller river channels. Their design was widely used on inland waterways in the medieval period. They would be either poled, rowed or sailed as conditions allowed. Like the sailing ship near Huntingdon Bridge, these boats are shown being unable to pass the Hemingford Grey mills and the dam at the entrance to the backwater.

The mill buildings

The map marks the location of the Hemingford Grey (P), Hemingford Abbots (Q), Houghton (R) and Hartford mills (S). One waterwheel is shown at each of the mills but in all probability, this is a mapping convention. Evidence suggests that there were at least two waterwheels at Houghton because there is a reference to a 'flood mill' on the north-east channel at Houghton in the report of the Commissioner's site visit (TNA DL3/23, 010):

> Also, they viewed the Abbot's corn mills on the north channel of the Ouse (at Houghton). There were three mills under one roof, one of which is a flood mill which will grind at high water for profit such that the miller will often not draw up the flood gates in time to stop the meadows, pastures and cornfields of the King's tenants of Godmanchester from drowning.

The height of the river striking the paddles of a waterwheel must be carefully controlled; if it is too high the wheel will not turn, and if it is too low, it will turn with little power. It is therefore safe to conclude that the 'flood mill' must have required a separate waterwheel to that of the 'normal' mill and would have been set so it could be used when the river level was high. That the miller seemed to be in no hurry to raise the flood gates suggests that perhaps the 'flood mill' was preferable to the 'normal' mill, perhaps because its wheel generated more power. And that the Abbot profited from the floods with his use of the flood mill, added greatly to the grievances and losses suffered by the Godmanchester farmers.

The Hemingford Grey mill building is shown on the map with four gables (P) and Robert Fuller testified that 'now there be 4 mills where before were but 2 mills' (TNA DL3/23, 015). However, the number of gables cannot be equated with the number of mills (or pairs of stones) at the other locations because, as has been seen, the Commissioners recorded three mills at Houghton 'under one roof' with only one gable being shown (R). Likewise, one mill is shown at Hartford (S), although the Domesday Book recorded two.

Godmanchester's mills are not shown, which initially seems surprising. However, they were only briefly mentioned in the petition and there is no indication in any of the documentation that they were seriously affected by the actions of the Prior, Abbot or Earl of Kent. The map shows the mills at Hartford, Houghton and Hemingford Abbots sited on channels taken off the main river. However, Hemingford Grey Mill is shown straddling the main river. This fits with the documentation and graphically explains the background to the 1274 *Quo Warranto* Plea, *i.e.* by controlling the entrance to the backwater (M), the miller could regulate the water reaching the mill.

How does the map aid an understanding of the development of the landscape?

Figure 6.2 is a LiDAR map with the same annotations as the 1515 map. Watercourses present in 1515 have been highlighted. There is a strong correlation between the two maps, which provides invaluable evidence for the development of the landscape. Starting in the west, the 1515 map confirms that Cook's Stream was the only stream on Westside Common which connected to the main river, and that was via an archway built into the causeway (D). This adds to the understanding of the outcome of the 1276 Inquest. The importance of Cook's Stream and the other channels on Godmanchester Westside Common to manage the level of water in the main river, returning any excess downstream of Hartford Mills, also stands out clearly. The Hartford Backwater, marked by a deviation in the parish boundary is shown (T), and the cuts connecting the different branches of Cook's Stream (U), are all still there today.

Moving to the central section, the role of the map in identifying the location of Hartford Mill (S), on a leat to the north of the downstream of two islands, which have now been reclaimed, and form part of the river's north bank (V) has already been discussed (see page 45). The map confirms the location of the

'Houghton Gulls' (F) leaving the main channel at what is now Rhymers Weir, and the Abbot's Leat (G). These are shown as artificial cuts and add significantly to understanding the development of the multi-channel form of the river, *i.e.* it is largely the result of watermilling. The 1515 map also shows that there was no connection between Cook's Stream and any of the channels on the Hemingford meadows, *i.e.* a key component of the multi-channel landscape, Fishers Dyke, post-dates this period. The course of Gumcester Drain (J) is distorted but shown accurately in relative terms. Its valley, with a marked change in direction, can be picked out on the LiDAR (W). The stream shown to the east of Gumcester Drain (X) exists in the landscape today only as a deep field ditch/drain. It may have been given prominence on the map because it marks the parish boundary between Hemingford Abbots and Godmanchester. It also flows into Gumcester Drain, as do the 'Houghton Gulls' and the Abbot's Leat, contributing to the flooding on Eastside Common. Much of the ridge and furrow shown on the 1515 map (I) has been destroyed by post-1960s sand and gravel extraction, but some is still discernible. The map shows the division of the main channel into the north-east and south-east streams at Houghton and confirms that what is now Trout Stream was Houghton Mill's tail race (Y). In the east, there is confirmation that what is now Battcock's Island (L), then known as Abel Holt (see above) had been created by 1515. The obstruction to Hemingford Grey Backwater is prominent (M) and it is joined by Trout Stream, as it still is today (Y).

In conclusion, the 1515 map fulfilled its brief to help the Chancellor and Council of the Duchy understand the area. Its legacy is an immeasurably better understanding of the valley landscape than could ever have been established from the court documents alone. It helps corroborate documents written in the 13th century and confirms post-1515 changes to the landscape. It also allows an evaluation of the landscape impact of the events leading up to the 1515 court case, and the Inquiry's decree. Overall, the Court's rulings had a limited long-term impact on the form of the river. The dam on Gumcester Drain was removed, a new *lawesyard* was built across the entrance to the Abbot's Leat, and management of the 'Houghton Gulls' was stipulated. These actions were successful in stopping the excessive flooding of Godmanchester Eastside Common. But the major and lasting change was that the channel leading from the 'Houghton Gulls' became a permanent feature of the landscape. At some point the gulls were replaced by a weir, known today as 'The Rhymers' (see Fig. 6.2, page 91). A 'rimer' is 'a post in a weir or lock, in or on which a paddle works up and down' with its first recorded use in 1794 (Oxford English Dictionary). This probably explains its name. It is labelled 'Long Overfall' in 1834 (R1/478), with 'The Rhymers' first appearing on the 1888 1:2500 OS map. Downstream of Houghton, the basic channel configuration which had been established at the end of the 13th century, continued unchanged.

There were then only a few years before the Dissolution of the monasteries between 1536–40 with a nation-wide re-allocation of the lands, property and possessions of the religious houses. The once powerful Abbot of Ramsey was pensioned off and the great estates of the Abbey were divided. The manor of Houghton and Wyton became the property of the Crown, and that of Hemingford Abbots had a rapid succession of owners, all variously connected as loyal servants of the Crown. The Priory of Huntingdon was in a parlous state before the Dissolution. At the resignation in 1532 of its Prior, William Gidding, Bishop Longland wrote to Thomas Cromwell that 'the house was left almost as poor as Job by his negligence' (VCH c, 1926). Whether the Hartford watermill was still functioning by this date is unclear.

CHAPTER SEVEN

The Age of Locks: a 17th century technical solution

The Dissolution to 1620

The period from the Dissolution of the Monasteries in the late 1530s to the early 17th century was one of very mixed fortunes for watermilling on the River Great Ouse (Fig. 7.1). The secularisation of the ecclesiastical estates, a period of royal control for some estates, along with a shuffling of ownership for several of the other manors and their mills, combined to bring a new order of political and economic allegiances along the river. In 1534 Hemingford Grey became the property of Sir Richard Williams, alias Cromwell, Thomas Cromwell's nephew. There were now four mills here, leased to John Keche, and then to Peter Smyth in 1540, whose estate retained the lease until 1610 (VCH f 1932, 309–314). Cromwell held the Hemingford Grey manor very briefly until 1542 when he exchanged it with the Crown for the manor of Upwood and other lands. The three mills 'lying under one roof' at Houghton passed from Ramsey Abbey to the Crown at the Dissolution. The Abbey's one or, more probably, two fulling mills of Hemingford Abbots, adjacent to the Houghton mills but on the south side of the river, receive no mention after 1515 when they were described as 'decayed' (TNA DL3/23, 010). No mills are recorded for Hemingford Abbots in 1540 (PRO 1967, 241), and as there is no further record, it would appear that they were defunct or demolished by that date (PRO 1967, 250). The mills at Hartford make a similar disappearance from the records. They had survived the Dissolution because the 1540 list for the assets of Huntingdon Priory at Hartford records 'rents from a messuage, lands, site of the manor and a watermill' (PRO 1967, 250). The manor of Hartford was granted to Richard Williams, alias Cromwell, in 1542 as part of an exchange for the manor of Brampton, but what then became of the watermill is not known. The last record of activity of Hartford mills is a pre-Dissolution note of the annual rental in 1517 as: 'from the same tax collector for rent on the watermills along with the private (stretch of) water in the same place for the aforementioned tenancy periods, 40 shillings' (BMS HUNTN 20).

The mills in the boroughs of Huntingdon and Godmanchester continued without change, but the nearby mills at Brampton saw new owners. The de Grey family had held the manor throughout the 15th century, but it was taken by the Crown in 1538 and sold to Richard Williams, alias Cromwell, who held it briefly until 1542 before returning it in an exchange to the Crown as mentioned above. By this time there were four mills of which one was a fulling mill. In the early 17th century Brampton and its mills would be granted to the Earls of Manchester.

Upstream of Brampton the documentary evidence for watermilling in the second half of the 16th century is limited. Buckden Mill continued to operate and there is reference to a sale of land in Offord Cluny in 1650 with an account that indicated the positions of mills (VCH h 1932, 319–322). This would suggest that Offord Mills also continued to operate after the Dissolution, but how many mills, their precise location, or their relationship to Buckden Mill, is not known. The St Neots Mills located in Little Paxton had passed with the St Neots manor to the Crown at the Dissolution. In 1547 they were granted to Robert Payne and then later his son, when in 1604 a malt mill is also recorded (VCH j 1932, 337–346). The manor was bought by the Montagu family in 1631 who would become the Earls of Sandwich. Four mills are mentioned in 1697 (Willan 1946, 121). However, if the neighbouring three mills at Little Paxton granted to Sawtry Abbey in the 12th century were still in operation at the start of the 16th century, they do not appear to have survived the Dissolution. St Neots Priory was pulled down after the Dissolution, but the watermill survived. In 1584 it was leased to Edward Catley who agreed to repair and maintain it (Tebbut 1966, 5). Eynesbury Abbey was granted to Sir Richard Williams who granted a horse-mill to Stephen Bull in 1540 but there is no mention of watermills, adding weight to the argument that the two mills mentioned in the Domesday Book had long disappeared (VCH e 1932, 272–280). On the other side of the river, Eaton Socon appears to have thrived, with its three mills of 1485 increasing to four by 1625 (VCH b 1912, 189–202).

Yet another round of commissions and litigation

In 1532 the Statute of Sewers had been passed, an Act designed to give permanent powers to the appointing of commissioners to address drainage and navigation issues on rivers – with note to where blockages were caused by mills or fish weirs. In several rivers, mills were demolished soon after the Act became law (Langdon and White 2017, 144) but despite the long history of mills blocking the Great Ouse and causing flooding, this river seems to have been spared the Act's attentions. This was most probably because the 1515 case had been seen to address the flooding problems, having concluded by giving the Godmanchester bailiffs the legal powers to prevent the floods. However, whether these legal powers had solved the flooding problems, or whether the administration of the legal powers was practical, would be seen in the years to come. From 1587 a new series of commissions took place. It seems to have been very much 'business as usual' between the men of Godmanchester and their neighbouring millers of Houghton, Hemingford Grey and Brampton. Tensions between millers and farmers persisted and direct conflict would flare up again.

A Commission of Sewers in 1587 investigated the water channels between Brampton, Huntingdon and Godmanchester mills, and the amount of water reaching Huntingdon mills. In their depositions the witnesses, experienced

7. The Age of Locks: a 17th century technical solution

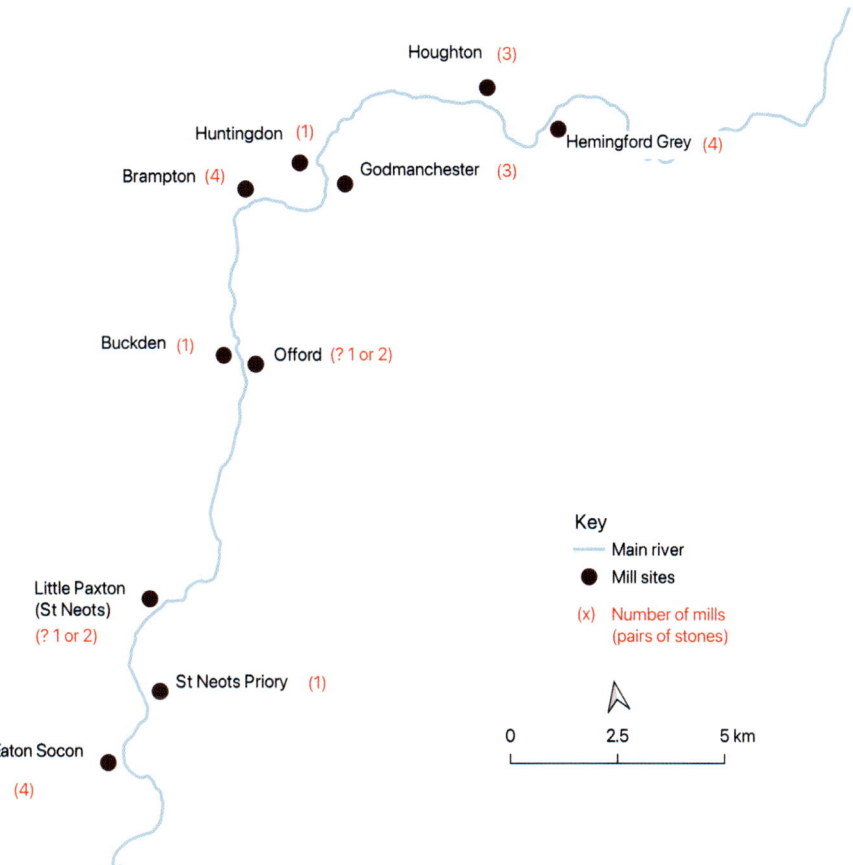

FIGURE 7.1. The location of watermills on the River Great Ouse in 1600

and elderly mill workers, stated that no new channels had been made. They were agreed that the Huntingdon mills were reliant on water downstream from Brampton mills, and as this supply was variable, the Huntingdon mills could 'stand dry for three weeks together so that they could not grind two bushels a week'. (Two bushels of wheat yields approximately 84 pounds of flour, a small quantity that could normally be milled in about two hours.) A previous tenant of Huntingdon mills said he had been 'weary of the lease and gave it away for want of water' (KG/D/3/2). This commission was followed by a letter of 1st July 1591 from Lord Burleigh (William Cecil, 1st Baron Burghley) as Lord High Treasurer and acting for the Queen, in response to a complaint from Richard Chessum, Her Majesty's farmer of Brampton Mills (KG/D/3/3). Lord Burleigh ordered the inhabitants of Godmanchester to restore a gull (channel) to its former course in accordance with an order of the Bishop of Lincoln as the 1587 Commissioner. Godmanchester bailiffs, Thomas Maille and William Smythe, drafted their reply of 24th July, boldly defending their action on the grounds that the order had never been set down in writing or engrossed, and that Brampton was taking more water than it should (KG/D/3/4). Specifically, they claimed that the number of mills at Brampton had been increased from two to four and that Chessum had raised the water level 13 inches higher than the normal level of the river to supply his mills, but to the detriment of Godmanchester's mills. The gull, or gulls, they 'cut down' (lowered) must have been upstream of Brampton Mills, so it was probably the complex of channels in the south-west corner of West Meadow (see Fig. 5.7, page 70). No other relict channels bypass Brampton Mills, unless they have been destroyed by later development, leaving no trace. Lord Burleigh threatened the Bailiffs with a summons to court at Westminster unless they restored the gulls, an offer the Godmanchester men appeared willing to accept. Unfortunately, the outcome of the dispute is not known.

The Bishop of Lincoln was back in Huntingdonshire for another Commission of Sewers in 1591 to hear the case against Robert Tryce, a Godmanchester man, the 'holder' of Hemingford Mills (Fox 1831, 206). He had allegedly raised the height of the dam at the Hemingford Grey Backwater – in the same place, Abel Holt now owned by Robert Sisson, and in the same way as the Earl of Kent in the 1515 Duchy case. All the towns and villages upstream from Hemingford Abbots to Offord Cluny claimed their lands were flooded as a result. The decree of 1515 was recited, along with the rights of Godmanchester to control or remove such obstructions. The Commission duly ordered the dam 'to be taken away to the bottom of the river'. Tryce appears next as a commissioner in 1595–96 in a 'Deposition as to the decay of the Queen's mills at Houghton' (TNA E178/1070). The mill seems to have fallen on hard times. The Inquisition heard that George Sandeforde, tenant of Houghton Mill, had let the leat silt up and had allowed the mill house and mill buildings to become dilapidated. There were 'three great breeches' in the 'dams' (which in this context almost certainly means the raised banks of the river) and rushes were growing in the channels because Sandeforde had not been scouring them as he was required to do. The Crown's interest was that this neglect meant a loss of revenue. Godmanchester and Hemingford Grey would also be affected because blocked watercourses would restrict flow downstream, and breeches would lead to flooding. Repairs to the water courses were estimated at six pounds and repairs to the 'going gears, flood hatches, mill house and timber work and thatch' at £24.

Tryce re-appears in 1606. He was the holder of both Houghton and Hemingford mills when his fellow townsmen of Godmanchester petitioned Sir Ralph Gardener, Chancellor of the Duchy of Lancaster, about his outrageous behaviour. Despite Tryce agreeing to the Godmanchester men opening the Houghton gulls to prevent the meadows and cornfields from flooding, he then shut the gulls. This resulted in the loss of the hay crop and the flooding of the grazing pastures so that cattle had to be penned in the cornfields. In his position as a Justice of the Peace, Tryce had 'procured a special Sessions where he proffered a Bill of Riot against the 14 Godmanchester men, having arranged a jury of his friends, kinsfolk and tenants'. Moreover, he purloined – 'gotten unto his hands' – the Godmanchester copies of the Duchy decrees which gave the men the right to open the gulls (KG/D/3/5 and KG/D/3/6). Evidently, he found it difficult to reconcile the conflicting interests of a Godmanchester citizen with those of a Hemingford and Houghton miller.

7. The Age of Locks: a 17th century technical solution

A review into the return of the Navigation

At the beginning of the 17th century the focus shifted, at last, from the centuries' old problems of mills and floods, to those of mills and navigation. In 1608 there was a special Commission when The Crown (James 1st) ordered an 'Inquisition as to the obstruction of the navigation of the river between Huntingdon and King's Lynn by the King's mills'. (TNA E178 3912). The Commission recited that it was by 'special petition of the inhabitants of Huntingdon' who sought the restoration of the navigation above St Ives, which was blocked by the Hemingford Grey and Houghton mills. Huntingdon had also requested that the Crown grant them these mills for a fee-farm rent so that the borough could then control the river. Here was a very different petition to that of 1515 when Huntingdon, with Godmanchester, complained about the lack of navigation. This time it would seem Huntingdon had a solution in mind. Possibly a radical one. Were they considering adapting these mill sites, or perhaps even demolishing the mills, to allow for navigation, and then off-setting the fee-farm rental of the mills against their new income from river trade? The 1608 Commission was not adversarial, nor was it apportioning fault. It was acknowledging a problem – a problem that had existed for nearly 350 years and one which continuing legislation had failed to resolve – then seeking to address it and, in so doing, looking forward.

The Commissioners found the river to be 'landed up' and rush beds growing everywhere. Those people responsible for scouring the river were not fulfilling their duties. The mills at Houghton needed £160 or more of repairs – up considerably on the 1595 estimate. At Hemingford Grey, the fulling mill had been out of service for nine years and, overall, the mills were 'in great decay' requiring over £200 to make them 'tenantable'. The Commissioners also reported that a dam had been built across the 'high stream (main river) … two furlongs above Hemingford Mills'. In this context a dam must refer to a weir, the purpose of which would have been to control the water reaching the mills. 'Two furlongs' places this dam roughly halfway between the mills and the entrance to the backwater (see Fig. 5.3, page 67) and it would clearly have been another significant barrier to river traffic. Then came a sharp assessment of the sustainability of the mills – something hitherto unrecorded, although undoubtedly observed. This is that [the mills] 'will and do more harm to the Country than they do good by drowning the meadows at every flood and surge of water, and [also that] they will not grind in the summertime above seven bushels of grain in 24 hours so that they are not worth the holding' (TNA E178 3912). Here was the old, recurring problem; by keeping the river levels high enough for profitable milling, especially in the summer when flow was reduced, any sudden heavy rain would cause flooding, resulting in economic loss for the farmers. What is not mentioned, but can be understood in this document, are the complaints raised in the 1515 Duchy case, that the mill owners' actions were for their 'singular profit against the common wealth' (TNA DL3/23, 010).

However, there was now a solution to the seemingly intractable problem of navigation, and one which the commissioners repeated; 'the said Navigation cannot be effected except there be sluces made there'. They went on to describe the benefits to Huntingdon plus the neighbouring counties and their towns. 'All mode of commodities [could] be brought up to Huntingdon as are now at St Ives'. If sluices were built, the carriage of goods from King's Lynn to Huntingdon would be three shillings and sevenpence – the price it currently cost for just the three miles from St Ives to Huntingdon. Further afield, transport from London to Huntingdon would be reduced from 50 shillings by land to ten shillings by water. The Commissioners, Sir Oliver Cromwell (uncle of Oliver Cromwell), Sir Richard Payne, William Dyer, Drew Burton and Robert Cromwell had presented a convincing business case for the restoration of the navigation with sluices to by-pass the Hemingford Grey and Houghton mills.

Construction of sluices: 1620 onwards

The varied terminology for the constructions to enable navigation can be confusing, but Summers (1973, 59) and Chisholm (2003, 183–200) have helpfully clarified what was meant by a 'lock', 'staunch' or 'sluice' on the Great Ouse in the 17th century. In its simplest form a staunch was a wooden barrier across the river. It consisted of a detachable horizontal guide bar, vertical bars called rimers and wooden boards called paddles that were set against the rimers. When it was not being used the water level was the same on both sides of the structure. When the boards were put in place the staunch raised the level of the river over the shallows on the upstream side to a sufficient height to allow the passage of river traffic. Some of the paddles were then lifted, creating a 'flash' of water, and the river traffic passed through the structure on this surge. The boards were then put back in place, the staunch was 'set' and the river was back to its natural level. Staunches were relatively straightforward to construct but their operation required four to five hours to raise the river level sufficiently for vessels to pass. During some of this time a nearby mill upstream could not operate because the water in its tail race would be too high, and a downstream mill would not have enough water to turn its wheel. The staunches were also dangerous for the vessels passing through on the 'flash': the downstream river traffic had to be controlled and steadied, and the upstream boats had to be hauled against the force of the 'flash'.

The disadvantages of staunches, or flash-locks as they were also known, meant that a different solution for bypassing the mills was needed. This was to be the 'pound lock', locally known also as a sluice – the type of lock seen most frequently on canals and rivers today. Pound locks were first used in England in 1564 on a small section of the River Exe (Satchell 2017, 21), with those on the Great Ouse being some of the earliest built elsewhere. Figure 7.2 is a 17th century diagram showing how they worked. First, a channel was cut round the mill and then the pound lock was constructed in this channel. The 'pound' where the water was stored had pairs of gates at either end, which vessels could enter, with the water level being raised or lowered once the gates had been closed. Thomas Surbey, an engineer, described and drew the pound lock at Godmanchester in 1699, confirming this arrangement (Hughes 1996, 103). He noted that, 'The lock is all timber.

7. The Age of Locks: a 17th century technical solution 103

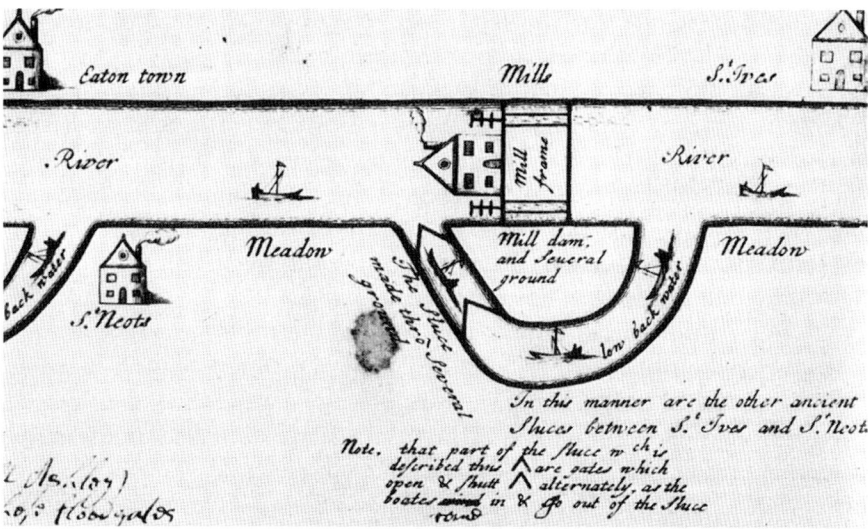

FIGURE 7.2. Map of the Great Ouse c. 1689, showing a pound lock

The boats that pass here draw two-foot water, and are in length twenty-eight feet, in breadth nine feet nine inch, depth three foot.' Pound locks were more complex and expensive to build than flash-locks but they used less water, mills could still operate unless river levels were very low, and they were safer. A confusion is that when some structures originally built as staunches/flash-locks were rebuilt with a pound lock alongside they retained their name, *e.g.* St Ives Staunch which, despite having a pound lock since 1838 is still called The Staunch. Others built in the 19th century with pound locks were called staunches, *e.g.* Brownshill Staunch. Also, 'sluice' was, and still is, also used to describe a barrier that can be raised or lowered regardless of whether it incorporated a lock, or not.

Construction of the first sluices (locks) on the Great Ouse was underway by 1618. There was now a new era with effective navigation above St Ives. The developments were part of a national trend towards river improvement, stimulated by the emergence of a market-led economy, a growing population and the Crown needing state income (Ash 2017, 2–3). In 1617 John Gason obtained a 21-year licence, as detailed in Letters Patent from the Crown, empowering him to make rivers navigable for an annual payment of £2. In return he was entitled to all profits from the venture, principally the tolls charged for vessels to pass through the staunches and sluices. The Letters Patent for Gason introduced the authority for compulsory purchase of land when 'first compounding and agreeing with the owners [and then] no person to refuse a reasonable composition (compensation)' (Willan 1946, 3, 29–30). Gason sold the rights over the rivers in Cambridgeshire, Huntingdonshire and Bedfordshire to Arnold Spencer and Thomas Girton. Their aim was to make the Great Ouse navigable upstream as far as Bedford. The scheme was known as the 'Navigation' and Spencer and Girton, who carried out the improvements, were the 'Undertakers' as they undertook the work. Between 1618 and 1626 Spencer and Girton built six sluices to bypass the mills at Hemingford, Houghton, Godmanchester, Brampton,

Offord and St Neots. (The Crown no longer owned the Hemingford Grey and Houghton Mills, having sold and granted them by 1615 and 1625 respectively.)

Navigation to Great Barford was achieved by these first six sluices by 1640 (Summers 1973, 50). Summers notes that the early years of river improvement were characterised by 'constantly changing ownership and perpetual disputes' (1973, 47) but Spencer remained a key player throughout this period and invested heavily, not just in the sluices but also in dredging the riverbed, scouring fords and digging ditches. Further progress was hampered, first by the Civil War in the 1640s, and then Spencer's financial difficulties which curtailed his ability to carry out further works before his death in 1658.

By the third quarter of the 17th century, many of the improvements upstream of St Neots had fallen into disrepair, while downstream of St Ives the river was affected by the draining of the Fens, 'The greatest single act of landscape transformation in modern times' (Pryor 2011, 384). Hermitage Sluice was built at Earith in 1651 by Cornelius Vermuyden, to divert water from the Great Ouse into the New Bedford River, the main artery of his drainage scheme (Fig. 7.3). This moved water downstream more quickly, but lowered river levels upstream, which made shallows more difficult to navigate. Summers (1973, 53) states that problems such as these remained unaddressed because of inefficient management. Given that the Navigation was under the control of Spencer's creditors for at least twenty years this seems more than likely, although the instability of the post-Civil War period and the opposition of landowners who wanted to reduce imports to keep local corn prices high were also important factors. An Act of Parliament in 1665 appointed an 'undertaker' to improve the river from Eaton Socon to Bedford but it was not until the Navigation was leased to Henry Ashley senior in 1674 that any improvement work took place. Development recommenced. First, the Navigation was restored and improved up to Great Barford, with sluices (pound locks) being built at Eaton Socon mills and Roxton, with staunches at Tempsford and Great Barford. In 1676 a staunch was built at St Ives to help vessels through the shallows made worse by the Fen drainage schemes. In 1680 work to re-build the sluice at Houghton was completed. In Bedfordshire, sluices were also built at Willington and Cardington, and staunches at Tempsford, Roxton, Great Barford and Lord's Holme, and by 1689 the Navigation to Bedford was complete (Fig. 7.3).

Disputes, agreements and concessions

Restoration of the Navigation by building sluices to bypass the mills was a considerable investment and achievement, but a long struggle. All parties were aware of the potential for disputes between the mill owners and those using the river for transport, so in 1640 certificates were signed by the inhabitants of Huntingdon and Godmanchester to demonstrate their agreement 'regarding the benefit' of the Navigation to their respective towns. The millers were more cautious with their agreement. Their certificate attested that 'the navigation is very little prejudicial to the mills' and added the proviso: 'if the gates of the said sluices be kept tight and that the watermen employed for the

7. The Age of Locks: a 17th century technical solution   105

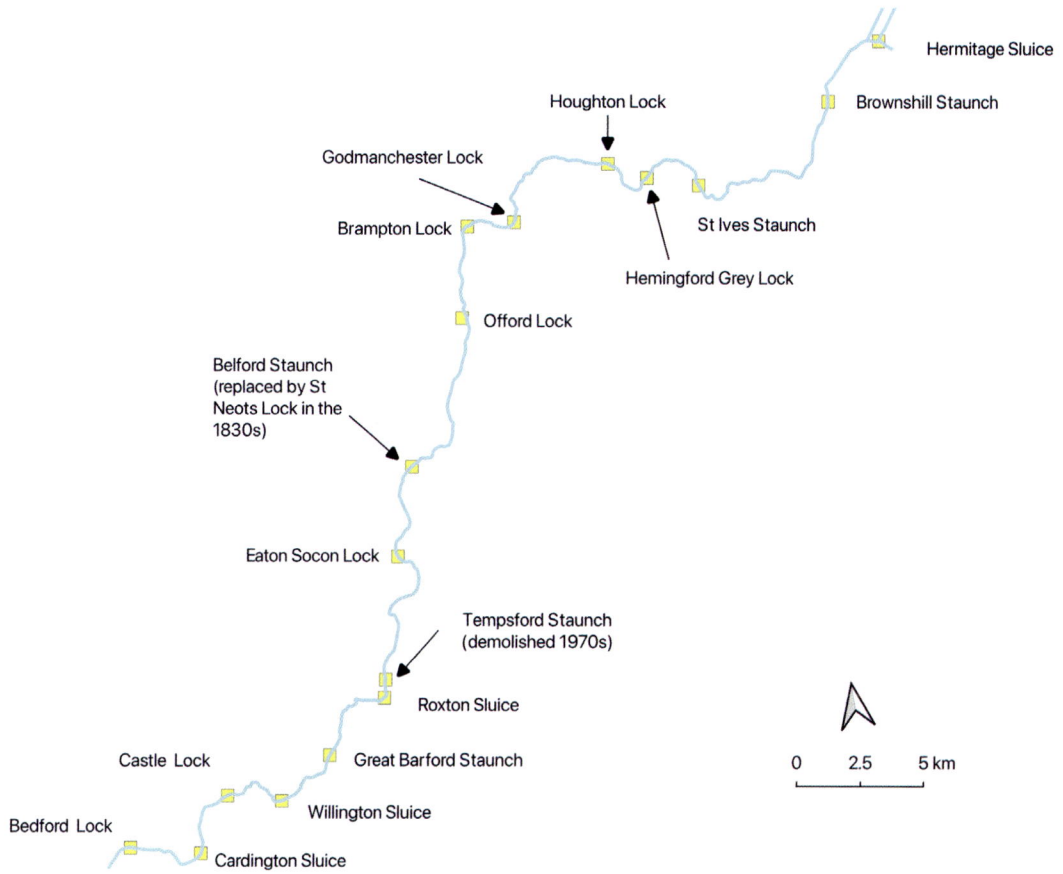

FIGURE 7.3. The River Great Ouse Navigation in 1700

carriage of commodities do duly shut the gates of the said sluices as they pass through' (Willan 1946, 43–44). Thus, the six sluices built by Spencer achieved co-operation between mill owners and the traders of Godmanchester and Huntingdon – something that had seemed impossible since the *Quo Warranto* Plea of 1274. However, the harmony on paper was in reality short-lived, and a fundamental disagreement quickly emerged which led to a new set of disputes.

Whether it was by legal right or long-standing practice, the millers fiercely defended their first claim to the water. In 1696 Thomas West, the miller at Eaton Socon, refused to let boats through the sluice without his permission, leading to long delays. In times of low water there are many examples of millers charging boats for water (Willan 1946, 24). Further practices include restrictions on how often the sluice could be used; for example, sometimes only one gang of lighters consisting of two boats might be allowed through every 12 hours. In summer, boats could be held up for days and so the watermen might then choose to load and unload their goods around the mill (which should have been free from toll), whereupon the millers might insist that their own men be given that job and be paid for it, or that the boatmen would need to pay for the use of the ground near the mill (Willan 1946, 110). These shenanigans explain why

Henry Ashley's son, Henry Ashley junior, who was in business with his father, tried to buy or lease some of the mills. He leased Offord mills in 1690 from the Bishop of Lincoln to gain control of Offord sluice, although complicated lease arrangements were against him, and he failed to achieve his aim. In 1697 he bought the six Eaton Socon mills. One of these was a fulling mill which he then converted to an 'oil mill' – to grind linseed to be made into cakes of cattle feed. Such a mill would presumably use less water than a fulling mill and allow more water for the locks and navigation (Willan 1946, 120–123). At other mills he came to agreements with their owners. In return for an annual payment the Earl of Manchester agreed to employ a 'fit person' to record the goods being taken through Hemingford Sluice, and to ensure that the miller provided sufficient water above and below the mills for river traffic.

Throughout the drafting and implementation of the 17th century Parliamentary Acts to authorise the Navigation, the Godmanchester Borough was assiduous in protecting the rights to the river it had achieved in the decrees of 1467 and 1515. The Duchy decree of 1467 had granted Godmanchester boats toll-free passage around the mills of Hemingford Grey, Houghton and Hartford, and in 1515 the townsmen had been granted the power to control the floodgates, of the same mills, when floods threatened the Godmanchester meadows if the mill owners did not open the gates quickly enough. With extraordinary success the Borough had these rights transferred into the new Navigation Acts and Henry Ashley's lease. The Act defined: 'all such boats of burthen as have been used or accustomed to pass … shall and may continue freely to go and pass.' And that specifically 'the freemen of Godmanchester have free liberty of passage with boats and lighters laden or unladen with goods which shall be for their own use or for any public use within the borough' (Fox 1831, 212). And, with regard to the control of gates so as to prevent flooding: 'it shall be lawful for the miller of the Godmanchester mills, or persons or officers appointed by the Bailiffs of Godmanchester for ever hereafter, upon every likelihood and appearance of any flood or outrage of water, to set open and keep open, or else to take off the gates of the aforesaid [Godmanchester] sluices, and also the gates of the sluices in and near Houghton, and also the gates of the sluices in and near the mill of Hemingford Grey, and lay them upon the lands by the side of the said sluices until the water be fallen and the flood well abated' (Fox 1831, 213–214).

Godmanchester's geographical control of the river was extended in 1719 in The Act for rebuilding the staunch at St Ives. At times of flood, the Godmanchester bailiffs were granted the power to affix a warrant to the staunch and/or the bridge at St Ives giving notice of their intention 'to take up and remove the said staunch and works'. If the owner or keeper of the staunch did not respond to the notice within half an hour, 'then in such case it may be lawful for the Bailiffs of Godmanchester to take up and remove the said aforesaid [staunch], and so to remain until the meadows shall be out of danger of being overflowed by the waters, doing as little damage to the said works [the staunch] as may be; the charge or expense thereof to be repaid and reimbursed by the owner of the works.' (Fox 1831, 218–219). The full implications of these powers granted to

7. The Age of Locks: a 17th century technical solution   107

Godmanchester and jealously used by them were to be seen nearly two centuries later in another protracted legal case as explained in Chapter 8.

Landscape impact

The landscape impact of the new sluices was largely confined to their immediate vicinity. For example, when Houghton Sluice was re-built in the late 1670s, it is recorded as being within a piece of land 'one rood' in area (Willan 1946, 57–58), *i.e.* a quarter of an acre, no more than the size of two tennis courts. However, it was often necessary to dig new channels to control the water entering the lock and to ensure its rapid discharge downstream. For example, landscape and map evidence suggest that Hemingford Grey Overfall Pit and its associated channels (Fig. 7.4) acted not only as a 'safety valve' to control the amount of water reaching the lock and mills, but also as a control mechanism for the level of water immediately downstream of the lock, to ensure a sufficient depth of water for vessels leaving and entering it. This is the most straightforward explanation for Overfall Pit having one entrance, a weir, but two exits, one discharging into the Hemingford Grey Backwater, and the other running parallel to the main channel, re-joining it immediately downstream of the lock. Figure 7.5 is a painting of Overfall Pit in 1908 when the mill was in operation. This construction is now very difficult to see; the weir feeding the Pit from the main channel is bricked up and the Pit itself is silted up and overgrown with reeds (Fig. 7.6).

FIGURE 7.4. Overfall Pit and its associated channels

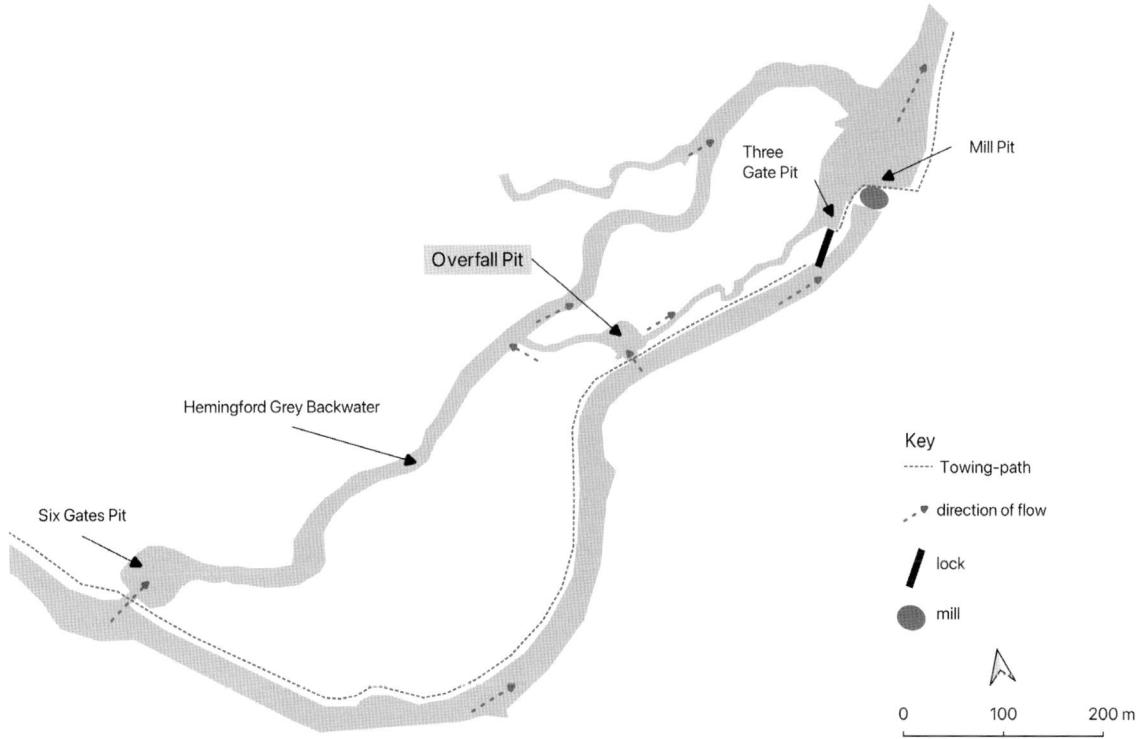

FIGURE 7.5. (opposite) Overfall Pit 1908 watercolour by Garden William Fraser (1856–1921)

The creation of towing-paths, known as 'halingways', had a significant impact on the landscape at the time. The towing-paths were essential to the Navigation because without being towed, usually by a pair of horses, vessels could not move upstream, and at times of low flow they might also need help with the downstream journey. It was the responsibility of the undertaker to create these towing-paths by negotiating agreements with the landowners, tenants and tithe owners. This was a complicated process and inevitably led to many disputes. One example of this is an award in 1691 to Ashley senior to establish a towing-path for four miles upstream of Great Barford, which involved 18 separate payments for damages (Willan 1946, 26). The award was for a towing-path three feet wide, marked out with stakes.

The scene of a string of barges, hauled by a pair of horses, as drawn by John Pettrey Hunter in 1835 (Fig. 7.7) was a common one. This was described in the 1890s by Foster (1891, 170–171):

> The gangs of lighters, as Ouse barges are called, are made up just in the same way as they were in the last century. First comes the fore-lighter, with the name of the owner painted on the bows. Then comes the house-lighter, so called because a part of it makes a cabin for the men. Then come two decked-lighters, that is, lighters with moveable covers, then an open lighter, and lastly the smallest lighter called the boat, which is sometimes used to transport the horses from one side of the stream to the other. This lengthy and heavy gang is drawn up stream, when loaded, by two horses, but coming down stream empty, one horse is sufficient, and the animals ride by turn in the fore-lighter.

FIGURE 7.6. (opposite) Overfall Pit, December 2022

FIGURE 7.7. St Ives, Huntingdonshire c. 1835 by James Pettrey Hunter (1791–1867)

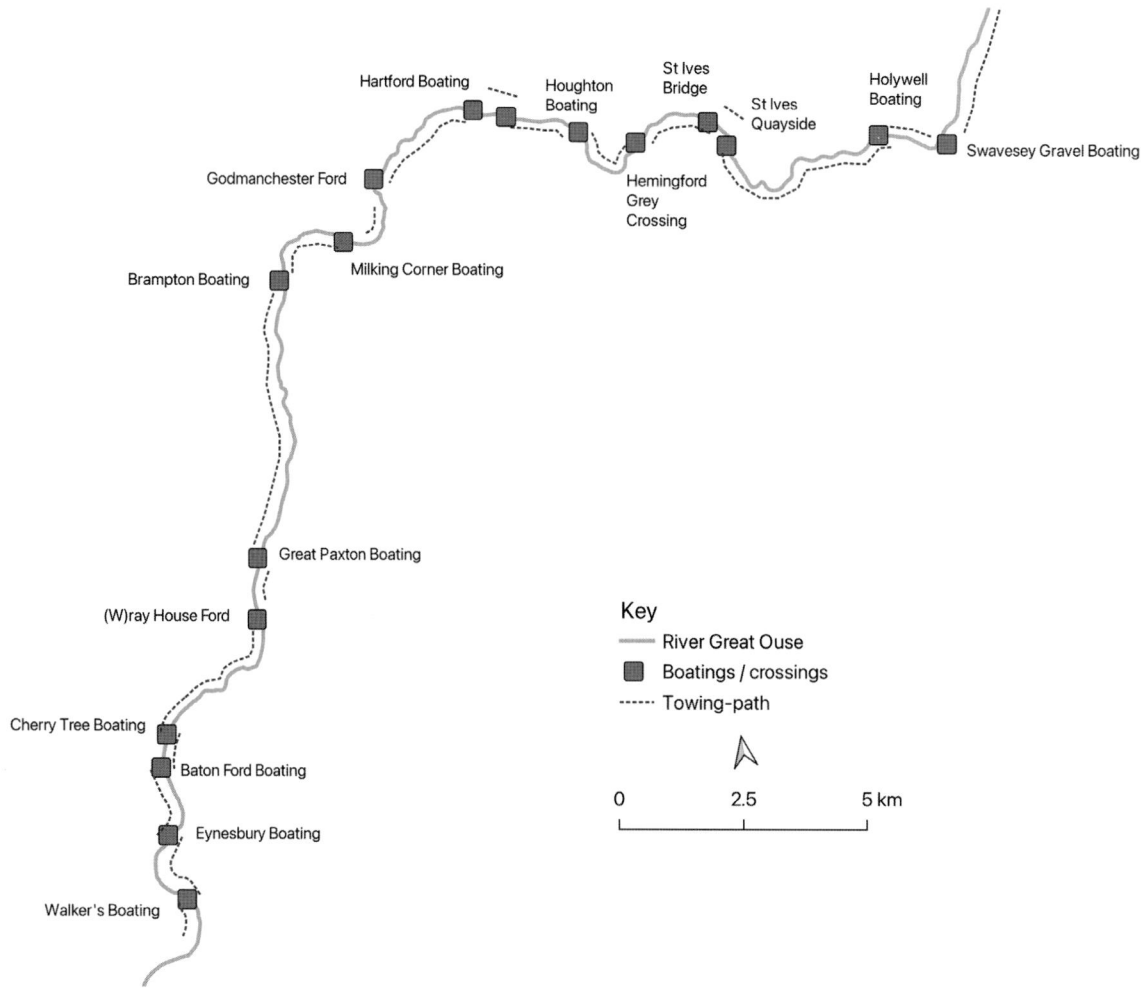

FIGURE 7.8. The towing-path, 1834

The 1834 Lenny and Croft map shows the towing-path on the Cambridgeshire section of the Great Ouse crossing from one side of the river to the other 17 times (Fig. 7.8). At some places this was because the towing-path was obstructed by riverside settlement, *e.g.* at Godmanchester (Godmanchester Ford). At others, crossing the river avoided the need to bridge watercourses, *e.g.* the south-west corner of Godmanchester West Meadow (Brampton Boating). Sometimes it was because it had not been possible to reach agreement with the landowners. Crossing the river was only possible where it was either shallow enough to ford, or was safe enough to take the horses across in a boat. Three places where the towing-path crosses the river are labelled 'Ford', and 11 are labelled 'Boating'. An account of a walk from Hemingford Abbots to Houghton written by Wimperis (1895) explains that 'Boatings' were places where the river was fordable: 'Presently we found the towing-path came to an abrupt termination, and in front of us a railway embankment barred our way. We were fairly puzzled, as we

7. The Age of Locks: a 17th century technical solution

FIGURE 7.9. Raised bank, Hemingford Abbots Meadow, 2024

knew the barge horses could not get over that, and we did not find out till a subsequent visit that there was a ford across the river at this point, and that the towing-path changed to the opposite side' (Wimperis 1895, 412). However, it is unlikely that Lenny and Croft would have used 'Ford' and 'Boating' if they were synonymous. It is therefore probable that a 'Boating' was a place where the river could be forded at certain times of the year, but when the water level was higher it was safe to transport the horses across in a boat. The double-crossing point at St Ives was particularly challenging. The towing-path from Fenstanton to St Ives was on the south bank of the river. Generally, it was possible for the horses to cross to St Ives Quay on the north bank with only a short stretch of deep water to swim (Skeeles 1933, 69). The barges were then hauled along the Quay. At the bridge, the towing line was cast off so that the barges could be manoeuvred under the arches (Summers 1973, 132–133). The horses crossed the bridge, back to the south bank where the towing-path then continued upstream on Hemingford Grey Meadow.

It is unsurprising that the towing-path has left little, if any, lasting impact on the landscape. Nineteenth century paintings, like Figure 7.7, show a strip of land next to the river. Such a path would leave next to no visible trace. In a few places the towing-path was on a raised bank next to the river. An example is the towing-path immediately west of Houghton, which can still be seen in the landscape (Fig. 7.9). This stretch of raised bank may have been constructed so that towing could continue when the surrounding meadows were flooded. However, it is more likely that the bank was raised as part of the river control measures in the 13th to 16th centuries, with the towing-path subsequently constructed on top of it. Most of the bridges that were built to allow the towing-path to cross tributary watercourses have fallen into disrepair and/or been demolished.

CHAPTER EIGHT

Continuity, disputes and cooperation: 1700–1850

At the beginning of the 18th century, watermilling on the River Great Ouse in Cambridgeshire was concentrated at eight locations, all recorded in the Domesday Book in 1086 (Fig. 8.1). This continuity of location is explained by two main factors. Firstly, the water engineering of mill-leats, tail races, weirs, sluices and locks, developed since at least the 10th century, proffered significant advantages and represented a major investment of time and money. Secondly, agreements for these, often hard won, had been secured between the millers and the other main users of the river and its floodplain – boatmen, farmers and fishermen - thus reducing conflict and enabling (some) cooperation. None of the water mechanisms, nor their long-established rights, could be quickly or easily replicated at new locations on the river. Such factors are also found to be significant on other lowland rivers; for example, Oliver (2013, 227) has identified patterns of use on the Thames that required – and were reinforced by – capital works and associated legal rights. By the mid-19th century, the beginnings of specialisation and diversification can be seen and, in keeping with Huntingdonshire's pre-eminent position in watermilling in the Middle Ages, several of the mills on the Great Ouse were amongst the most advanced and well run in the country (Howes 2020, 10). However, in contrast to the Middle Ages, some of these later mill buildings and their equipment have survived, making it easier to evaluate their impact on the past and present landscape.

Developments

The Eaton Socon Mill was rebuilt, still as a watermill, as late as 1847, across the original mill stream. In contrast, the St Neots Mill, near Little Paxton, was an example of 19th century diversification. Known as Okestubbe Mill, it was rebuilt in 1799 by its new owner, Owsley Rowley, who came to St Neots from Godmanchester. Initially, it was let to Mr Hobson, the miller at Eaton Socon, but in 1804 it was converted from a corn mill to a paper mill, the first to make use of a new machine invented by Henry Fourdrinier that produced a continuous roll of paper (Howes 2020, 18). Henry set up the paper mill with his brother, Sealy, and a business partner, John Gamble. The very high development costs led to their bankruptcy, but the paper mill survived to be a successful and profitable enterprise. It remained powered solely by water until

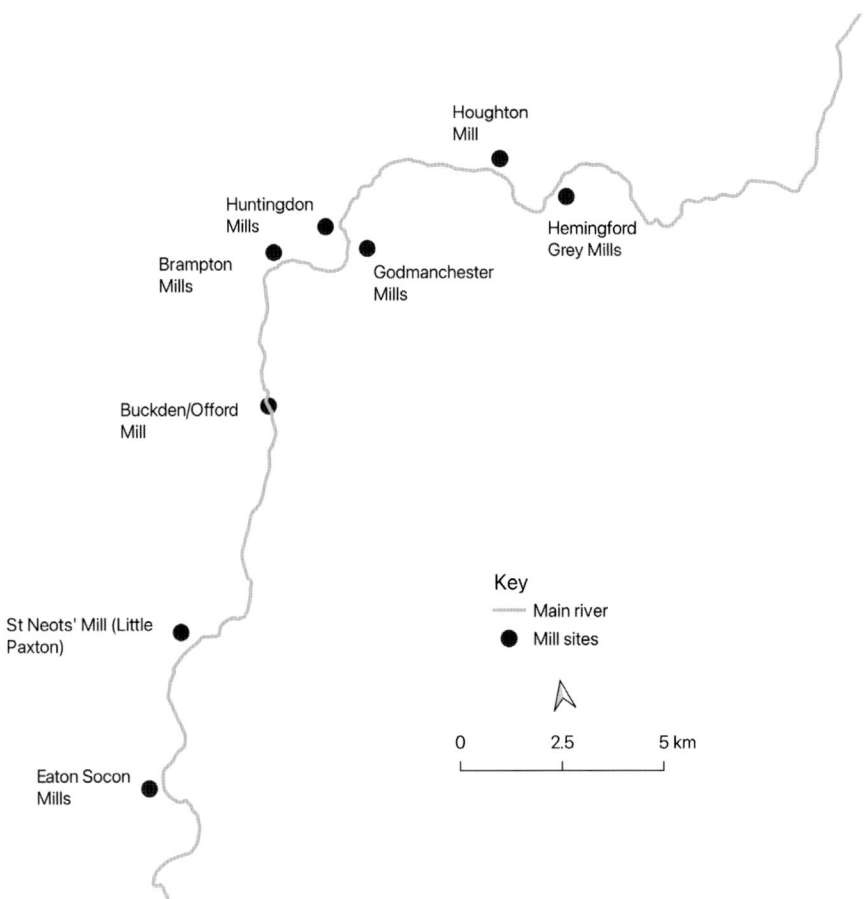

FIGURE 8.1. Watermill sites on the Great Ouse in Cambridgeshire, 1700–1850

1851 when steam power units were introduced. Uncertainty about the location of Offord Mills has already been discussed, but it is certain that there was a watermill at Buckden in this period because it is shown on the Jefferys map of 1768 (KHAC4/4347), the Offord Cluny Inclosure map of 1806 (KDMC/344) and the Buckden Inclosure map of 1813 (KDMC/312). The mill was powered by two undershot waterwheels and had ten pairs of stones. The fortunes of the mills at Brampton and Huntingdon in the 18th-19th centuries are described in the section below. Godmanchester Mill operated throughout this period as a timber clad, four-storey mill with three pitched roofs. Houghton Mill, the only watermill on the Great Ouse still in operation today, although only for demonstration purposes, was rebuilt following a major fire in 1754. This is the building that survives, with 19th century modifications (see Fig. 1.2, page 3). These years were very profitable for Houghton Mill, with Potto Brown taking over the business from his father in 1822. Brown, together with his business partner, Joseph Goodman, specialised in producing high quality flour, using machinery and techniques that he introduced following visits to France and

Germany. In 1852 he brought his sons into the business, and he retired in 1862 (Howes 2020, 24).

Disputes

Despite the many legal agreements set up over the centuries to sort out the varying claims to the river and the floodplain, the lawyers were busy as disputes rumbled on and the various parties involved needed reminders of their responsibilities. A good example is revealed in an indenture of covenants dated January 1787 (KBR2/BOX1/6) between Henry Dobson (tenant of Brampton Mills), John Earl of Sandwich (owner and proprietor of Brampton Mills) and the 'Mayor, Alderman and Burgesses of Huntingdon', the owners and proprietors of the Huntingdon Mills. It records that the agreement reached in 1741 between these parties and Thomas Warner of Huntingdon (tenant and occupier of Huntingdon Mills) should be respected. Unfortunately, the 1741 agreement has not survived but a deed of covenant dated March 1837 (KBR2/BOX1/13) described it in some detail. The 1837 document was occasioned by the Earl of Sandwich's purchase of the Huntingdon Mills from the Borough at a public auction on 8th October 1836. It refers to 'several disputes, controversies and suits' that had arisen between Thomas Warner, the tenant/occupier of Huntingdon Mills, and the 'landowners, commoners and inhabitants of Brampton Parish' in the late 1730s. The main dispute was that Thomas Warner had deepened Bromholme Brook and Portholme Brook to increase the supply of water to the Huntingdon Mills (Fig. 8.2). This prevented the movement of cattle across the meadow to the pastures on Portholme owned by Brampton's farmers; 'they had always had a right to a fordable way'. In summary, the 1741 agreement was that the owners of the Huntingdon Mills were to build a bridge across each of the two brooks; erect four 'strong and substantial' flood gates between Portholme and Watermills Close; to keep the above in good repair 'for forty years'; 'pen up' the flood gates to keep the level of water in the main river high enough to allow boats or lighters into Brampton Sluice; and scour out the brooks without widening them or damaging the land on either side. Huntingdon Mills had to give six days' notice prior to scouring out the brooks because work on Bromholme Brook, Brampton Mills' tail-race, would require its closure. Two days were allocated to carry out the works and any overrun was charged at five shillings a day. The 1837 deed of covenant transferred these responsibilities to the Earl of Sandwich.

The impact of Thomas Warner's actions to increase water supply to the Huntingdon Mills can still be seen in the landscape. The probable origin of Portholme Brook as a drainage channel for Bromholme Field was discussed in Chapter 3. It is now silted up and dry for most of the year, but its course can be followed on the ground, marked by a line of trees and a shallow depression that is occasionally water-filled (Fig. 8.3). The 1787 and 1837 documents detail how it was exploited to provide water for Huntingdon Mills by 1741, but unfortunately

116 *The Watermills and Landscape of the River Great Ouse, Cambridgeshire*

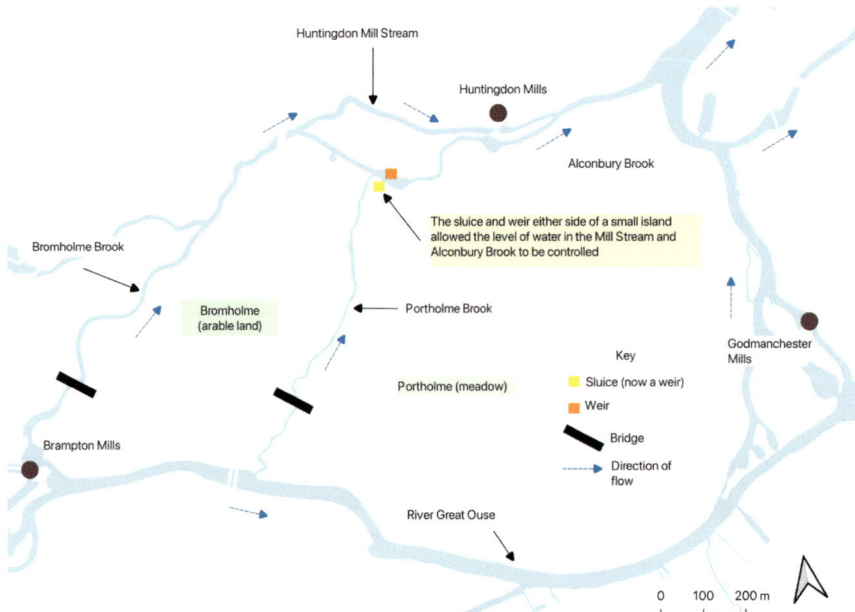

FIGURE 8.2. Huntingdon Mills and Portholme Brook

FIGURE 8.3. (below) Portholme Brook, April 2022

8. Continuity, disputes and cooperation: 1700–1850

do not record when this operation had begun. The earliest map showing Portholme Brook is from 1730 (KAcc4577/2/11), although its confluence with Alconbury Brook is drawn inaccurately. It is also shown being crossed by a bridge, whereas contemporary documentation records this was a ford. Given that the use of Portholme Brook to increase the supply of water to the Huntingdon Mills would have been a major undertaking (it would have required the building of a sluice or weir downstream of its confluence with Alconbury Brook because the entrance to the mill-race is upstream of the confluence), in all probability it was not until the late 1730s that it was incorporated into the watermilling system. A plan of the Earl of Sandwich's lands on Portholme from 1757 (KHAC0/223/1) shows the brook as a major feature, crossed by a bridge, confirming that the 1741 agreement had been implemented by then. The 1886 OS map records a sluice and a weir capturing the flow from Portholme Brook, the former today replaced by a weir (Fig. 8.4). Finally, the bridge Warner was required to build is still there (Fig. 8.5).

Although no further concerns regarding the management of Portholme Brook are found in the records, other disputes, not dissimilar to those in the 13th century and earlier, continued to surface from time to time. For example, in 1876 (KHINCH/10/12) John Ingram, the Mayor of Huntingdon, and 31

FIGURE 8.4. The weir immediately downstream of Portholme Brook's confluence with Alconbury Brook, April 2022

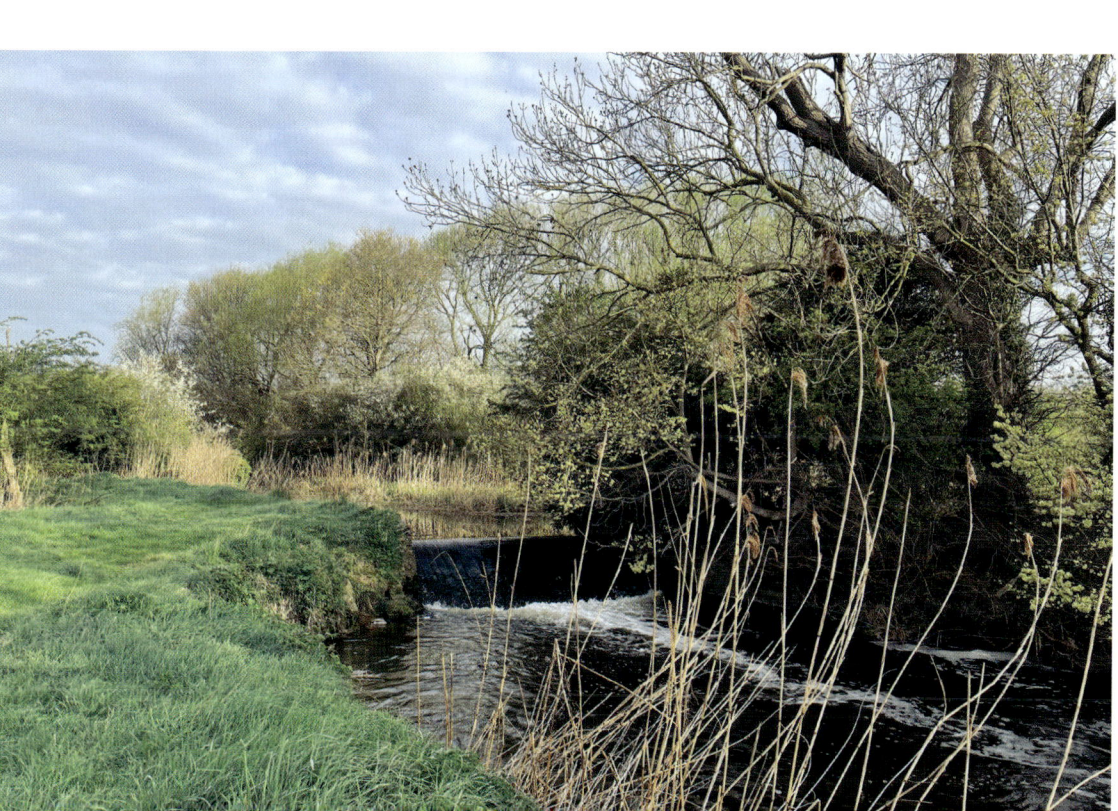

other people, wrote to the Earl of Sandwich to use his influence to compel the Borough of Godmanchester to clean out the Godmanchester Backwater, which they blamed for flooding on Portholme.

Cooperation

It was not always about conflict – there were also examples of cooperation between the millers. In a book of reminiscences, Bird (1911, 52–53) described how in the middle years of the 19th century the miller at Godmanchester hoisted a red flag when his mill was working to alert, he thought, Huntingdon Mill. He suggested that this 'had something to do with the regulation of the water'. However, given that the Huntingdon Mill was supplied by a mill-leat coming off Alconbury Brook (Fig. 5.5, page 69), it would not have been significantly affected by the Godmanchester Mills taking water from the Great Ouse, whereas the Brampton Mills would have been, and vice versa, so perhaps Bird's reminiscence is incomplete. Yet the legal disputes described above show that Brampton Mills affected the operation of Huntingdon Mill, so a flag for the three mills alerting each other does make sense.

Landscape change

The development of watermilling between 1700 and 1850 did not result in major landscape change. Bromholme Brook and Portholme Brook were deepened but this did not alter the river pattern. The channel from the Huntingdon Mill Stream to Alconbury Brook (see Fig. 5.6, page 69) may have been cut during this period. However, although it first appears on the Jefferys map of 1768, there is no certainty that it does not pre-date 1700 because, as a relatively small feature, it would not necessarily have been included on earlier maps, especially as they were mostly small-scale. Other changes are almost all associated with the building and rebuilding of the locks and had a localised impact.

However, one very significant landscape feature did appear in this period. This is Fishers Dyke, which runs from the eastern branch of Cook's Stream to join the pit below Rhymers Weir (Fig. 8.6). Its exact date of construction is not known. It is not on the Jefferys map of 1768 but is on the Godmanchester Inclosure map of 1803 (KDMC/325), so must have been cut at some point between these two years. The first half of the Dyke separates land allocated to Lady Olivia Sparrow from land allocated to Henry Sweeting in the Inclosure Act, and so may be contemporaneous with the Act, *i.e.* the early 1800s. The second half of the Dyke crosses Godmanchester Eastside Common. It takes water out of the eastern branch of Cook's Stream into the Hemingford Abbots Backwater via the cut from Rhymers Weir. It may have been constructed to reduce the volume of water reaching Houghton Mill in times of flood by preventing Cook's Stream from discharging into the main river, but with Rhymers Weir and Four Gates Pit (the 'Houghton Gulls' and the Abbot's Leat on the 1515 map) it is hard to

8. Continuity, disputes and cooperation: 1700–1850   119

FIGURE 8.5. The bridge crossing Portholme Brook, April 2022

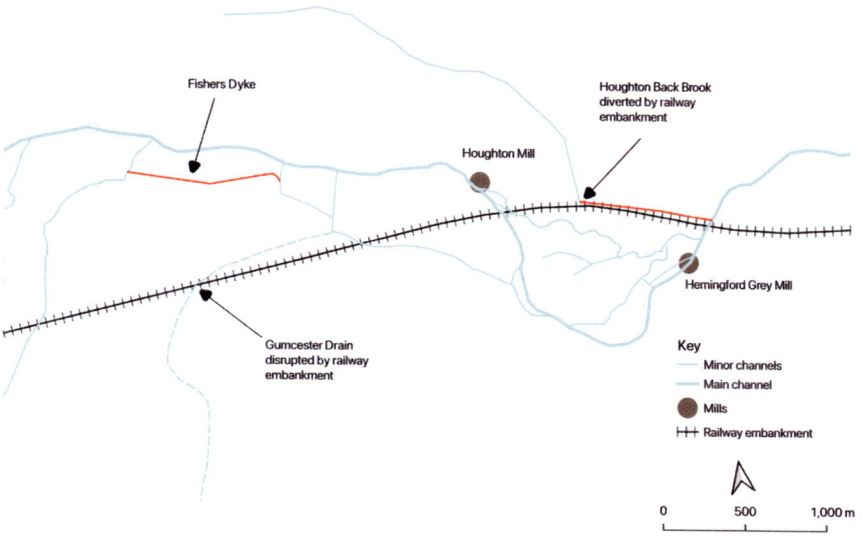

FIGURE 8.6. Fishers Dyke and the railway embankment location map

see why it would have been necessary. A more likely explanation is that it was constructed to alleviate flooding on the Godmanchester meadows both to the east and west of Cook's Stream. In times of flood, the volume of water in the main river would act as a barrier, preventing Cook's Stream from discharging into it. This would cause the water in Cook's Stream to back up, and as it did so it would rise above its banks and spill onto the floodplain. The Lenny and Croft

FIGURE 8.7. The weir at the entrance to Fishers Dyke, 2024

map of 1834 labels the entrance at the western end of the Dyke as an overfall, *i.e.* a weir, which it still is today (Fig. 8.7). Set at the appropriate height, this would act as a safety valve for water unable to get into the main channel, taking it across to Hemingford Abbots Backwater and stopping the meadow from flooding. The significance of Fishers Dyke is that it connected – for the first time – the channels of Godmanchester Westside Common with the channels of Hemingford Abbots Meadow, *i.e.* it was the first time that what had been two separate systems of tributaries were joined up. As such, it was, and still is, a key component of the multi-channel landscape.

Road and railways make their mark on the watermilling landscape

The early history of the Godmanchester causeway on the south side of Huntingdon Bridge was discussed in Chapter 4. The Prior of Huntingdon had responsibility for its repair, recorded in 1276 as 'perpetual repairs' (Fox 1831, 365). The causeway was elevated above the flood meadow and crossed the backwater which served Hartford mills. Flood gates were positioned within one of its seven arches to control the level of the backwater. As well as being a local road connecting Huntingdon and Godmanchester, the causeway carried the national road of Ermine Street, later known as the Great North Road and then the Old North Road. The Prior had assiduously minimised his expenditure on the causeway by limiting its use. He had the road chained at both ends except in times of flood. At all other times travellers had to use a parallel roadway over the meadow to the east. The Prior's 'perpetual maintenance' of the causeway came

FIGURE 8.8. The remains of the trestle bridge crossing Houghton Mill's tail race

to an end with the Dissolution, and as generally happened with many roads, local parish or borough maintenance proved insufficient – especially for those roads that received out-of-parish use. The causeway was replaced by new arches in 1637 and named after Robert Cook who had donated funds after escaping drowning in the backwater (see also Chapter 4). Flood gates in the arches to control the backwater were no longer necessary because Hartford Mills had become redundant by the mid-16th century. The 1768 Jefferys map of Huntingdonshire (KHAC4/4347) shows the new causeway (Cook's Bridge) and the eastern 'dry weather' route still in existence, the latter crossing the backwater (Cook's Stream) via either a bridge, or more likely a ford. Across the country, the 18th century revolution in road travel brought enormous improvements in road construction; in 1784 the Royston to Wansford Bridge Turnpike Trust built a new causewayed road across the backwater and on to Huntingdon Bridge. There were two eight-arched brick bridges with an embankment between. The whole road was 572 yards long, 60 feet wide with a footpath of 10 feet (523 m, 18.3 m, 3 m). It was sited between the route of the old causeway and the eastern track. The plaque commemorating Robert Cook was re-positioned in the new brick arches – which are still known as Cook's Bridge.

The impact of the railway on the watermilling landscape was much more extensive than that of the roads. The challenge presented by the complex watermilling channels to the construction of the railway line from St Ives to Godmanchester in 1847 has already been discussed but it is also important to note the lasting impact of the railway line on the watermilling landscape here (Fig. 8.6). Today there are a few dwindling remains of posts of the wooden trestle bridges that carried the railway across the river and its channels (Fig. 8.8), whereas the long stretches of earthed embankments that raised the railway above the flood level of the meadows are a strong feature of the landscape. (These now serve as a refuge for grazing livestock during floods). Two watercourses were altered by the construction of the railway. Houghton Back Brook, that had been exploited as Houghton Mill's tail race in the medieval period, was diverted by the embankment to rejoin the main river further downstream. At the western end of Godmanchester Eastside Common the embankment disrupted the course of Gumcester Drain. This watercourse had been repeatedly referred to in the litigation from the 13th century through to the 16th century, but after the construction of the railway in 1847 it was virtually eliminated from the landscape.

CHAPTER NINE

Decline and romantic appreciation: 1850 to the present day

By the mid-19th century, it was clear that the use of waterpower for grinding grain would soon be superseded by the new superior technology of steam power. For most of the existing watermills across the country which did not convert to steam power, it was only a matter of a few decades before they would decline economically and eventually become redundant. Their disused buildings were relatively easy to demolish, clear away or build over, but it was more difficult to erase complex systems of water channels. And where such channels were not required for a replacement steam mill, or for drainage or navigation purposes, they were left alone. Backwaters in every sense of the term. This scenario is particularly evident along the Great Ouse in Huntingdonshire; although many of the watermill buildings have now gone, most of the pre-1850 landscape of the watermilling industry remains *in situ*. Some smaller channels have silted or dried up due to lack of use and/or maintenance, but otherwise there have been few alterations or adaptations from that date. Weirs, sluices and locks have been maintained to help control the flood risk and allow river navigation. Since the 1960s the river valley landscape has been interrupted by large scale gravel extraction. However, the extraction sites respected the existing river channels – natural and artificial – to prevent the quarries from flooding. Consequently, the landscape heritage of the watermills has remained largely intact.

The demise of watermilling

The demise of the watermills was relatively swift. From the late 18th century, the new technologies of the Industrial Revolution drastically changed Britain. Large numbers of people migrated to urban centres in search of better employment, and at the same time there was a rapid increase in population. The census of 1801 recorded 8.3 million people in England and Wales, almost doubling to 15.9 million in 1841. Consequently, there was a growing demand from the cities for flour. The trade restrictions of the 1815 Corn Laws had limited grain imports to protect British farm prices, but home-grown supply could not meet demand and shortages ensued. In 1846 the unpopular Corn Laws were repealed. With the arrival of large quantities of overseas grain, an economically efficient milling process on a much greater scale quickly developed. Steam mills were built at the ports and the new railway system transported the flour to the urban centres. The new mills developed the use of rollers rather than stones for grinding.

This technology had the advantages of producing a whiter, longer-lasting flour which customers preferred. In Huntingdonshire the milling firm of Brown and Goodman had built a modern steam mill in St Ives in 1854 and planned a bigger steam mill at Godmanchester. Bateman Brown, son of Potto Brown, remembers that they sited the mill in Godmanchester for crusading political and religious reasons, explaining:

> We should not have increased our business merely for the sake of increasing our money, and we were perfectly aware that, from a commercial point of view, London or some other large port would have been the place to build another mill, but our main object was as stated to strengthen both the Nonconformists and the Liberal party in the County town, so the mill was built and opened in 1863 (Brown 1905, 94).

The huge eight-storey Godmanchester steam mill dominated Huntingdon and the riverside landscape. As was intended, the building certainly made a strong statement, yet it was not so commercially selfless as Bateman Brown had indicated. Brown and Goodman were enterprising, innovative and financially successful. Their Godmanchester mill, like the company's other steam mill at St Ives, operated 16 pairs of stones and used an automated, streamlined milling process. But when the Godmanchester mill was upgraded with rollers, its output exceeded that of the two mills, and so St Ives was closed in 1898. By that time, the Godmanchester mill was one of the most technologically advanced in Europe.

A cluster of new steam mills was built in the town of St Neots. A steam-powered corn mill started operating at Brookside in 1855. On part of the old Priory site, downstream of the town bridge, a small steam-powered roller mill was working from the latter part of the 19th century within the curtilage of Day's Brewery. And on Bedford Street, the large brewing and milling firm, Paine and Company, had their 'St Neots Steam Flour Mills', where, from 1840, a beam engine powered ten sets of stones.

Along the river there were mixed fortunes for the old rural watermills. Those at Huntingdon and Godmanchester had closed by the mid-1880s because their proximity to the Godmanchester steam-powered corn mill (both were within approximately 800 m) made them no longer viable. The mills at Brampton and Hemingford Grey continued as water-powered, despite their proximity to the Godmanchester and St Ives steam mills. But the watermill at Houghton was the exception and it clearly prospered. It was the original part of the Brown and Goodman milling empire and now benefitted from the company's size and expertise: in 1880 its three wheels were working ten pairs of stones. The mills at Offord/Buckden converted their ten pairs of stones to rollers in 1887 and in the mid-1890s replaced the waterwheels with two water-powered turbines and a steam engine. Little Paxton corn mill was converted to a paper mill in 1804, and in 1851 changed from water to steam power. At Eaton Socon the construction of a large three-storey replacement watermill across the original mill stream in 1847 bucked the trend towards modern steam power, but in 1903 its waterwheels were replaced with water-powered turbines (Howes 2020, 28).

The development of the railways was a major influence on the economic success of the mills along the Great Ouse, particularly for those mills sited close to the railway lines. Transport of grain to the mills and the distribution of flour to the urban centres was faster and more efficient by rail than by water. The towns of Huntingdon and St Neots were well placed on the East Coast Main Line which had opened in 1850. The Offord/Buckden mills shared this advantage with a private siding to the main line. But the railway to the east – between St Ives and Godmanchester, opened in 1847 – did not bring the same benefits. Less than five miles long it had been very expensive to build because of the complicated and challenging topography of river channels. The line had to cross and recross the network of backwaters and leats of the watermilling landscape. Only light locomotives could be used on the weak, wooden trestle bridges which limited trains to a single-track crossing at 40 mph, at times reduced to only 10 mph. The Godmanchester steam mill had its own sidings on this railway, but by then the railway was connected by a new bridge across the river that linked to the East Coast Main Line at Huntingdon just half a mile away.

Disputes recur and force the closure of the locks

The Navigation continued to thrive until the third quarter of the 19th century when its fortunes declined rapidly due to competition from the ever-expanding rail network. For example, toll receipts fell by over 50 per cent between 1855 and 1862. However, the cost of water transport for heavy, bulky loads such as paper, coal and iron remained economic in comparison with the cost of rail transport and various attempts were made to keeping the Navigation going. In 1893 it was bought by Leonard T. Simpson, a wealthy stockbroker, and his brother who invested heavily in repairing and renewing the locks as well as introducing a fleet of steam-powered commercial boats. Initially, there was a revival in trade and commercial use of the river, but the maintenance costs were considerable, and Simpson was unable to secure agreement on levying economic tolls for the use of his locks. He faced opposition from Bedfordshire and Huntingdonshire County Councils whose aim was to remove the Navigation from private control, *e.g.* challenging his right to increase the 1d toll at St Ives staunch, despite it having been set in 1720. The Councils also tried to establish whether there was a public right of navigation on the Great Ouse and whether the new owner was liable to maintain the St Ives Staunch (KBLC/5/5/1).

Simpson had meanwhile encountered further opposition which threatened the viability of his new enterprise. The Godmanchester Corporation actively continued to exercise their right to open the Godmanchester, Houghton and Hemingford floodgates in times of flood should their lands be threatened by the floods. This right had been confirmed in the 1515 Duchy of Lancaster court case, and although at that time the decree had referred to the mill floodgates and overflows, Godmanchester Corporation had later managed to have it applied to the gates of the pound locks built from the 17th century, and then St Ives

Staunch. However, it is unclear if Simpson had any inkling of Godmanchester's powerful rights before he acquired the Navigation, nor, if he had, whether he would have agreed to such terms. (They had not been specified in the 1892 Particulars or Conditions of Sale for the Navigation (HINCH/10/72).)

Simpson seemed genuinely bewildered by the ferocity of the Godmanchester action against him and was astonished at the town's determination to control the lock gates, resulting in wanton damage to the locks. The Earl of Sandwich offered to mediate between the Godmanchester Corporation and Simpson. In a letter of December 1894 Simpson wrote to the Earl:

> During the last two years I have expended a very large sum in restoring the navigation between St Ives and Bedford, a work which it seems to me must be of considerable benefit to the County of Huntingdon. One would therefore have thought that I should have received some support or encouragement from the various bodies controlling the areas benefited. But as far from receiving any support or encouragement, I have been met on all sides with the most determined and continuous opposition, and have thereby been put to great and, as events have proved, unnecessary expense (KHINCH 10/81).

In 1894, after his re-built lock gates at Godmanchester had been damaged three times, Simpson took legal action against the Mayor and Corporation to secure compensation. The transcript of the 1895 case in the High Court reveals the persistence and zeal of the Corporation in regularly forcing open the lock gates against flood waters or lifting them off their hinges. There are many pages of evidence of this ancient practice spanning nearly 250 years from the Corporation's accounts and Minute Books, one example reading: '1819; Childs a bill 3/7d. Fields & Bister drawing Gates etc and Fisher 12 journeys and bills etc for same and for watching the gates and taking them off £5-7s-6d' (KHAC1/1737, 232). The most complete run of records is from 1736 to 1835. Each entry sets out who was paid, the type of intervention – 'drawing, looking after, mending, watching, shutting, opening, taking care' – and its cost. Payments are recorded for 65% of these years. It is more likely that the records for the years without interventions are simply missing, but it is possible that the gaps reflect years in which the river did not flood. A run of dry years, although increasingly uncommon in our current changing climate, is not unknown. A typical entry is for 1748: 'For drawing the Staunch and the Gates 2/6 (two shillings and six pence); Spent at St. Ives drawing the Staunch 1/6; Pd. Thos. Shaw for looking after the Staunch 3 days and four nights 9/; Pd. Hy. Press for drawing Houghton and Hemingford Sluice Gates 10/' (KHAC1/1737, 227). Quite often the payment is to cover the cost of beer for the workers, *e.g.* 1766: 'Beer for the men opening the sluice gates 2/' (KHAC1/1737, 228).

The court case heard engineers give their expert opinion on the futility of such actions in controlling flood waters and the accumulative damage incurred on the gates and locks. When the river was in flood, a colossal amount of force was required to push open the gates against the torrent of water, or lift them off using a crane with a grappling mechanism known as a 'crab'. Each of the gates weighed about 32 hundred weight (1,635 kg). William Thornber, Engineer of the Ouse Navigation, having recently moved from a similar post in charge of the Rochdale Canal, stated that the flood water 'would pull the gates to pieces. No gate could stand it. There is not such a thing known anywhere else … The water also scours out an immense pit below the foundation of the lock. At Godmanchester there is about 16 feet of water beneath the lock tail' (KHAC1/1737 83–85). Simpson's court case failed, and he responded by nailing up all the lock gates. However, he persisted with legal actions and the case eventually reached the House of Lords where it was decided that Simpson did have the right to close the locks (KHAC1/1737) – which he promptly did. No-one could afford to purchase the Navigation from Simpson, who wished to recoup his losses. Consequently, by 1909 the Navigation stopped at St Ives and by the 1930s it was completely derelict to Bedford (Summers 1974, 187). Navigation along the river was again, as it had been from the 13th to the mid-17th century, sectional from mill dam to mill dam.

Pretty as a picture: the painted watermills along the Great Ouse

The demise of the navigation and the industrial river transport heralded a new era. In the late 19th and early to mid-20th century the watermills brought unexpected fame to the river landscape in Huntingdonshire – particularly along the stretch of river between St Ives and Huntingdon. The two working watermills at Houghton and Hemingford became central features in a new appreciation of the area. The landscape was 'discovered' by artists when they declared it 'a most picturesque and paintable stream, simply abounding in picture-making material' (Hissey, 1898).

Many of the artists who came to work along the Great Ouse in the villages around St Ives were following well-established patterns of landscape painting – particularly those of the Picturesque movement begun almost a century earlier. In 1801 Samuel Jackson Pratt described the attributes of the local landscape in both Picturesque and Pastoral terms:

> The view from the Bridge as you enter St Ives from London or Cambridge, opens a scene of beauty that commands attention. The admired steeples of St Ives and Hemingford, the pure river winding before you, the anglers on the willow-shaded banks, the clack of the water-mill, the mill house, the playful variety of green unfolding the diversity of autumn, many hundreds of acres of the richest meadow ground covered with herds. (Pratt 1801, 453)

When the artists came to this area from 1880 – a place hitherto artistically unknown and unrecognised – they found scenes in and around the villages that incorporated all the required elements for gentle, pastoral landscapes. Here were broad flower-filled meadows interlaced with pretty backwaters, a slow river, quaint small villages of thatched cottages, historic market towns, medieval bridges and churches, and the old wooden watermills at Houghton and Hemingford Grey. Hilaire Belloc felt a nostalgic romanticism: 'it is contented everywhere, and as you go you are in the middle of a thousand years' (Belloc 1908).

Watermills had been a favourite subject of the 17th century Dutch landscape painter Jacob van Ruisdael (1628–1682) and then his pupil Meindert Hobbema (1638–1709). In flat Dutch and Flemish landscapes with great skies, very similar to those of Huntingdonshire, they frequently placed 'the old watermill' as a focal point of their scenes. Many subsequent artists depicted watermills in their landscape views, but it must be John Constable (1776–1837) who brought them so powerfully to the forefront. What was the attraction of the watermill to these artists, and why did the subject, especially in the later 19th century, become so popular with the art-buying public?

Rural watermills were common, familiar features along most rivers – as they had been for centuries. They were industrial buildings of utilitarian design built with local materials and maintained only as necessary, often in a weatherbeaten, worn and patched way. As such they blended into the landscape as rustic, unkempt, almost organic structures. In and around the watermill there was a buzz of activity as the miller, mill-workers and mill-wrights combined to keep the great mechanisms of water wheel, gears and grinding stones in slow steady action. A watermill grinding the village's grain into flour for the daily bread was basic to everyday life, and a constant along with the village church, the Manor and the farm. But the most remarkable feature of a watermill was, and is, its power – seen, heard and felt. Within the mill is the rumble of machinery and stone, and outside is the roar and fall of water from the wheels and the dams. The continuous circular motion of the water wheel, cogs, gearing and stones is spectacular and mesmerising. A watermill is probably a perfect example of sustainable use of natural resources in its harnessing of the power of water. The writer A.C. Benson romanticised Houghton mill as

> a big, timbered place, with a tiled roof, odd galleries and projecting pent-houses, all pleasantly dusted with flour, where a great wheel turned dripping in a fern-clad cavern of its own, with the scent of the weedy river-water blown back from the plunging leat. River and leat and back-water here ran clear among willow-clad islands, all fringed with meadow-sweet and comfrey, butterbur and melilot (1908, 157)

Until the 19th century, artists frequently titled their watermills as 'old', mainly because those mills that they had chosen to paint were old, both in age and looks. New or modern mills were generally not considered artistic subjects. But by the late 19th century all the watermills were of olden times, having been superseded by new technology, and so they were seen as evocative symbols of a pre-industrial age. Icons of nostalgia. In 1880, the watermills at Houghton and Hemingford Grey were still in use, and would continue so for about another 50 years but, in the rest of the county, watermills were rapidly converting to the use of steam power. Thus, the small stretch of river between Huntingdon and St Ives was a time warp 'with the Great Ouse meandering sleepily by the old weather-beaten mill … [the area] is all the more interesting to people who want to escape the tall chimneys and pulsing looms. Hemingford is much what it was in Cromwell's day' (*The Advertiser* 1906, 7). The old working watermills were seen as survivors, keeping modern life at bay. For those people who felt that industrialisation and the machine age were taking society in the wrong direction, as well as those city dwellers who remembered their families' pastoral lives of just one or two generations ago, the watermills were a poignant symbol of a lost way of life – a rural idyll.

The paintings and drawings of this period c.1880–1930 can be a valuable source of evidence for the historian following the development of the river and riverside landscape, but caution is needed because some artists painted their contemporary landscape more faithfully than others. And others imagined it. The exquisite watercolours of Garden William Fraser (1856–1921) are an exceptional, and invaluable record of the area. He painted the landscape in minute detail with photographic accuracy. He frequently chose unremarkable scenes of no distinctive beauty or fame such as a backwater or weir and, very importantly, was not selective in what he included in the scene; he drew everything. For example, his painting of Overfall Pit helps significantly with today's understanding of the function of this water control feature given that its entrance is now bricked up and no longer visible from the river, and that the pit is completely overgrown with vegetation. His 1891 painting of the new Staunch and Lock at St Ives shows many more clear details of the mechanism than do the photographs of the time. The landscape work of other artists (specifically relating to mills and the river) ranged from general depictions of the mill buildings – usually seen from the mill pool – to scenes of pleasure boating. It being a very flat landscape, any panoramic or distant scenes had a limited capacity for overall landscape details such as the connections of minor watercourses. William Watt Milne (1865–1949) painted the watermills with great energy and strong colour, frequently populating his scenes with industrious workers nearby, either with carts, or in boats, or carrying flour sacks. But his work is in complete contrast to that of Garden Fraser and offers almost no reliable evidence to the landscape historian. It is frequently a total distraction. His oil paintings were often done in two parts – the main body of the painting worked *en plein air* in order to capture the light, mood, vitality and impression of the scene, and then the background finished in the studio when fillers and embellishments of considerable artistic licence were added. A comparison of Figures 9.1 and 9.2 illustrates this point. Both paintings are of Houghton Mill. The former is by Garden William Fraser and shows great attention to detail. The latter is by William Watt Milne and displays considerable artistic licence, even to the inclusion of distant (non-existent) hills.

The artists' words about the river landscape and the mills are, in several cases, as valuable to the historian as their images. The first national announcement about the artistic value of the Great Ouse in Huntingdonshire came in an article in the *Art Journal* of 1881 entitled 'Little Known Sketching Grounds' written by Wilfrid Meynell and illustrated by George Gordon Fraser (1859–95, brother of Garden Fraser) (Meynell 1881, 9–12). It described the merits of the

FIGURE 9.1. Houghton Mill by Garden William Fraser (1856–1921)

river scenery on a boat trip from Bedford to King's Lynn. Ernest Wimperis (1835–1900) wrote of the summer of 1890 he and his friend Keeley Halswelle (1832–1891) spent sketching along the river in a specially commissioned punt so that they could access all the backwaters (Wimperis 1895, 413–415). In these and other articles, diaries and letters, the artists describe the river landscape from a new view-point – that of a post-industrial state, the merits of which were unrecognised by the local inhabitants. Especially, the artists explain the river's decay and disuse – which to them were some of its most attractive features; 'It still possessed all the appointments of a navigable stream, such as a towing path with its bridges, locks, and fords, and these in what to an artist is their most serviceable form – that is to say, somewhat neglected, decayed, and overgrown'. And when Wimperis announced that the area's scenery contained 'Constables ready-made', what better invitation could be given to bring other artists to paint here? A colony of artists was established in the Hemingford, Houghton and nearby Holywell villages (Flanagan 2010). Many more visited regularly. The watermills were painted so frequently and their images hung in city galleries and drawing rooms that they became nationally recognisable as iconic landmarks of this part of Huntingdonshire.

9. Decline and romantic appreciation: 1850 to the present day   131

FIGURE 9.2. Houghton Mill by William Watt Milne (1865–1949)

The place was declared a beauty spot, so tourists soon followed, and along with them came all the usual promotional paraphernalia. This was quite a novelty for an area unvisited before. As with the Thames, guide books for the Great Ouse were necessary. *The Ouse* by A.J. Foster (1891) is a historical guide to the river and *Ouse's Silent Tide* by C.F. Farrar (1921) is a narrative of a canoe trip from source to sea with much history and anecdote interspersed. Farrar describes the end of the commercial river:

> its traffic has now vanished. Yet I remember in the sixties when twenty barges would lie below Bedford Bridge with cargoes of wood for 'Green's Wharf' or Hobson's Wharf, grain for Pigott's Brewery, bricks for extensions to Howard's Works and the Embankment (Farrar 1921, 13)

For Farrar, like Wimperis 30 years earlier, the river had been freed from industry and its gentle dilapidations allowed romanticism and leisure. Paddling his canoe around the Hemingford Abbots backwater he observes:

> Below Wyton the river divides into two branches, one passing by flood gates on the right and circling round by pleasant ways to Hemingford Abbotts the other, the main stream, passing on to Houghton Mill – quite a beauty spot of the Ouse … where I would fain dream away a summer (Farrar 1921, 153)

As the tourists wrote home from their boating, fishing and camping holidays, the watermills featured on many a photo and postcard. For the mills it was a romantic golden sunset after almost a millennium of industry.

The demise of watermilling on the Great Ouse

Hemingford Grey Mill (Fig. 9.3) had two internal waterwheels driving six pairs of stones. One of these wheels, known as the 'Town Mill', probably because the machinery it drove was used exclusively for the villagers or local farms, fell into disrepair very early in the 20th century. In 1920 a Tattersall's 'Midget' roller flour mill powered by a diesel engine was introduced, along with a 'Smut and Separating' machine which cleaned the grain before it was ground. These two pieces of modern machinery allowed the mill to remain profitable. But there was then a long slow decline in the mill's activity. By the 1950s only one of the waterwheels remained and this had not been used for many years. In its later years the mill was grinding animal feed rather than flour. The Mill continued working until 1958 when it was acquired by the Great Ouse River Board. The mill and most of its adjacent buildings were demolished to make way for a new sluice, designed to improve flood control on the river (Howes 2020, 31). The mill house survives.

Houghton is the oldest, largest and only working watermill on the Great Ouse, although now operational for demonstration purposes only. It ceased commercial production in 1928 and only narrowly escaped demolition. Huntingdon Corporation blamed the disrepair of the lock gates for the low levels and insanitary state of the river. The Great Ouse River Board bought the mill and proposed that it be demolished. They first removed the two waterwheels in 1931 and replaced them with sluice gates, as part of a flood protection scheme. After local and national protests, including letters to *The Times*, the mill was saved by its picturesque fame and a determined group of villagers who bought the building in 1934 and then leased it to the Youth Hostel Association. The mill closed as a youth hostel in 1982 and was bought by the National Trust for one pound – the maintenance costs of the wooden building being prohibitive to the trust body that owned it. It was opened to the public in 1983, with the milling machinery run by an electric motor. In December 1996 the National Trust made a successful bid to the Heritage Lottery Fund to reinstall one of the waterwheels. This had significant implications for the flow of water through the mill:

> Over many lengths of the Great Ouse, channel configurations exist where the natural river channel has been amended to facilitate milling activities, navigation and flood control measures. Nowhere is the situation more complicated than over the reach of the river which includes Houghton Mill (Noble 1994, 2)

The solution was a new drop gate sluice alongside the reinstated waterwheel and a new flood relief channel, a penstock taking water from the mill dam to an electricity generating turbine, and new flood defences (Fig. 9.4). The restoration took 18 months to complete and was officially opened in June 1999.

9. *Decline and romantic appreciation: 1850 to the present day* 133

FIGURE 9.3. Hemingford Grey Mill, early 20th century

FIGURE 9.4. Houghton Mill (west side), 2024

Godmanchester Mill closed in 1884 and was demolished in 1927 (Fig. 9.5). Huntingdon Mill is shown as 'disused' on the 1886 OS map. Brampton Mill stopped working not long after the First World War and was derelict by 1924. It is now a restaurant with a decorative water wheel as a reminder of its past. The Buckden/Offord mill continued to be powered by water-powered turbines

FIGURE 9.5. Godmanchester Mills, early 20th century

FIGURE 9.6. Buckden Mill Buildings, 2024

and steam until it closed in 1965 and was converted into residential apartments (Fig. 9.6). The steam powered mill at Little Paxton closed in 1988 and the site has been developed with nearly 200 new houses. The access road is vulnerable to flooding and requires regular expensive maintenance. The Eaton Socon mill continued working, powered by water-powered turbines, through to the 1960s. The mill building is now a pub and restaurant (Fig. 9.7).

9. Decline and romantic appreciation: 1850 to the present day

FIGURE 9.7. Eaton Socon Mill Buildings, 2024

FIGURE 9.8. Platinum Jubilee celebration, Hemingford Abbots Backwater, 2022

The industrial landscape, once dominated by these watermills, has now changed its role to serve the interests of leisure and recreation (Fig. 9.8). Only the meadows are still worked; they are managed traditionally by being farmed for hay and then grazed. Crossed by paths and trails they are enjoyed by a multitude of visitors. In 1934 the Great Ouse Catchment Board bought the river navigation from Mr Simpson, but it was not until 1978 that all the locks were restored, and the navigation again reached Bedford. Boating of all kinds is now popular along the river and backwaters between St Neots and St Ives.

Houghton Mill is Listed Grade II* and Brampton, Buckden/Offord and Eaton Socon mills are Grade II. The mills' Listing recognises them as heritage assets, as nationally important buildings. Where they are within Conservation Areas, they contribute to that group heritage asset. But they should not be seen solely as a building – that is just a part of their story. When the mills were working there was a general understanding as to how and why they required not only the river to allow them to function, but a complex network of water channels around them. In a lowland river valley such as that of the Great Ouse in Huntingdonshire these channels extended over a large area. It is now imperative that the mills and their wider landscape are re-connected. The Listing details and reasons for designation need to incorporate the landscape that the mills shaped. Houghton Mill's landscape should be seen as integral to Houghton mill – a great survivor.

CHAPTER TEN

Modelling and managing the watermilling landscape

This chapter presents a four-stage model to summarise the major stages of the impact of watermilling on the landscape of the River Great Ouse. The stages show how the impact has changed over time, influenced by technological, socio-economic and political developments. As with any model, it is an abstraction of reality. None of the watermilling landscapes fit the model exactly. However, all almost invariably fit the general pattern. The process of developing the model helped identify and understand landscape impact. One example of this was the recognition of a deviation of a parish boundary when it leaves the main river to follow a smaller channel by-passing mills. This became a diagnostic feature of backwater development.

A model of watermilling landscape development

The model is set out in Figure 10.1. Stage 1 describes the period from the 10th century – and possibly earlier – through to the 1250s. Watermills of this period were generally sited on leats because they were too small to be located on the main river. These leats can still be seen in the landscape, *e.g.* at Houghton (page 48), or on the LiDAR, *e.g.* at Hartford (page 46). Here, it can be seen that the parish boundary bisected the main river. Stage 2 describes the period from the 1250s through to the end of the 16th century. Technological developments and an increase in demand from a growing population led to an expansion of watermilling activity. Larger mills were constructed, either on the main channel, *e.g.* at Hemingford Grey (i) (page 67) or on a modified leat, *e.g.* at Huntingdon (ii) (page 69). Backwaters and overspill channels were necessary, and these have left a very significant mark on the landscape, *e.g.* the Hemingford Grey Backwater (page 67). Parish boundaries were amended so that the mill owners had control over the backwaters, weirs and sluices that enabled them to regulate the water powering their mills. Stage 3, from the early 1600s through to the 20th century, saw the mills being bypassed by pound locks. These locks had only a local impact on the landscape, but most have survived, unlike the mills themselves. Stage 4 describes the post-watermilling landscape. With only a few exceptions the mill buildings have gone but most of the channels survive and are important to the water management of the floodplain. Boundary rationalisation in the 1970s has removed some, but not all, of the parish boundary deviations.

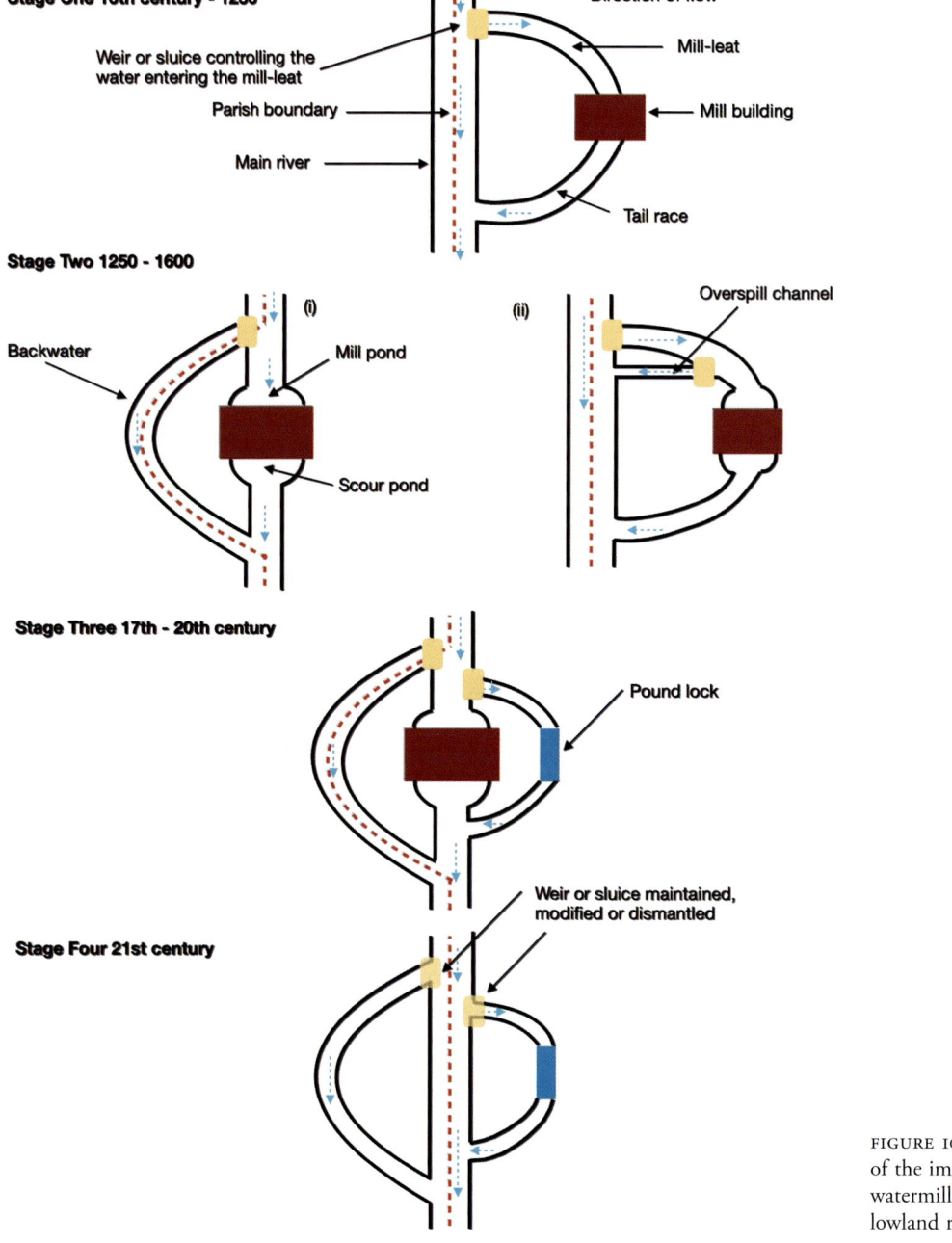

FIGURE 10.1. A model of the impact of watermilling on a lowland river landscape

This study has focused on the River Great Ouse in Cambridgeshire, but the model can be applied to other lowland river landscapes. For example, Elton on the River Nene had two watermills in 1086 and was the location of an early fulling mill, in the 13th century (VCH iii 1936, 154–166), owned by Ramsey Abbey. What is immediately striking on the 1886 OS map is the long, strange deviation

10. Modelling and managing the watermilling landscape 139

in the county boundary to the west of the main river (Fig. 10.2). Equally obvious is that this boundary deviation encompasses a backwater complex necessary to control the level of flow through the mill building, which was constructed across the main channel (Stage 2 (i)), and which is now bypassed by a lock (Stage 3). In 1974 this deviation was removed, and the county boundary now follows the main channel; all in all, making this a good illustration of the importance of historic maps for landscape research. Another example is at Olney on the River Great Ouse, upstream of the study area, in Buckinghamshire. On the 1882 OS map the parish boundary truncated the island in the river, as it still does today (Fig. 10.3). This was to encompass the weir and sluice controlling the entrance to the mill race that supplied the corn mill (a variant of Stage 2 (ii)). The weir maintained the level in the mill race and the sluice provided a safety valve if the river was too high.

The development of watermilling on the River Itchen between Southampton and Winchester further demonstrates the applicability of the model. The Domesday Book records ten mills at five sites along the 17 km stretch of the river between Woodmill in the parish of Bitterne and Winchester with an average value of 18s, *i.e.* above the national average of 11/ 7d = Stage 1 of the model. This is explained largely by its favourable physical geography, with the section between Worthy and Eastleigh being identified as historically anabranching by Lewin (2010, 274). In 1618 a survey was made with the aim of opening the river to navigation, restoring it to a 'decent approximation of a traditional centuries-old state of the river likely going back to the 1270s when population rise and improving damming techniques – especially for mills – seemingly began to close off rivers that had formerly been more receptive to navigation' (Langdon and White 2017, 150) = Stage 2 of the model. The outcome of the

FIGURE 10.2. Elton Mill: county boundary and backwater

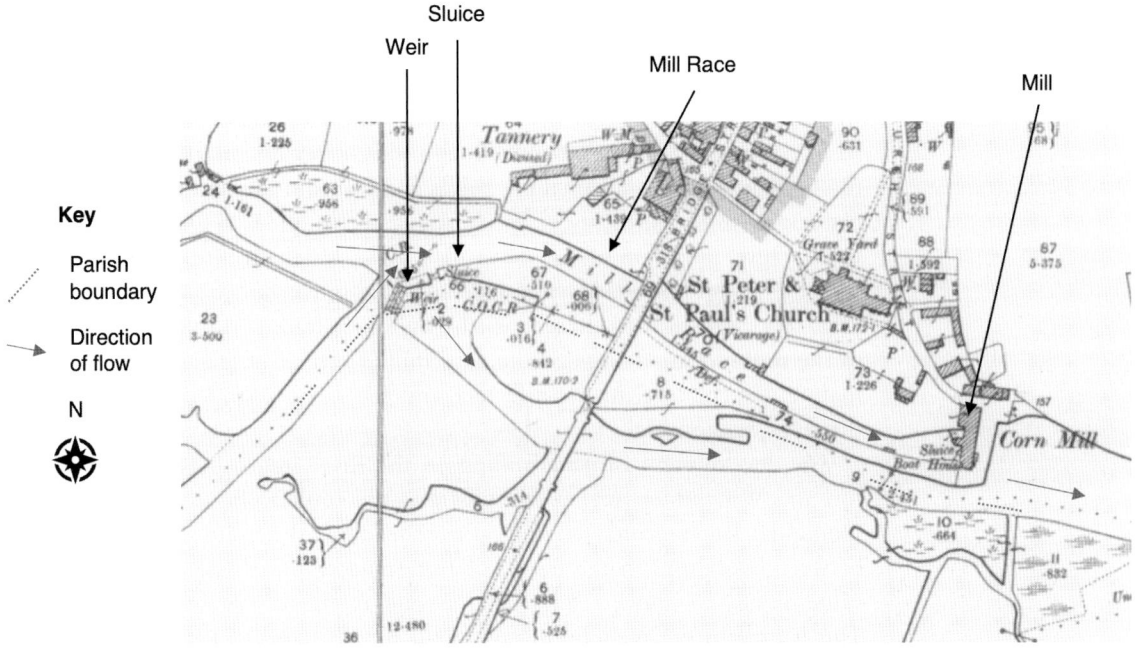

FIGURE 10.3. The Mill Race at Olney

survey was a scheme that suggested cuts around the mills, the mending of banks and the scouring of channels, and although locks were not mentioned it did lead to their eventual construction = Stage 3 of the model. Today, the river is an important corridor for leisure and recreation for Southampton through to Winchester = Stage 4 of the model. We also see another example of the 'parish boundary principle'. Upstream of Gaters Mill the parish boundary deviates back on itself for no apparent reason. The explanation can be seen on the 1895 OS map (Fig. 10.4). It was then known as Westend Mills and the parish boundary is following an overspill channel that was part of the backwater associated with the mill that South Stoneham needed to control. It is thought that this is one of the two mills recorded in the Domesday Book in North Stoneham and that it was transferred to South Stoneham by the change of boundary (VCH a, 1908).

Historic Water Polygons: identifying and recording watermilling landscapes

Rhodes (2007, 136) suggests that it is possible that the degree of human modification of lowland river systems has been previously underestimated, a view this study supports. The applicability of the four-stage model suggests that this is almost certainly the case for other lowland rivers, too. The implication is that landscapes previously unrecognised, or interpreted as natural, are frequently the result of watermilling activity over many centuries.

In 2018 Historic England published a national overview of Historic Watermill Landscapes (Alexander and Edgworth 2018). The report's authors begin their conclusions with the statement, 'Watermill landscapes are complexes of interrelated historic assets linking natural and artificial watercourses and a

10. Modelling and managing the watermilling landscape 141

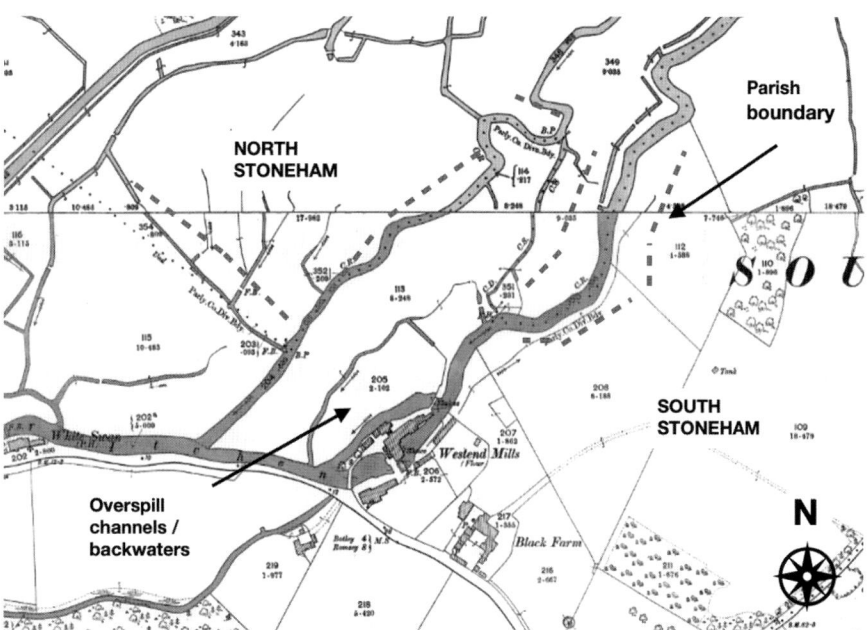

FIGURE 10.4. Westend Mills on the River Itchen

wide range of structures into a whole constituting far more than the sum of its parts' (2018, 65). This study of the Great Ouse provides numerous examples to support their conclusion. For instance, the Abbot's Leat, Rhymers, Trout Stream tail race and the Hemingford Abbots Backwater (see page 65) are not part of Houghton Mill's Grade II* Listing. However, they were an essential and integral part of Houghton's milling operation for many centuries and should be recognised and recorded as such.

One of Alexander and Edgeworth's recommendations was that better use should be made of the Local Authority Historic Environment Records (HERs) to record these landscapes. HERs underpin the work of Local Authority historic environment services and can help improve the protection, conservation and management of heritage assets by informing the planning process of significant heritage assets in a particular area. Alexander and Edgeworth concluded by stating that, 'In an ideal world it would be beneficial if high-level records and GIS polygons could be created for watermill landscapes that pulled together all the relevant subsidiary entries' (2018, 61).

Historic England followed up this recommendation by commissioning a project to develop a methodology for identifying the historic character of watercourses within a catchment, using the Dorset Stour as a case study (Firth and Firth 2020). The methodology developed was the Historic Water Polygon (HWP). This is a mappable area within which all the components – watercourses, weirs, sluices, ponds – of a landscape associated with a particular mill can be found. The authors of the report acknowledged that the boundaries of the HWPs would be imprecise and possibly overlap. However, HWPs have the advantage of locating all the interrelated components of the landscape, so that the mills themselves are no

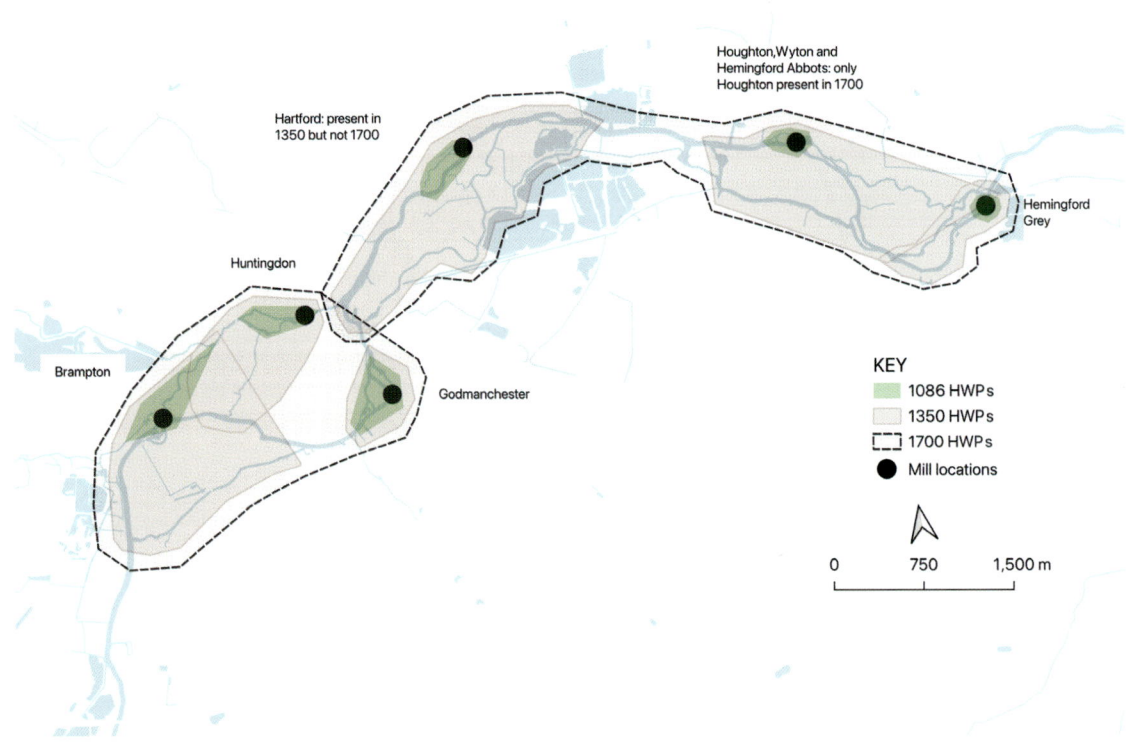

FIGURE 10.5. Historic Water Polygons: Brampton to Hemingford Grey, 1086–1700

longer recorded and viewed in isolation. Once defined, the HWPs can be stored in a GIS, which allows comparison with other spatial data, *e.g.* geology, settlement, and farming, all of which are relevant to understanding the history, development and functioning of the watermills. The methodology was subsequently successfully applied to the rivers Culm in Devon, the Eden in Cumbria and the Thames in Oxfordshire (Firth and Firth 2021).

We have applied this methodology to the watermilling landscape in our study area, extending the technique to look at the HWPs at different stages in the landscape's development (Figs 10.5 and 10.6). In 1086 none of the HWPs overlap, illustrating the relatively local, and minor, impact on the landscape of the Domesday watermills. By 1350 many of the HWPs are significantly larger because of the development of the backwaters. There are several overlaps illustrating how the actions of one mill were directly impacting the others. Most notable is the stretch of river between Hartford, Houghton and Hemingford Abbots. The *Quo Warranto* Plea of 1274 details the Prior, the Abbot and Reginald de Grey as being responsible for the problems on the river cited by the complainants from Huntingdon and Godmanchester. What any one of these three did at one mill would have affected both the others at their mills. And this supports the argument that they must have acted together to some extent. The overlapping HWPs also illustrate why disputes occurred between the mill

10. *Modelling and managing the watermilling landscape*   143

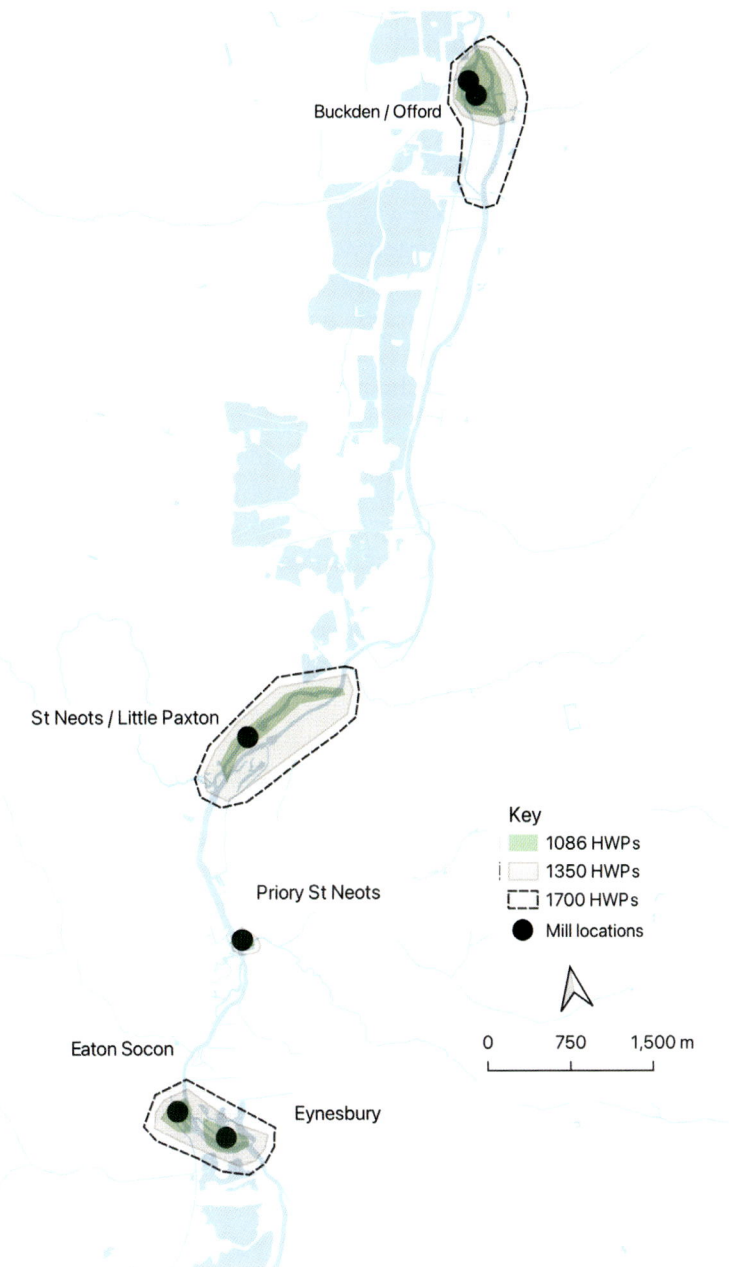

FIGURE 10.6. Historic Water Polygons: Eaton Socon to Buckden, 1086–1700

owners of Brampton, Huntingdon and Godmanchester. In 1086 these mills had been under the single ownership of the Crown but from the 13th century they were under separate ownership; all competing for the same resource. By 1700, the river between Brampton and Hemingford Grey had reduced to two HWPs, with Hartford, Wyton and Hemingford Abbots mills having closed. Upstream of Brampton the HWPs do not increase significantly in size, largely because there is a greater distance between the locations. This analysis successfully demonstrates the value of using HWPs to record watermilling landscapes. It also graphically illustrates how frequently the mill site is found to be much larger than originally anticipated.

Managing watermilling landscapes

The management of any landscape over a wide area is never straightforward. There are invariably conflicting uses. Mostert notes that the argument in favour of river basin management is simple – in order to manage the interrelations between 'society and ecology, land and water, and upstream and downstream' a basin-wide approach is needed (2017, 51). However, he notes that this is hard to achieve in practice. In writing about the River Great Ouse basin, he examines why this has been, and still is, the case, concluding that current strategies focus too little on community ambitions and social relations. That there is community interest is not in doubt, *e.g.* the Great Ouse Valley Trust was established in 2018 'to protect, promote and enhance the special landscape in the Great Ouse Valley in Cambridgeshire' (https://greatousevalleytrust.org.uk). The Trust is involved with a wide range of projects, from improving access to the riverbank, tree planting, monitoring water quality, and campaigning for the river and its floodplain to be protected by statutory designation, as either a single Conservation Area or a National Landscape. However, managing the needs of the different users of the river, and its different uses, will always be a challenge. This was articulated in the Environment Agency's 'River Great Ouse Waterway Plan' (2006), written primarily to meet the needs of boat users, whilst acknowledging the needs of the Great Ouse's many other uses – tourism, leisure (including sailing, rowing, angling, horse riding, walking), heritage, wildlife, agriculture, water supply and flood management.

It must also be acknowledged that there are specific management challenges for watermilling landscapes because of their geomorphological legacy. Downward and Skinner (2005, 138) note that although most of the redundant 19th century watermills were removed, their associated river structures, *e.g.* weirs and sluices, were not, and many of these are now beginning to fail. However, if these structures are removed, the river will adjust to the new physical circumstances, and landscape change will result. For example, if a weir or dam is removed, the river's velocity downstream will increase leading to bank erosion and possible flooding. Upstream, sediment will be removed leading to bed erosion. River levels will drop, in turn affecting water levels in backwaters. Downward and Skinner identify three management options: one, do nothing – the structures fail, and the river adjusts to the 'new normal'; two, allow managed failure – mitigate the worst effects, *e.g.* flooding; and three, maintain or modify the structures to conserve the landscape. Pessimistically, they conclude that 'Currently, guidance on such decisions is largely absent' (Skinner 2005, 139).

The issues facing watermilling landscapes on lowland rivers are urgent and are exacerbated by the increased risk of flooding resulting from climate change and settlement growth. The UK still subscribes to the European Water Framework

Directive (European Commission 2000), which means that River Basin Management Plans must focus on achieving 'good ecological status' (GES). This is defined as based on three criteria: ecology, water quality and hydrogeomorphology. Plans must aim to restore rivers to what they were like in the past.

Boardman and Foster (2023) examine these issues, with a case study of the River Rother. They note the European Commission's aim to achieve 25,000 km of 'free-flowing' rivers by 2030 with a focus on removing 'obsolete barriers'. The argument for removing barriers is principally that they are a problem for migrating fish, although their removal is also part of the broader aim of river restoration. In 2022, 325 barriers of various sorts were removed from European rivers. However, in the UK the construction of fish passes, such as that built in 2022 into the weir at Godmanchester on the site of the demolished watermill (Fig. 10.7) and the Environment Agency's installation of over 500 eel passes around weirs and dams have been a more usual strategy. Boardman and Foster show that the consequences of removing a barrier are very specific due to a range of factors, *e.g.* weir height, the geology of the bed and banks, and the sediment load of the river. The benefits and disbenefits of removal need to be studied for each barrier before an informed decision can be taken. For example, their investigation of three weirs on the River Rother showed that although removal would improve fish migration, there would be unintended consequences on biodiversity because the sand currently trapped by the weirs would be transported downstream, smothering the natural gravel bed and reducing species from 14 to 3. Their conclusion is that solutions will have to vary from river to river.

The future

Our research has led us to conclude that the River Great Ouse and its floodplain in Cambridgeshire – particularly on the stretch between Brampton and St Ives – is an exceptional example of a 'lowland watermilling landscape'. In 1086 its watermills, collectively, had the highest average value of any in the country, and it remained a watermilling 'powerhouse' throughout the Middle Ages and into the modern period. The history of these watermills is recorded in the landscape, and forms the principal features of this landscape but, until now, these features have been unrecognised as the product of a thousand years of watermilling history. Figure 10.8 is a striking illustration of this impact. It shows the river between Brampton and St Ives today, with the channels that have been dug, or modified, in red. The number of artificial channels demonstrates beyond doubt that the multi-channel form of the river is the result of human activity. Contrary to the 19th century paintings and photographs, the creation of this landscape has been no idyll. It has been adapted to extract maximum power from its water. Alongside the landscape evidence of these watermills there is a vast and, we consider, unique, record of detailed documentary evidence charting the development of the mills. This recounts the recurring friction, conflict and passion caused by the concentrated and competitive use of the river for economic gain.

FIGURE 10.7. (above) Godmanchester Fish Weir

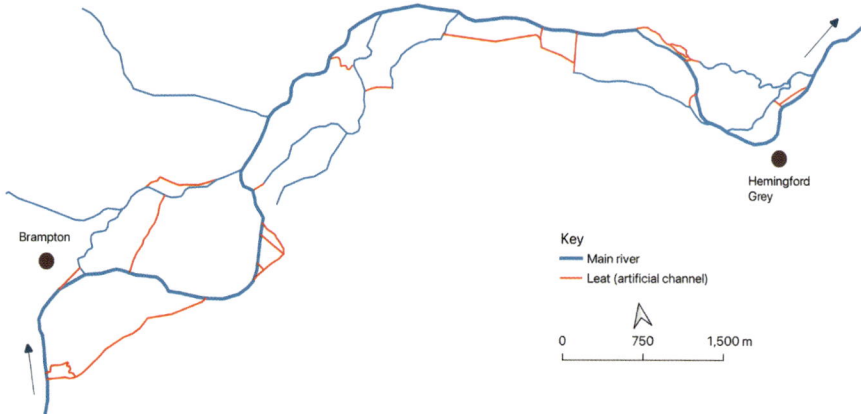

FIGURE 10.8. The river system today, showing the impact of the artificial channels dug to enable watermilling over a thousand-year period

We have shown that our findings apply to other lowland valley landscapes. In Chapter 2 we noted that Lewin had identified a relationship between 17 stretches of historically anabranching lowland rivers and medieval watermilling, including the river between Huntingdon and St Ives. Our preliminary analysis of the Great Ouse at Olney, the Nene at Elton and the River Itchen indicates that a detailed study of all lowland river systems will identify complex and significant landscapes like that of the Great Ouse valley. And it is also clear that the lasting impact of watermills on the landscape is not confined to these historically anabranching systems, *e.g.* Watts's study of 'Water Power in the Lower Culm Valley' (2016). Consequently, we fully support Alexander and Edgeworth's position that, 'it is apparent that many watermill landscapes require management and/or protection. The assessment of significance, and the degree of threat, will be the key factors in determining the best approach to be taken. There are, however, numerous practical considerations to be considered, increasing with the extent and complexity of the landscape' (2018, 57).

Regarding statutory protection, one option is Listing. Although this applies to buildings, not landscapes, it may offer some protection to the area in the immediate vicinity of the building. In February 2024 the National Heritage List for England (NHLE) contained 1,007 Listed Buildings indexed as watermills (6 Grade I, 103 Grade II* and 898 Grade II). The other option is Scheduling, which applies to archaeological sites and heritage assets not suitable for Listing. In February 2024 the NHLE contained 98 Scheduled Monuments indexed with watermills. Generally, these Listings cover an area larger than the immediate vicinity of the Monument and can be of some use in protecting aspects of a watermilling landscape. A typical example is Ellerton Priory in North Yorkshire, a Cistercian nunnery including its fishponds, water management system, mill, field system and Ellerton medieval settlement (https://historicengland.org.uk/listing/the-list/list-entry/1019154). However, the Scheduled area at Ellerton is small in comparison with the Historic Water Polygons identified on the Great Ouse and elsewhere. Thus Scheduling, because it is monument based, is insufficient for the much larger watermilling landscapes that have been identified and recorded. In February 2025 eight Parks and Gardens were indexed with watermills in the NHLE, all with relatively small Scheduled areas. (There are no Scheduled Monuments, or Parks and Gardens, indexed with watermills on the Great Ouse.) Listed or Scheduled assets 'at risk' can be placed on the Heritage at Risk register (HAR), which provides an additional level of protection, with some support and guidance for asset owners, although no financial support. In summary, Listing, Scheduling and the HAR may be of some use in protecting watermilling landscapes, but they are not – and cannot be – appropriate for the protection of the majority of the watermilling landscapes of the character that we have identified.

A Conservation Area is an 'area(s) of special architectural or historic interest, the character or appearance of which it is desirable to preserve or enhance' and the *Planning (Listed Buildings and Conservation Areas) Act 1990* requires every Local Authority to identify and designate such areas (https://www.legislation.gov.uk/ukpga/1990/9/contents/enacted). In March 2025 there were 11,168 Conservation Area in England, and Alexander and Edgeworth's estimate still stands: 'it is clear that several hundred Conservation Areas include watermills, and no doubt significant elements of the associated landscapes. Others will incorporate relict watermill landscapes and those where the mill itself is long gone' (2018, 59). In Conservation Areas, special considerations apply to planning permission and other development control procedures. However, the asset must be recognised for this to apply. For example, the Houghton and Wyton Conservation Area Character Assessment (HDC, 2012) records the Mill itself, which is a Grade II* Listed building, but none of the water channels we have identified as being significant to its history are recorded as assets. Also, it ends at the parish boundary – the Abbot's *rivulus* – *i.e.* it covers only a small part of the AD 1300 Historic Water Polygon, so the landscape cannot be considered as a whole. This is often although not always the case with Conservation Areas.

The National Planning Policy Framework (NPPF) outlines planning policies for England, emphasizing the protection and enhancement of the natural, built, and historic environment with a focus on sustainable development (NPPF 2024). This includes a requirement for Local Authorities to maintain an Historic Environment Record (HER), which is crucial for recognizing (*inter alia*) the significance of landscapes, including watermilling landscapes. The Framework distinguishes between 'Designated Heritage Assets' with statutory protection, such as Listed Buildings, and 'Heritage Assets' that merit consideration in planning decisions and can be locally listed. This is a helpful distinction because it allows a Local Authority to identify a watermilling landscape as an asset that should be considered when planning decisions are taken. The NPPF requires Local Planning Authorities in England to prepare a Local Plan, which sets out the strategic planning policies for their area over at least a 15-year period. Once approved, the development control process manages consents and permissions for development to go ahead. Thus, the planning system has the potential to protect watermilling landscapes, but planners need to be aware of the significance of these landscapes.

The Environment Agency's River Basin Management Plans (RBMPs) and Flood Risk Management Plans (FRMPs) present both opportunities and threats to watermilling landscapes. For example, the Great Ouse Catchment Flood Management Plan includes a proposed action for the Houghton–Hemingford–St Ives stretch of the river to 'Develop environmental enhancement projects to improve the natural state of the rivers and their habitats' (Environment Agency 2011, 25). Depending on how this action is implemented it could protect the watermilling landscape, *e.g.* ensuring that backwaters do not silt up, or damage it, *e.g.* by removing weirs. Some watermilling landscapes contain protected sites like SSSIs, *e.g.* Portholme, Godmanchester Eastside Common and Houghton Meadows on the River Great Ouse, but their protection is solely for their ecological value.

From this complex planning and regulatory framework, a range of options for the preservation and management of watermilling landscapes emerges. Alexander and Edgeworth (2018, 63) favour a combination of Listing, Scheduling and inclusion as elements of historic Parks and Gardens, and Conservation Areas. However, they acknowledge that most individual assets will not, on their own, merit designation. Rather, it is when they are combined as elements of a whole watermilling landscape that they achieve significance. They suggest that this is where the NPPF could help, *e.g.* watermilling landscapes being recognised in Local Plans. Examples of how this approach can be put into practice are presented in Historic England Research (Firth and Firth 2021, 26–31), *e.g.* a Green

Recovery Challenge Fund project, led by the National Trust at Killerton in Devon, identified and recorded the watermilling landscape as HWPs, which contributed to the design and consenting process for a Landscape Recovery Project.

Following this approach, we will put our research findings forward for inclusion in the Cambridgeshire Historic Environment Record so that there is up-to-date evidence about the heritage assets and environment of watermilling along the Great Ouse in Cambridgeshire. An application will then be submitted to Historic England proposing Scheduling of the watermilling landscape and its components. Meanwhile, the relevant Local Planning Authorities will be notified so that they are aware of this research and consider the landscape's value in relation to their Development Control processes. They will also be asked to consider inclusion of the historic importance of the Great Ouse watermilling landscape in the relevant Conservation Character Assessments and current Local Plans. We will be advocating that this landscape formed by watermilling over almost a millennium, together with its documented history and cultural associations is an irreplaceable heritage asset that deserves recognition and protection.

Primary sources

Bedfordshire IX.9. Ordnance Survey, 25 inch to the mile. Surveyed: 1882, Published: 1884. https://maps.nls.uk/view/114481680 [accessed 27 February 2025].

BMS HUNTN 20. Transcript of the Accompt Book of the Priory of St Mary's, Huntingdon, Michaelmas 9th Henry VIII to Midsummer following. Norris Museum, St Ives.

FN1254 Francklin MSS. Bedfordshire Archives, Bedford.

HINCH 10/72 Sale Particulars; Property known as The River Ouse Navigation comprising all the rights of levying tolls authorised by Acts of Parliament; about 31 miles in length, from its mouth at Earith to the town of Bedford. Cambridgeshire Archives, Huntingdon.

Huntingdonshire XXI.12. Ordnance Survey, 25 inch to the mile. Surveyed: 1886, Published: 1888.

Huntingdonshire XXV.4. Ordnance Survey, 25 inch to the mile. Surveyed: 1886, Published: 1888. https://maps.nls.uk/view/114490208 [accessed 27 February 2025].

Huntingdonshire 52/37. Ordnance Survey, 1:25 000. Published: 1949. https://maps.nls.uk/view/196192140 [accessed 27 February 2025].

KAcc4577/2/11 Gordon, W. (1730) *Map of Huntingdonshire*. Cambridgeshire Archives, Huntingdon.

KBLC/5/5/1, 2, 3, 4 Huntingdonshire County Council v Leonard T. Simpson. Cambridgeshire Archives, Huntingdon.

KBR2/BOX1/6 Indenture of covenants to shut down sluices and floodgates belonging to Brampton Mills (1787). Cambridgeshire Archives, Huntingdon.

KBR2/BOX1/13 Deed of covenant for the repair of certain bridges across Bromholme and Portholme Brooks (1837). Cambridgeshire Archives, Huntingdon.

KDMC/312 Buckden Inclosure Map. Cambridgeshire Archives, Huntingdon.

KDMC/325 Godmanchester Inclosure Map. Cambridgeshire Archives, Huntingdon.

KG/A/3/8 Henry V: Appointment of Commissioners to set up a floodgate at Hartford. Cambridgeshire Archives, Huntingdon.

KG/A/1/12 1426 Henry VI: Priory of Huntingdon-Grant to Robt. Dobson. Cambridgeshire Archives, Huntingdon.

KG/A16/1 Godmanchester Borough Records Former Box 16. Cambridgeshire Archives, Huntingdon.

KG/D/3/2 Depositions or answers of elderly millers, mill-wrights and mill-labourers 1587. Cambridgeshire Archives, Huntingdon.

KG/D/3/3 Letter from W. Burgliegh to the Bailiffs and Inhabitants of Godmanchester ordering the inhabitants to restore the gull lying between [Brampton?] Mill and Richmonds Gull to its former course, 1st July 1591. Cambridgeshire Archives, Huntingdon.

KG/D/3/4 Two drafts of a letter of reply to W. Burgliegh defending their actions re the course of the river Ouse, 24th July 1591. Cambridgeshire Archives, Huntingdon.

KG/D/3/5 Petition from the Bailiffs and Inhabitants of Godmanchester to the Duchy of Lancaster asking for a writ of Privy Seal to be issued against Richard Trice for taking the townsmens deeds and agreements re the gulls. Cambridgeshire Archives, Huntingdon.

KG/D/3/6 Third order of the Court of the Duchy of Lancaster in the case of Godmanchester vs Trice. Cambridgeshire Archives, Huntingdon.

KHAC0/223/1 Survey of Estates of John, Earl of Sandwich 1757. Cambridgeshire Archives, Huntingdon.

KHAC1/1737 The appeal from the House of Lords by Leonard Taylor Simpson. Cambridgeshire Archives, Huntingdon.

KHAC4/4347 Jefferys, T. (1768) *'Printed map of Huntingdonshire' scale: two inches to one mile (1:31680)*. Cambridgeshire Archives, Huntingdon.

KHINCH/10/12 Petition to 7th Earl of Sandwich 1876. Cambridgeshire Archives, Huntingdon.

KHINCH 10/81 Letter; Leonard T. Simpson, Tonbridge, Kent, to 8th Earl of Sandwich. Cambridgeshire Archives, Huntingdon.

KDMC/344 Offord Cluny inclosure map 1806. Cambridgeshire Archives, Huntingdon.

KHP64/26/1 Gt. Paxton & Toseland Inclosure Award & Map 1811. Cambridgeshire Archives, Huntingdon.

KPGMD/2913/Z/9/B 1524, Henry VIII, judgement v the Abbot of Ramsey who had dammed the Ouse and caused flooding. Cambridgeshire Archives, Huntingdon.

Pettis's Ancient History of St. Ives. Norris Museum, St Ives.

PRO, 1967. List of the Lands of Dissolved Religious Houses (Lists and Indexes Supplementary Series vols. 1 to 7, Kraus Reprint 1967). No. III vol I Bedfordshire – Huntingdonshire. Huntingdonshire Archives Reference Library. (Also available at https://archive.org/stream/listoflandsofdis01newy/listoflandsofdis01newy_djvu.txt [accessed online 26 February 2025].

R1/478 Lenny & Croft (1834) *Plan of the River Ouze*. Bedfordshire County Archives.

TNA DL3/23 Petition to the Duchy of Lancaster 1515, Bills and depositions.

TNA MPCC 1/9 'Huntyngdon & Godmanchester'. Plan of the River Ouse and waterways between Huntingdon and St Ives bridge.

TNA SC/8/171/8518 'Petitioners: Prior and monks of St Neots. Addressees: King and council', 1285–1310.

TNA E178/1070 'Deposition as to the decay of the Queen's mills', 1595–1596.

TNA E178 3912 'Inquisition as to the obstruction of the navigation of the river between Huntingdon and King's Lynn by the King's mills' 1608–1609.

Bibliography

Alexander, M. and Edgeworth, M. (2018) *Historic Watermill Landscapes: A national overview*. Historic England ref: Research Report Series no. 17–2018.

Allcroft, A.H. (1908) *Earthwork of England*. London, Macmillan.

Allen, M., Blick, N., Brindle, T., Evans, T., Fulford, M., Holdbrook, N., Lodwick, L., Richards, J.D. and Smith, A. (2018) *The Rural Settlement of Roman Britain: an online resource*. York, Archaeology Data Service https://doi.org/10.5284/1030449 [accessed 5 December 2024].

Ambler, J. and Langdon, J. (1994) Lordship and Peasant Consumerism in the Milling Industry of Early Fourteenth-Century England. In *Past & Present*, No. 145, 3–46. Oxford, Oxford University Press.

Ash, E.H. (2017) *The Draining of the Fens*. Baltimore, John Hopkins University Press.

Aston, M. (1985) *Interpreting the Landscape*. London, Routledge.

Ault, W.O. (ed.) (1928) *Court Rolls of the Abbey of Ramsey and the Honor of Clare* New Haven, Yale University Press.

Banfield, L. (2023) *Making Flour the German Way in Roman Britain*. Oxford, BAR Publishing.

Belloc, H. (1908) The River Ouse in *The Morning Post* (June).

Bennett, R. and Elton, J. (1899) *History of Corn Milling Vol. II Watermills and Windmills*. London, Simpkin, Marshall and Company Ltd.

Benson, A.C. (1908) *At Large*. London, Smith, Elder, & Co.

Bird, F. (1911) Godmanchester Mill Memories in *Memorials of Godmanchester*. Peterborough, Peterborough Advertiser Company.

Blair, J. (1994) *Anglo-Saxon Oxfordshire*. Stroud, Sutton Publishing Ltd.

Blair, J. (2007) *Waterways and Canal-Building in Medieval England*. Oxford, Oxford University Press.

Boardman, J. and Foster, I. (2023) Are 'free-flowing rivers' a good idea? The challenge of removing barriers from our rivers. *Geography* 108 (3), 121–129.

Bond, C.J. (1979) The Reconstruction of the Medieval Landscape; the Estates of Abingdon Abbey. *Landscape History*, 1:1, 59–75.

Bond, J. (2007) Canal Construction: An Introductory Review in Waterways and Canal-Building. In *Medieval England*, ed. J. Blair, 153–206. Oxford, Oxford University Press.

Bos, K., Schuenemann, V., Golding, G., Burbano, H., Waglechner, N. and Coombes, B. (2011) A draft genome of Yersinia pestis from victims of the Black Death. *Nature* 478, 506–510.

British Geological Survey (1975) 1:50 000 Drift Edition for Huntingdon.

Brown, B. (1905) *Reminiscences of Bateman Brown, J.P.* Peterborough, The Peterborough Advertiser.

Burn-Murdoch, B. (2009) *The Shaping of St Ives*. Cambridge, Friends of the Norris Museum.

Camden, W. (1610) *Britain, or, a Chorographicall Description of the most flourishing Kingdomes, England, Scotland, and Ireland*. London. https://www.visionofbritain.org.uk/travellers/Camden [accessed 5 December 2024].

Campbell, B. (2016) *The Great Transition*. Cambridge, Cambridge University Press.

CHER (Cambridgeshire Historic Environment Record) 02420 https://www.heritagegateway.org.uk/Gateway/Results_Single.aspx?uid=MCB3048&resourceID=1000 [accessed 30 May 2025].

Chisholm, M. (2003) Conservators of the River Cam, 1702–2002. *Proceedings of the Cambridge Antiquarian Society XCII*. The Cambridge Antiquarian Society.

Darby, H.C. (1934) Domesday Woodland in East Anglia. *Antiquity* 8(30), 211–215.

Darby, H.C. (1972) *The Domesday Geography of Eastern England* (3rd Edition). Cambridge, Cambridge University Press.

DeWindt, A.R. and DeWindt, E.B. (eds) (1981) *Royal Justice and the Medieval English Countryside: The Huntingdonshire Eyre of 1286, the Ramsey Abbey Banlieu Court of 1287, and the Assizes of 1287–88*, 2 vols. Toronto, Pontifical Institute of Mediaeval Studies.

DeWindt, E. (1976) *The Liber Gersumarum of Ramsey Abbey: A Calendar and Index of B.L. Harley MS 445*. Subsidia Mediaevalia, Volume 7. Toronto, Pontifical Institute of Mediaeval Studies.

Doody, J.P. (2008) Portholme Meadow. A Celebration of Huntingdonshire's Grassland. In *The Huntingdonshire Fauna and Flora Society*, 60th Anniversary Report, 9–16.

Downward, S. and Skinner, K. (2005) The Geomorphological Legacy of English Freshwater Mills. *Area* 37 (2), 138–147. https://www.jstor.org/stable/20004443 [accessed 2 December 2024].

Dugdale, W. (1693) *Monasticon Anglicanum Vol. 3*. London.

Dunn, C. (1977) *Huntingdon: A Portrait of the Town*. Buckingham, Barracuda Books.

Edmondson, G. and Mudd, A. (2004) Medieval occupation at 'Danish Camp', Willington. *Bedfordshire Archaeological Journal* 25, 208–221.

Environment Agency (2006) *A Better Place For All: River Great Ouse Waterway Plan*. https://assets.publishing.service.gov.uk/media/5a74853040f0b616bcb1723f/gean1205bkbr-e-e.pdf [accessed 19 February 2025].

Environment Agency (2011) *Great Ouse Catchment Flood Management Plan*. https://assets.publishing.service.gov.uk/media/5a7c39a4ed915d7d70d1d6c9/Great_Ouse_Catchment_Flood_Management_Plan.pdf [accessed 19 February 2025].

European Commission (EC) (2000) *Water Framework Directive* https://environment.ec.europa.eu/topics/water/water-framework-directive_en [accessed 7th October 2024].

Evans, C. *Late Iron Age & Roman Resource Assessment*. https://researchframeworks.org/eoe/resource-assessments/late-iron-age-and-roman/#section-1 [accessed 18 April 2024].

Fagan, B. (2000) *The Little Ice Age*. New York, Basic Books.

Farrar, C.F. (1921) *Ouse's Silent Tide*. Bedford, The Sidney Press.

Firth, A. and Firth, E. (2020) *Historic Watercourses: Developing a method for identifying the historic character of watercourses*. Historic England ref: HE 7244.

Firth, A. and Firth, E. (2021) Historic Watercourses and Climate Change: mapping the history of rivers and floodplains. *Research* 19. Historic England.

Firth, E. and Firth, A. (2023) *Mapping Historic Floodplain Meadows along the Rivers Swale, Ure and Ouse*. Floodplain Meadows Partnership.

Flanagan, B. (2010) *Artists along the Ouse 1880–1930*. London, Burlington Press.

Foster, A.J. (1891) *The Ouse*. London, Society for Promoting Christian Knowledge.

Fox, R. (1831) *The History of Godmanchester*. London, Baldwin and Cradock.

Gibbard, P.L., West, R.G. and Hughes, P.D. (2018) Pleistocene glaciation of Fenland, England, and its implications for evolution of the region. https://royalsocietypublishing.org/doi/10.1098/rsos.170736 [accessed 5 December 2024].

Goddard, A.R. (1901) The Danish Camp on the Ouse, near Bedford. In *Saga-Book*. Vol. 3. London, Viking Society for Northern Research.

Gould, D., Creighton, O., Chaussée, S., Shapland, M. and Wright, D.W. (2025) Where Power Lies: Lordly Power Centres in the English Landscape c. 800–1200. *The Antiquaries Journal* 104, 72–106.

Great Ouse Valley Trust. https://greatousevalleytrust.org.uk [accessed 5 December 2024]

Green, C. (2000) Geology, relief, and Quaternary palaeoenvironments in the basin of the Great Ouse. In *Prehistoric, Roman, and Post-Roman Landscapes of the Great Ouse Valley*, ed. M. Dawson, 5–16. York, Council for British Archaeology.

Green, H.J.M. (1977) *Godmanchester*. Cambridge, Oleander Press.

Hackney, G. (2020) The Value of Huntingdonshire Mills at Domesday. *Mill News* April 2020 https://www.spab.org.uk/sites/default/files/images/MillsSection/Mill%20News%20April%202020%20final%20low%20resolution_compressed%20extreme.pdf [accessed 31 May 2024].

Haigh, D. (1984) Rescue Excavations at Cow Lane, Godmanchester, Cambs. during 1984. *Proceedings of the Cambridge Antiquarian Society* 73. https://doi.org/10.5284/1073140 [accessed 17th October 2024].

Hart, C. (2000) The Danes. In *An Atlas of Cambridgeshire and Huntingdonshire History*, eds T. Kirby and S. Oosthuizen, Section 30. Cambridge, Anglia Polytechnic University.

Hart, W.H. and Lyons, P.A. (eds) (1884–93) *Cartularium Monasterii de Rameseia* Vol. I. London.

HDC (2012) *Houghton and Wyton Conservation Area Character Assessment*. Huntingdonshire District Council https://assets.publishing.service.gov.uk/media/5a74853040f0b616bcb1723f/gean1205bkbr-e-e.pdf [accessed 19 February 2025].

Henderson, E.F. (1896) Confirmation of the Charters Act 1297 25 Edw.I c.16 https://en.wikisource.org/

wiki/Confirmation_of_the_Charters_Act_1297 [accessed 15th September 2024].

Higham, N.J. and Ryan, M.J. (2015) *The Anglo-Saxon World*. New Haven and London, Yale University Press.

Hissey, J.J. (1898) *Over Fen and Wold*. London, Macmillan and Co.

Hodgen, M. (1939) Domesday Water Mills. *Antiquity* 13(51), 261–279.

Holt, R. (1988) *The Mills of Medieval England*. Oxford, Blackwell.

Howes, H. (2020) *The Water and Steam Mills of Huntingdonshire's Great Ouse*. Reading, The Mills Archive Trust.

Hughes, P. (1996) Some Civil Engineering Notes from 1699. *The Local Historian* 26, 2. Salisbury, British Association for Local History.

Hyer, M. and Hooke, D. (eds) (2017) *Water and the Environment in the Anglo-Saxon World*. Liverpool, Liverpool University Press.

Illingworth, W. (1812) *Rotuli hundredorum temp. Hen. III & Edw. I in Turr' Lond', Vol. I*. London, Record Commission.

Illingworth, W. (1818 i) *Placita de Quo Warranto Temporibus Ewd. I. Ii. Iii*. In *Curia Receptae Scaccarij Westm. Asservata* London, Record Commission.

Illingworth, W. (1818 ii) *Rotuli Hundredorum, temp. Hen. III & Edw. I in Turr' Lond'*, Vol. II. London, Record Commission.

Jesmond Dene Old Mill http://www.jesmonddeneoldmill.org.uk/mill/technology.html [accessed 5 December 2024].

Keith, S. (2017) A study of 'Domesday Watermills' in the Cambridgeshire landscape. *Proceedings of the Cambridge Antiquarian Society* CVI, 49–60.

Keith, S. (2020) Letters to the Editor. *Mill News* July 2020. https://www.spab.org.uk/sites/default/files/images/MillsSection/Mill%20News%20164%20July%202020%20low%20resolution_compressed.pdf [accessed 31 May 2024].

Langdon, J. (2004) *Mills in the Medieval Economy: England 1300–1540*. Oxford, Oxford University Press.

Langdon, J. and White, J. (2017) An Early Seventeenth-Century River Environment: The 1618 Survey of the Itchen. *Proceedings of the Hampshire Field Club Archaeological Society* 72, 142–165.

Lewin, J. (2010) Medieval Environmental Impacts and Feedbacks: The Lowland Floodplains of England and Wales. *Geoarchaeology: An International Journal* 25(3), 267–311.

Lewis, C. (2016) Disaster recovery: new archaeological evidence for the long-term impact of the 'calamitous' fourteenth century. *Antiquity* 90, 777–797.

Lodwick, L. (2017) Arable farming, plant foods, and resources. In *The Rural Economy of Roman Britain,* T. Brindle, A.T. Smith, M.G. Allen, M.G. Fulford, and L. Lodwick, 11–84. London, Society for the Promotion of Roman Studies. https://doi.org/10.5284/1090307. [accessed 19 February 2025]

Lucas, A. (2014) *Ecclesiastical Lordship, Seigneurial Power and the Commercialization of Milling in Medieval England*. London, Routledge.

Lyons, A. (2019) *Rectory Farm, Godmanchester, Cambridgeshire: Excavations 1988–95, Neolithic monument to Roman villa farm*. Cambridge, Oxford Archaeology East.

Makaske, B. (2001) Anastomosing rivers: a review of their classification, origin and sedimentary products. *Earth-Science Reviews* 53, 149–196.

Maxwell Lyte, H.C. (1895) Calendar of Patent Rolls, Edward I: Volume 2, 1281–1292 (1287–8, membranes). *British History Online* https://www.british-history.ac.uk/cal-pat-rolls/edw1/vol2/pp289-304 [accessed 15 November 2024].

Maxwell Lyte, H.C. (1914) *Edward III Vol. XV*. London, Fisher Unwin.

McNulty, J. (2013) *The Chartulary of the Cistercian Abbey of St Mary of Sallay in Craven: Volume 1*. Cambridge, Cambridge University Press.

Meynell, W. (1881) Little Known Sketching Grounds. *Art Journal*. London, J.S.Virtue and Co. Ltd.

Mostert, E. (2017) River basin management and community: the Great Ouse Basin, 1850–present. *International Journal of River Basin Management* 16(1), 51–59, https://doi.org/10.1080/15715124.2017.1339355 [accessed 5 December 2024].

National Library of Scotland OS maps https://maps.nls.uk/os/ [accessed 5 December 2024].

National LiDAR Programme https://www.data.gov.uk/dataset/f0db0249-f17b-4036-9e65-309148c97ce4/national-lidar-programme [accessed 5 December 2024].

National Planning Policy Framework (2024) Ministry of Housing, Communities & Local Government. https://assets.publishing.service.gov.uk/media/67aafe8f3b41f783cca46251/NPPF_December_2024.pdf [accessed 19 February 2025].

National Trust. *Landscape Recovery Project at Killerton*. https://www.nationaltrust.org.uk/visit/devon/killerton/landscape-recovery-project-at-killerton [accessed 5 December 2024].

Noble, D. (1994) Installation of Waterwheel at Houghton Mill. In *Houghton Mill, Cambridgeshire: National Trust Heritage Lottery Fund application*, submitted 20 December 1996. Accessible via Norris Museum, St Ives.

NRA Anglian 93 *The Great Ouse*. Peterborough, National Rivers Authority.

Oliver, S. (2013) Liquid materialities in the landscape of the Thames: mills and weirs from the eighth century to the nineteenth century. *Area* 45(2), 223–229. https://www.jstor.org/stable/24029874 [accessed 5 December 2024].

Oosthuizen, S. (2007) The Anglo-Saxon Kingdom of Mercia and the Origins and Distribution of Common Fields. *The Agricultural History Review* 55(2), 153–180. British Agricultural History Society.

Oosthuizen, S. (1993) The Origins of Hemingford Grey. *The Records of Huntingdonshire* 3(1), 2–7. The Huntingdonshire Local History Society.

Oxford English Dictionary, s.v. 'rymer (n.1),' July 2023, https://doi.org/10.1093/OED/1050507510. [accessed 19 February 2025].

Pelham, R.A. (1944) The Distribution of Early Fulling Mills in England and Wales. *Geography* 29(2), 52–56.

Perrins, R.J. (2023) Westside Common, Land adjacent to the River Great Ouse, Godmanchester, Cambridgeshire. Application Ref: COM/3311859 (The Planning Inspectorate).

Pounds, N.J.G. (2006) *A History of the English Parish: The Culture of Religion from Augustine to Victoria*. Cambridge, Cambridge University Press.

Pratt, S.J. (1801) *Gleanings in England*. London, Longman.

Pryor, F. (2010) *The Making of the British Landscape*. London, Penguin.

Raftis, J.A. (1957) *The Estates of Ramsey Abbey: a study in economic growth and organization*. Toronto, Pontifical Institute of Mediaeval Studies.

Reynolds, T. (2000) The Palaeolithic of the Ouse Valley. In *Prehistoric, Roman, and Post-Roman Landscapes of the Great Ouse Valley*, ed. M. Dawson, 35–44. York, Council for British Archaeology.

Rhodes, E. (2007) Identifying Human Modification of River Channels. In *Waterways and Canal-Building in Medieval England*, ed. J. Blair, 133–152. Oxford, Oxford University Press.

Rippon, S. (2001) Adaptation to a changing environment: the response of marshland communities to the late medieval 'crisis'. *Journal of Wetland Archaeology* 1, 15–39. Oxford, Oxbow Books.

Rynne, C. (2018) Water and Wind Power. In *The Oxford Handbook of Later Medieval Archaeology in Britain*, ed. C. Gerrard and A. Gutiérrez, 491–510. Oxford, Oxford University Press.

Satchell, M. (2017) Navigable waterways and the economy of England and Wales: 1600–1835. *The Online Historical Atlas of Transport, Urbanization and Economic Development in England and Wales c.1680–1911* https://www.campop.geog.cam.ac.uk/research/projects/transport/onlineatlas/ [accessed 15 November 2024].

Scaife, R. (2000) The prehistoric vegetation and environment of the River Ouse Valley. In *Prehistoric, Roman, and Post-Roman Landscapes of the Great Ouse Valley*, ed. M. Dawson, 17–26. York, Council for British Archaeology.

Shaffrey, R. (2024) A14 Cambridge to Huntingdon Improvement Scheme Specialist Analysis Report: the Querns and Millstones Overview. MOLA Headland Infrastructure https://archaeologydataservice.ac.uk/archives/collections/view/1003796/downloads.cfm?group=11418 [accessed 14th October 2024].

Skeeles, J. (1933) *NOTES on the History of Saint Ives from 1796 to 1930*. Norris Museum, St Ives. https://drive.google.com/file/d/12ikX0_6iCjZj6-0pbbxPVPxRPcstyeY1/view [accessed 5 December 2024].

Speed, J. (1611–12) *The counties of Britain: A Tudor Atlas by John Speed* (1988 edition). London, Pavilion Books.

Spoerry, P. (2000) Estate, Village, Town? Roman, Saxon, and medieval settlement in the St Neots area. In *Prehistoric, Roman, and Post–Roman Landscapes of the Great Ouse Valley*, ed. M. Dawson, 145–160. York, Council for British Archaeology.

Summers, D. (1973) *The Great Ouse: The History of a River Navigation*. Newton Abbot, David & Charles.

Sürmelihindi, G., Leveau, P., Spöti, C., Bernards, V. and Passchier, C.W. (2018) The second century CE Roman watermills of Barbegal: Unraveling the enigma of one of the oldest industrial complexes. *Science Advances* 4, https://www.science.org/toc/sciadv/4/9 [accessed 20 February 2025]

Tann, J. (1965) Some problems of Water Power – a Study of Mill Siting in Gloucestershire. *Transactions of the Bristol and Gloucestershire Archaeological Society* 84, 53–77.

Tebbutt, C.F. (1966) St Neots Priory. *Proceedings of the Cambridge Antiquarian Society* LIX, 85–89. Cambridge, Deighton Bell.

The Advertiser (1906) At the Art Gallery: Some Minor Pictures. *The Advertiser*. South Australia. https://trove.nla.gov.au/newspaper/article/5015212?searchTerm=some%20minor%20pictures# [accessed 26 February 2025].

The Hull Domesday Project https://www.domesdaybook.net [accessed 5 December 2024].

The Protection of Public Rights of Navigation, 2015. *Cal Pat Rolls 1370 Nov. 26* http://www.riveraccessforall.co.uk/docs/totally_compelling_evidence.pdf [accessed 15th September 2024].

Thomas, R. (2022) Abbot Ordric's Cut Revisited. *Oxoniensia* 87, 17–26.

VCH a (Victoria County History) (1908) *Parishes: North Stoneham*. A History of the County of Hampshire: Volume 3, Page, W. (ed.) London, British History Online https://www.british-history.ac.uk/vch/hants/vol3/pp478-481 [accessed 19 February 2025].

VCH b (Victoria County History) (1912) *Parishes: Eaton Socon*. A History of the County of Bedford: Volume 3, Page, W. (ed.) London. British History Online https://www.british-history.ac.uk/vch/beds/vol3/pp189-202 [accessed 15 November 2024].

VCH c (Victoria County History) (1926) *Houses of Austin canons: The priory of St Mary, Huntingdon*. A History of the County of Huntingdon: Volume 1, Page, W., Proby, G. and Norris, H.E. (eds) London, British History Online https://www.british-history.ac.uk/vch/hunts/vol1/pp393-395 [accessed 19 February 2025].

VCH d (Victoria County History) (1932) *Parishes: Buckden*. A History of the County of Huntingdon: Volume 2, Page, W., Proby, G. and Inskip Ladds, S. (eds) London. British History Online https://www.british-history.ac.uk/vch/hunts/vol2/pp260-269 [accessed 30 May 2024].

VCH e (Victoria County History) (1932) *Parishes: Eynesbury*. A History of the County of Huntingdon: Volume 2, Page, W., Proby, G. and Inskip Ladds, S. (eds) London. British History Online https://www.british-history.ac.uk/vch/hunts/vol2/pp272-280 [accessed 15 November 2024].

VCH f (Victoria County History) (1932) *Parishes: Hemingford Grey*. A History of the County of Huntingdon: Volume 2, Page W., Proby, G. and Inskip Ladds, S. (eds) London. British History Online https://www.british-history.ac.uk/vch/hunts/vol2/pp309-314 [accessed 15 November 2024].

VCH g (Victoria County History) (1932) *Parishes: Houghton*. A History of the County of Huntingdon: Volume 2, Page W., Proby, G. and Inskip Ladds, S. (eds) London. British History Online https://www.british-history.ac.uk/vch/hunts/vol2/pp178-181 [accessed 30 May 2024].

VCH h (Victoria County History) (1932) *Parishes: Offord Cluny*. A History of the County of Huntingdon: Volume 2, Page, W., Proby, G. and Inskip Ladds, S. (eds) London. British History Onlinehttps://www.british-history.ac.uk/vch/hunts/vol2/pp319-322 [accessed 15 November 2024].

VCH i (Victoria County History) (1932) *Parishes: St Ives*. A History of the County of Huntingdon: Volume 2, Page W., Proby, G. and Inskip Ladds, S. (eds) London. British History Online https://www.british-history.ac.uk/vch/hunts/vol2/pp210-223 [accessed 10 June 2024].

VCH j (Victoria County History) (1932) *Parishes: St Neots*. A History of the County of Huntingdon: Volume 2, Page W., Proby, G. and Inskip Ladds, S. (eds) London. British History Online https://www.british-history.ac.uk/vch/hunts/vol2/pp337-346 [accessed 23 February 2025].

VCH k (Victoria County History) (1932) *The borough of Huntingdon*. A History of the County of Huntingdon: Volume 2, Page, W. (ed.) London. British History Online https://www.british-history.ac.uk/vch/hunts/vol2/ pp121-139 [accessed 15 November 2024].

VCH l (Victoria County History) (1936) *Parishes: Brampton*. A History of the County of Huntingdon: Volume 3, Page, W., Proby, G. and Inskip Ladds, S. (eds) London. British History Online https://www.british-history.ac.uk/vch/hunts/vol3/pp12-20 [accessed 15 November 2024].

VCH m (Victoria County History) (1936) *Parishes: Elton*. A History of the County of Huntingdon: Volume 3, Page, W., Proby, G. and Inskip Ladds, S. (eds) London. British History Online https://www.british-history.ac.uk/vch/hunts/vol3/pp154-166 [accessed 8 October 2024].

VCH n (Victoria County History) (1989) *A History of the County of Cambridge and the Isle of Ely*: Volume 9, Wright, A.P.M. and Lewis, C.P. (eds) London. British History Online https://www.british-history.ac.uk/vch/cambs/vol9/pp386-392 [accessed 30 May 2024].

Walters, W.D. (1973) *Changing Rural Population Distribution in Bedfordshire and Huntingdonshire, 1086–1279*. Unpublished D Phil thesis, Indiana University.

Watts, M. (2002) *The Archaeology of Mills and Milling*. Stroud, Tempus.

Watts, M. (2016) Water Power in the Lower Culm Valley. *Transactions of the Devon Association for the Advancement of Science* 148, 227–254.

Watts, M. (2017) Watermills and Waterwheels. In *Water and the Environment in the Anglo-Saxon World*, eds M. Hyer and D. Hooke, 167–186. Liverpool, Liverpool University Press.

West, E., Christie, C., Moretti, D., Scholma-Mason, O. and Smith, A. (2024) A Route Well Travelled. The Archaeology of the A14 Huntingdon to Cambridge Road Improvement Scheme, *Internet Archaeology* 67. https://doi.org/10.11141/ia.67.22 [accessed 19 February 2025].

Whitcomb, L. (1947) Anastomosing vs Braided Streams. *Proceedings of the Pennsylvania Academy of Science* 21, 64–68.

White, G.J. (2012) *The Medieval English Landscape, 1000–1540*. London, Bloomsbury.

Willan, T.S. (1946) The Navigation of the Great Ouse between St. Ives and Bedford in the Seventeenth Century. *Bedfordshire Historical Record Society* Vol. 24. Luton, The Society at Streatley.

Wimperis, E.M. (1895) Favourite Sketching Grounds, The Hemingfords. *The Leisure Hour*. Religious Tract Society.

Winchester, A. (2000) *Discovering Parish Boundaries*. Oxford, Shire Books.

Woodger, A. (1990) The Danes in Huntingdonshire. *The Records of Huntingdonshire Vol. 2, No. 9*. Huntingdonshire Local History Society.

Index

Numbers in *italic* denote pages with figures.

Abbot's Leat (*rivulus*) 19, 64, *65*, 66, 84, 89, 90, 118, 141
Abel Holt 52, 88, 92, 94, 100
Abingdon 6
Aethelberht of Kent 4, 28
Ailwin, Earl 28, 47
Alconbury Brook 37, 70, 117, *117*
Alexander, M. and Edgeworth, M. 10, 140, 141, 146, 147, 148
Ambler, J. and Langdon, J. 5, 7, 37, 54
Anabranching rivers, historically 8, 9, 18, 19, 66, 139, 146
Anastomosing rivers 8, 18, 39, 155, 158
artists 127–132
    Constable, John 128
    Fraser, Garden William *108*, 129, *130*
    Fraser, George Gordon 129
    Halswelle, Keeley 130
    Hobbema, Meindert 128
    Hunter, John Pettrey 109, *109*
    Milne, William Watt 129, *131*
    van Ruisdael, Jacob 128
    Wimperis, Edmund Morison 110, 130–1
Ashley, Henry 104, 106, 109
    Henry, jnr 106
Aston, M. 6, 7, 22

Back Brook *34*, 35
backwater (definition) 25
    Brampton 70, 71–2
    Godmanchester 70–1
    Hartford 67–70, *68*
    Hemingford Abbots 62–6, *65*, 82, 120
    Hemingford Grey 19, *34*, 35, 66–8, *67*, 83, 94, 100, 107, *131*, *135*, 137
    Huntingdon 70–1
    Little Paxton *43*, 72, 77
Barbegal 27
Battcock's Island *49*, 52, 64, 92, 94
Bedford(shire) 1, 4, *22*, 31, 32, 50, *53*, *55*, 56, *57*, 63, 103, 104
    Lock *105*
Belford Staunch *105*
Benedictines 29, 54
Bennett, R. and Elton, J. 4

Bitterne 139
Black Death 79, 81, 83
Blair, J. 1, 8, 32
Boardman, J. and Foster, I. 11, 145
Boatings 110–11
    Baton Ford *110*
    Cherry Tree *110*
    Milking Corner *110*
    Walkers *110*
Bond, C.J. 6, 29, 62
boundary 137, *137*
    Commission 77
    County 138–9, *139*
Brampton 17, 18, 27, 28, 50, 62, 97, *142*, 143
    Backwater 70, 71–2
    bailiffs 88
    Boating *110*
    Fulling mill 81
    mills 33, *34*, 38, *51*, 61, 70, 81, 98–100, 114–17, 124, 133, 136, *142*
Bromholme Brook 33, 50, 115, 118
Brown, Bateman 124
    Potto 114
    Brown and Goodman 124
Brownshill Staunch 103, *105*
Brudenell, Robert 85
Buckden 14, *20*, 30, *38*, 39, 43–4, *44*, 50, 72, 98, *99*, 114, 124, 125, 133, *134*, 136, *143*
Bugel Moor Brook 75, 76, *76*
Bull, Stephen 98
Burleigh, Lord, aka Cecil, William 99–100
Burton, Drew 102

Cardington 104
    Sluice *105*
Castle Lock *105*
Catley, Edward 98
Chessum, Richard 99
Chesters 27
Civil War, The 104
Coningsby, Humphrey 85
Cook, Robert 121
Cook's Stream 19, *34*, 35, 68–70, *68*, 82, 90, 93–4, 118–19
Corn Laws 123

County Councils
    Bedfordshire and Huntingdonshire 125
Cow Lane 90
Cromwell
    Oliver 102, 129
    Oliver, Sir 102
    Robert 102
    Thomas 95, 97
    Williams, Sir Richard, alias 97–8
Crown, The 83, 95, 97, 100–1, 103–4, 144

dam 45, 63, 64, 71, 85, 86–9, 92, 94, 100
Danelaw 21, 28, 30
Darby, H.C. 5, 21
Day's Brewery 124
de Grey, family 97
    John 62
    Reginald 35, 62, 63, 66, 67, 142
de Vere, Aubrey *38*, 56, 58
Dissolution of the Monasteries 95, 97–8, 121
Dobson, Henry 115
Domesday (Book, Survey) 1, 4, 5, 6, 7, 9, 14–15, 21, 22, 28, 30, 33, 37, *38*, 39, *40*, *41*, 43, 44, 50, 51, 52, *53*, 54, *55*, *57*, 58, 61, 71, 72, 93, 98, 113, 139–40
Dounby Click Mill 23
Downward, S. and Skinner, K. 8, 144
Drawing place, the 80, 88
Duchy of Lancaster 83, 86
    Chancellor, Gardener, Sir Ralph 100
    commission 85–7
    Court of 83–6, 94, 100
    Decree of 1427 106
    Decree of 1515 88–9, 100, 125
    map of, 1515 89–94, *91*
Duchy of Lancaster, 1515 Commissioners 85, 88, 90
    Bonham, Sir Thomas 85, 88
    Corner, John 85
    Mordaunt, Sir John 85
    Petition 16
    Walwyn, Sir William 85, 88
Duchy of Lancaster 1515 witnesses
    Dalton, William 88
    Fuller, Robert 88, 93
    Hall, Thomas 88
    Pelle, John 88
Dyer, William 102

Earith 104
Eastleigh 139, *135*
Eaton Socon 1
    Lock 104, *105*
    mills 30, *38*, 39, 40, *41*, 50, 61, 72, 77, 98, *99*, 106, 113, *114*, 124, 134, *135*, 136, *143*

Ellerton Priory 147
Elton 81, 138, *139*, 146
Environment Agency 144
Ermine Street 90, 120
exclusa(e) 63, 64, 67, 83–4
Eynesbury
    Abbey 98
    Boating 110
    mills 30, *38*, 39, 40–1, *41*, 50, 62, 72, 98

Fens, the
    drainage of 104
Fenstanton 111
Firth, A. and Firth, E. 10, 22, 141, 142, 148
fish and eel passes 145, *146*
Fishers Dyke 94, 118 *119*, 120, 120
flood mill 93
flooding 81–7, 89, 93, 98, 100–1, 106
ford 110
Four Gate Pit 64, *65*, 118
Fourdrinier, Henry 113
Fourdrinier, Sealy 113
Fox, R. 1, 2, 3, 4, 15, 63, 67, 69, 84, 100, 106, 120
Fuller, Stephen 81
fulling mill(s) 47, 61, 65, 71, 75, 76, 81, 82, 86, 87, 88, 89, 97, 98, 101, 106, 138

Gamble, John 113
Gason, John 103
Gater's Mill 140
Geographic Information System (GIS) 11
Gidding, William 95
Girton, Thomas 103
glacial
    diversion of drainage 18
    period 19, 20
Godmanchester 85–7
    backwater 70–1
    bailiffs 83–6
    Borough and corporation 81–2, 89, 126
    causeway 69, 120–1
    Charter 62, 83
    control of gates 86, 89, 100, 106–7, 125–6
    Drain (Gumcester Drain) *34*, 35, 50, *51*, 64, 82, 84–6, 88–92, 94, *119*, 122
    Durogivutum 21, 27
    Eastside Common 94, 118, 122, 148
    fee-farm rent 82–3
    Fish Weir *146*
    histories 1–2, 5–6, 30
    Lock *105*
    millers 106

mills 30–3, *31*, *38*, 51, *51*, *91*, 97–8, 103, 114, *114*, *134*
　steam mill 124–5
　West Meadow 100, 110
　Westside Common 93, 120
Goodman, Joseph 114
Gordon, Willam 12, 43
Great Barford 104, 109
　Staunch 105
Great Ouse Valley Trust 144
Great Paxton 30, 41–2, *42*, 110
Green, H.J.M. 5–6, 20, 30, 70

Halingway *see* towing path
Haltwistle 27
Hartford
　backwater 67–70, *68*
　Boating *110*
　mills *38*, 45, *46*, 62, 80–5, 88, 89, 90, 92, 93, 94, 95, 97, 121, 142, 143
Hemingford Abbots 88, 110, 111, 130, 131, 135, 142, 143
　backwater 62–6, *65*, 82, 120
　bridge 86–7, 90
　fulling mill 81, 85–7, 89, 97
　meadow *111*, 120
　mill *38*, 47–9, *49*, 52, 81, 88, 92–4, 95, 97
Hemingford Grey 9, 18, 37, 88, 130
　backwater 19, *34*, 35, 66–8, *67*, 83, 94, 100, 107, 131, *135*, 137
　Lock 105, *106*
　meadow 2
　mills 10, *38*, 39, 52, 56, 58, 80–2, 89, 92–3, 97, *99*, 101, 106, 103, *114*, 124, 127–32, *133*, 142
　Overfall Pit 107, *107*, 108, *129*
Hen Brook 41
Hermitage Sluice 104, *105*
High Court 126
Historic England 9, 141
　Conservation Areas 147, 149
　Heritage Assets 148
　Listing 136, 141, 147
　Scheduling 147
Historic Environment Record (HER) 141, 148
Historic Water Polygon (HWP) 10, 140–4, *142*, *143*, 147–8
Hobson, Mr 113
Hodgen, M. 4, 5, 21, 39
Holt, R. 7, 37, 53, 61, 81
Holywell 57, 73, 81, 130
　Boating *110*
　windmill 81
horse mill 98
Houghton 79, 88, 110, 130

Back Brook *119*, 122
Boating *110*
gulls 84–6, 89–90, 94, 118
Lock *105*
Long Overfall 95
meadows 148
mill(s) 1, *3*, 24, 28, 30, 35, *38*, 39, 51–2, 62–6, *65*, 82, 84, 86, 88, 90, 92–3, 97, *99*, 100–1, 103, 114, *114*, 124, 127–9, *130*, *131*, 132, *133*, 136
Howes, H. 10, 39, 42, 113, 115, 124, 132
Hundred Rolls (*Rotuli Hundredorum*) 2, 15, 16, 42, 47, 61, 66
Huntingdon, 85–6, 88
　backwater 70–1
　bailiffs 85–6
　bridge 90, 92, 101, 120–1
　Charter 83
　fee-farm rent 83, 101
　mills *38*, 50, 51, 80–2, 85, 97–9, *99*, 114–15, *116*, 117, 131, *133*
　population 21
　Prior and Priory 9, 12, 67, 68, 69, 81, 83, 95, 97
Hyer, M. and Hooke, D. 9

Ickham 27
Inclosure Map 13
　Buckden 114
　Godmanchester 118
　Great Paxton and Toseland 42
　Offord Cluny 114
Industrial Revolution 123
Ingram, John 117

Jefferys, Thomas, map of 12, 45, 47, *69*, 70, 118, 121
Judith, Countess *38*, 40

Keche, John 97
Keith, S. 9, 38, 53
Kent, Earl of 81–2, 88–9, 92–3, 100
　tenants of 82
King's Lynn 86–7, 90, 102, 130

landscape 123–4
　Dutch and Flemish 128
　historic watermilling 123, 136–7, 140–8
　modelling impact of watermills 137–40, *138*
　romantic 127
Langdon, J. 7–8, 37, 62, 63, 66, 68
lawesyard 83–4, 89, 92, 94
Lee's Brook 33, *34*, *70*, 71
Lenny and Croft, map of 13, 44, 71, 72, 110, 111, 119
Lewin, J. 8, 19, 139, 146

LiDAR 11, 30, *46*, *48*, *91*, 137
lighters 109
Lincoln, Bishop of 99–100, 106
Little Paxton
    backwater *43*, 72, 77
    mills 40, 41–3, *43*, 98, *99*, 113, *114*, 124–5, 134
lock
    flash lock 81, 92, 102–3
    pound lock 102, *103*
Longland, Bishop 95
Lord's Holme 104
Lucas, A. 9, 29, 30, 56

Maille, Thomas 99
Malcolm IV of Scotland 41, 42
malt mill 98
Manchester, Earl of 98, 106
mill-leat *25*, *26*
mill pond *25*
molendini 62
Montagu family 98
multi-channel *17*, 18, 19, 33, 35

National Landscape 144
National Planning Policy Framework 9, 148
National Trust, The 1, 39, 132, 149
navigation 88
    impeding of and disputes 79–91, 98
    restoration 101, 103–4
    rights of 79–80, 125–7
non-conformism 124

Offord Cluny 14, 18, 30, *38*, 39, 40, 43–4, *44*, *45*, 50, 72
oil mill 106
Okestubbe Mill 113
Old River (Chubb Stream) 73, *75*, *75*, 76
Old Windsor (Kingsbury) 28
Olney 139, *140*, 146
one mill = one wheel = one pair of stones 32, 37–9

Paine and Company 124
parish boundaries 7, 22–4, 42, 43, 44, 66–7, *67*, 68, 72, 94, 137, *138*, *139*, 139, *140*, 140, 148
Paxton (see also Great Paxton and Little Paxton) 5, *38*, 40, 41–3
Payne, Richard 102
Payne, Robert 98
Pettis, Edmund 74–6, *74*, *75*, 76
picturesque 127
ploughlands 14, 21, 22, 53, 56, 57
population
    census 123
    Huntingdon 21
Portholme *31*, 32, 88, 148
    Brook 19, 33, *34*, 35, 115, *116*, 117, *117*, *119*, 148
pre-watermilling landscape 33, *34*, 35

Quo Warranto Plea 2, 15, 62, 63, 66, 67, 93, 105, 142

railway
    East Coast Main Line 125
    embankment 110, *119*
    St Ives to Godmanchester Line 121, 125
    transport
    trestle bridge 121, *121*, 125
Ramsey Abbey 97, 138
    Abbot of 9, 12, 62, 63, 64, 67, 81, 85–6, 88, 95
    tenants of 82 88
Ranulph, Abbot 72
relict channel *20*, 33, *45*, 47, 52, 56, 71, 73, 100
Rhodes, E. 8, 18, 19, 140
Rhymers Weir *65*, 94–5, 118
Richard the miller 48
ridge and furrow 21, 33, 90, 94
rimers 94, 102
riot 84, 100
river
    Culm 142
    Eden 142
    Exe 102
    Itchen 139, *141*, 146
    Nene 81
    New Bedford 104
    Rother 145
    Stour (Dorset) 141
    Thames 131, 142
River Great Ouse 102, 104, 113, 123, 129, 138, 145
    discharge 18
    Great Ouse Catchment Board 135
    Great Ouse River Board 132
    physical geography 17–18
rivulus 63, 64, *65*, 148
Roman period 20, 27
Rowley, Owsley 113
Roxton 104
    Sluice *105*

St Ives *109*
    Bridge *110*
    Easter Fair 83
    Prior's Mill 73
    Quay 110
    Saint Audrey Lane *74*, *75*, 76
    staunch 103, *105*, 126, 129

steam mill 124
    watermill 72–6, *74, 75, 76*
St Neots 87 104
    Brookside 124
    Prior and Priory 40, 41, 79, 98, *99*
    mills 98, 104, 113
    Steam Mills 124
sand and gravel extraction 94, 123
Sandeforde, George 100
Sandwich, Earl of 83, 98, 115, 117, 126
Sawley 64
Sawtry Abbey and Abbot 41, 42, 43, 62, 98
scour pond *25*
Sewers, Statute of 98
    Commission 98, 100
single channel *17*, 19, 33
Simpson, Leonard T. 16, 125–7, 136
Sisson, Robert 100
Six Gates Pit 66, 92, *107*
sluice *25*, 26, 101–2
    gates 104, 106
Smyth, Peter 97
Smyth, William 81
Smythe, William 99
Southampton 139–40
Sparrow, Lady Olivia 118
Speed, John 11
Spencer, Arnold 103–5
stagnum 8, 63, 64, 66, 67, 71
Stanwick 27
staunch 102–3
steam
    steam powered mills 123–4, 134
Stoneham, North and South 140, *141*
study area *3*
Styward, Thomas 81
suit of mill 29, 49, 56, 73
Summers, D. 5, 17, 20, 32, 39, 63, 102, 104, 111, 127
Surbey, Thomas 102
Swavesey 20, *38*, 39, 40, 49
Sweeting, Henry 118

tail race *25*
Tamworth 25
Tempsford 104
    staunch *105*
The Times 132
Thornber, William 127
Thorney Abbey 37
Three Gate Pit *107*
tolls 84, 106, 125
Tottenhill glacial advance 18

tourists 132
towing path *107*, 110–1
trade, waterborne 79–81, 85–6, 89, 102, 106
trout stream 94
Tryce, Richard 100
Turnpike Trust 121

Upwood 97

Vermuyden, Cornelius 104

Warboys Windmill 81
Warner, Thomas 115, 117
watermills
    clusters 58–9, *58*
    earliest evidence 27
    proximity to towns 55
    value 37, *38*, 52–9, *53, 54, 55, 57*
Watermills Close 115
waterwheel
    breast-shot 25
    horizontal *23*, 25
    overshot 25
    undershot *24*, 25, 27
    vertical *24*, 25
Watts, M. 7, 25, 27, 28, 30, 37, 61
weir *25*, 26
West, Thomas 105
Westend Mills 140–1, *141*
Wharram le Street 29
Wharram Percy 29
wheat 20–1
Willan, T.S. 5, 98, 103, 105, 106, 107, 109
William I, King of England *38*, 58
Willington 31, 32, 104
    Sluice *105*
Winchester 139–40
windmill(s) 37, 49, 61, 72, 73, *74, 75, 76*, 81
Wistow Windmill 81
Worthy 139
Wray House Ford *110*
writers
    Belloc, Hilaire 127
    Benson, A. C128
    Farrar, C.F. 131
    Foster, A.J. 131
    Meynell, Wilfrid 129
    Pratt, Samuel Jackson 127
Wyton 30, *38*, 47, *48*, 50, 52, 58, 61, 66

Youth Hostel Association 132